CULTURES OF PRINT

Cultures of Print

ESSAYS IN THE HISTORY
OF THE BOOK

David D. Hall

University of Massachusetts Press
Amherst

Essay Index

Copyright © 1996 by David D. Hall
All rights reserved
Printed in the United States of America
LC 96-18430
ISBN 1-55849-048-5 (cloth); 049-3 (pbk.)
Designed by Jack Harrison
Set in Adobe Caslon by Keystone Typesetting, Inc.

Library of Congress Cataloging-in-Publication Data
Hall, David D.
Cultures of print : essays in the history of the book / David D. Hall.
p.   cm. — (Studies in print culture and the history of the book)
Includes bibliographical references and index.
ISBN 1-55849-048-5 (alk. paper). — ISBN 1-55849-049-3 (pbk. : alk. paper)
1. Books and reading—United States—History—17th century.
2. Books and reading—United States—History—18th century.
3. Books and reading—New England—History—17th century.
4. Books and reading—New England—History—18th century.
5. Books—United States—History—17th century.
6. Books—United States—History—18th century.
7. Books—New England—History—17th century.
8. Books—New England—History—18th century.
I. Title.   II. Series.
Z1003.2.H35   1996
002'.0973—dc20   96-18430
                                                            CIP

British Library Cataloguing in Publication data are available.

This book is published with the suppport and cooperation of the
University of Massachusetts Boston.

Permission to reprint has been graciously granted by the American
Antiquarian Society for "On Native Ground: From the History of
Printing to the History of the Book," "The Uses of Literacy in New
England, 1600–1850," and "Readers and Reading in America: Historical
and Critical Perspectives"; by Carol Armbruster for "The Politics of
Writing and Reading in Eighteenth-Century America"; and by the Johns
Hopkins University Press for "The World of Print and Collective
Mentality in Seventeenth-Century New England."

For my father,
lifelong reader

Contents

CULTURES OF PRINT

Introduction

T H E "history of the book" is an odd-sounding phrase, seemingly too nebulous and sweeping to exert interpretive power. The essays brought together in *Cultures of Print* are, I hope, demonstrations to the contrary. Predicated on the assumption that the better we understand the production and consumption of books, the closer we come to a social history of culture, these essays employ a variety of strategies in giving weight to an otherwise enigmatic phrase.[1] For the most part the setting is colonial America, but because the practices and representations described in these essays originated in early modern Europe, the frame of reference is recurrently transatlantic.

This frame is all the more appropriate because it was European scholarship that set in motion the history of the book. Taking this scholarship as my model, I have also depended on an overlapping body of work that investigates popular culture in the early modern period. The premise behind much of this work is an argument about authority and agency in matters of culture. Acknowledging the authority exerted

---

1. All but one of these essays have been previously published. The original place and date of publication are indicated in a note added to each. I remark on the situation of book history in America and on the project, now under way, of a collaborative "history of the book in America," in "The History of the Book in the United States: Prospects and Perspectives," in *Histoires du Livre: Nouvelles Orientations,* ed. Hans Erich Bodeker (Paris, 1995), 47–60.

I

by the learned, the clergy, a centralizing civil state, or an urban bourgeoisie, historians like Natalie Zemon Davis have nonetheless insisted
that ordinary people retained a strong element of agency or independence. Accordingly, the task of describing popular culture has involved
these historians in a kind of double vision, a perception both of what
the powerful were providing and of how those at the margins reworked
or resisted these seemingly authoritative messages. Another way of
enacting this double vision has been to discern the intermediaries
(printers and booksellers, for instance) who carved out a space between
center and periphery, high and low. A third possibility—one that owes
much to cultural anthropology—is to focus on certain locations that
permit or encourage transgressive practices. Here too the historian
must employ a form of double vision, in this instance of boundaries
that alternatively seem sharply etched and fluid.

I was led to book history by scholarship that employed all of these
strategies in describing printers, booksellers, "cheap books," and literacy. For example, in Natalie Davis's "Printing and the People," she
argued that in the hands of French Protestants in the early modern
period, printing served to "challenge traditional hierarchical values."
Explicating the scene of the village *veillées* where people gathered to
hear books read aloud, she proposed that illiterate peasants, far from
being excluded from the new world of printing by an inability to read,
were "active users and interpreters" of the information that came their
way. Although Robert Darnton's starting point was not popular culture, his account of the "literary underground" in prerevolutionary
France made it appear that printers worked both inside and outside the
regulation and patronage provided by an absolutist civil state. In the
same vein, though almost as an afterthought, Peter Burke characterized printers as cultural intermediaries. The work of Margaret Spufford on chapbooks in Restoration England and of Bernard Capp on
English almanacs in the seventeenth century documented the vast pro-
fusion of these inexpensive pamphlets and exposed the surprising mixture of lore—the debris, as it were—they contained.[2]

2. Natalie Zemon Davis, "Printing and the People," in *Society and Culture in Early Modern
France* (Stanford, Calif., 1975), 189–226; Robert Darnton, *The Literary Underground of the Old
Regime* (Cambridge, Mass., 1982); Peter Burke, *Popular Culture in Early Modern Europe* (New
York, 1978), 78; Margaret Spufford, *Small Books and Pleasant Histories* (Athens, Ga., 1982); Ber-
nard Capp, *English Almanacs 1500–1800* (Ithaca, N.Y., 1979). See also Robert Darnton, "What Is
the History of Books?" in *The Kiss of Lamourette: Reflections in Cultural History* (New York, 1990).

The essays in *Cultures of Print* address similar issues in early America and, in particular, the intellectual and religious history of Puritan New England. I do not have to wrestle with social and cultural divisions like those of early modern Europe, for the English immigrants who colonized New England in the seventeenth century were relatively homogeneous. But I do have to reckon with the assumption—strenuously argued at the outset of the 1970s by social historians—that the Puritan clergy stood apart from ordinary people, who paid them little heed. The mental world of these people was supposedly constrained by illiteracy and oral culture, or marked by an indifference to the substance of religion.

I challenged this assumption in my initial foray into book history, "The World of Print and Collective Mentality in Seventeenth-Century New England," an essay written for a conference held in 1977 to assess the situation of intellectual history, which at that moment seemed irretrievably displaced by a numbers-driven social history. No longer satisfied with the ideas-in-themselves approach that Perry Miller had taken in his magisterial study of the Puritan mind, but wanting to keep ideas as part of the story, I found a temporary way station in the concept of *mentalité* and longer-lasting possibilities in the then-emerging study of popular religion and the history of the book.

When I extended the argument of this essay into a full-scale study of popular religion (*Worlds of Wonder, Days of Judgment: Popular Religious Belief in Early New England*), book history was crucial to the story in several respects. One way of closing the distance between ordinary people and the clergy was to suggest, on the basis of court records and other kinds of evidence, that most of the colonists were literate in the sense of being able to read. Another means of indicating common ground was to sketch the circulation of certain narratives via sermons and conversations as well as via books. Everyone seemed to share a stock of stories, like the tale of Francis Spira and of kindred "wonders." Because these same stories embodied a patchwork of ideas partly inconsistent with orthodox theology, they offered an intriguing demonstration of the middle ground between learned and popular religion. For that matter, sermons and devotional literature incorporated elements of literary sensationalism more commonly associated with "cheap print." Printers and booksellers, though issuing much that was consistent with the main lines of Puritan belief, were practiced at exploiting every possibility for exaggeration. In the case of the almanac, tried-and-true conventions won out over a reformed version of this popular text. Book history thus provided a way out of the impasse into which intellectual history had fallen, for it brought together the official and the unofficial, learned and popular religion.

Historians of popular culture in early modern Europe were moving toward similar perceptions. A conference at Cornell University in 1982 was an important step in linking my nascent project with theirs. One lesson I learned from the Europeanists was that, in past times, reform-minded agencies of learned culture had worked hard to proscribe certain forms of popular belief and behavior. These agencies invented the all-too-enduring association of popular religion with those elusive entities, "magic" and "superstition." The reverse was also true: some elite constructions of popular culture could be deployed *against* modern or official culture, as in celebrations of the "folk." A cautionary lesson emerged from recognizing that the very category of folk was infused with these ideological crosscurrents: what we historians were describing as popular culture was not a direct product of the material circumstances of the people. In response to this lesson, Roger Chartier proposed the alternative notion of "appropriation" to signal the differing ways in which social groups took over and remade orthodox or official stories, texts, and practices.[3]

These lines of inquiry and reflection have culminated in a particular understanding of the term "culture," an understanding summed up by the British social historian E. P. Thompson in this manner:

> Culture is . . . a pool of diverse resources, in which traffic passes between the literate and the oral, the superordinate and the subordinate, the village and the metropolis; it is an arena of conflicting elements, which requires some compelling pressure—as, for example, nationalism or prevalent religious orthodoxy or class consciousness—to take form as "system." And, indeed, the very term "culture," with its cozy invocation of consensus, may serve to distract attention from social and cultural contradictions, from the fractures and oppositions within the whole.[4]

3. Roger Chartier, "Culture as Appropriation: Popular Cultural Uses in Early Modern France," and Jacques Revel, "Forms of Expertise: Intellectuals and 'Popular' Culture in France (1650–1800)," both in *Understanding Popular Culture: Europe from the Middle Ages to the 19th Century*, ed. Steven L. Kaplan (The Hague, 1984); Burke, *Popular Culture*, Pt. 1. See also Chartier, "Introduction," *The Cultural Uses of Print in Early Modern France*, trans. Lydia G. Cochrane (Princeton, N.J., 1987). I owe much as well to the reflections on high and low in Peter Stallybrass and Allon White, *The Politics and Poetics of Transgression* (Ithaca, N.Y., 1990).
4. E. P. Thompson, *Customs in Common* (New York, 1993), 6.

All of the elements of this statement were made visible in the history of the book. The significance of book history was that it forced a recognition of culture not as something uniform or imposed from above but—to repeat some of Thompson's language—fractured, local, and charged with oppositions.

To quote Thompson is to be reminded that, for him, the fundamental source of opposition was the struggle of labor against advancing capitalism. He emphasized the power of capital to transform labor, though he also saw the capacity of "custom" to offer resistance. My vision is different. The strand of culture that especially interests me is what I term the Protestant vernacular tradition. It is appealing because of its insistence on lessening the distance between the clergy and the people, as in making the Bible available in the vernacular and in calling for the participation of everyone in the practices of reading and speaking. Yet in certain situations the clergy and the learned who labored within this tradition became caught up in the "reform of popular culture" (to borrow Peter Burke's useful phrase) and the inscribing of fresh boundaries between high and low and between men and women. Inclusive and emancipating, the vernacular tradition was also disciplining and prescriptive. And as the history of Quakerism so interestingly reveals, modes of hierarchy and censorship figure even among the most "radical" versions of this Protestant culture. The story that I want to tell, therefore, is one of ongoing exchanges and negotiations, intermixed with episodes of proscription and withdrawal.

My interest in this tradition affects how I approach the politics of culture within the sweep of American history. Some historians have argued that in early America, hierarchy gradually gave way to democracy; others, carrying the story forward into the nineteenth century, have argued that democracy gave way to hierarchy. Though it may seem quixotic (if not also elitist) to ignore both the moral fable of democratization and its satanic twin, the fable of democracy corrupted by an elite, I have never found either of these stories plausible. The making and remaking of culture seem too dynamic and elusive to permit control by an elite that was never really unified, while what is designated as democracy is, from my angle of vision, always marked by forms of high and low. In the essays that follow, I implicitly privilege a series of events and processes that cannot be subsumed within the metanarrative of democratization: the Protestant Reformation; the Puritan movement in England and America and its radical offspring, the Quakers; the reaction against "enthusiasm" that, abetted by John Locke's insistence on the priority of reason, gradually carried one wing of English and American Protestantism away from the vernacular tradition; the renewal of that tradition in eighteenth-century evangelicalism; and the quickening currents of nationalism, capitalism, and romanticism in the nineteenth.

Amid change there was continuity. The persistence of the vernacular tradition is aptly captured in the long duration of the "steady sellers" I describe in "The Uses of Literacy." Another element of continuity was the adversarial relationship between the Protestant vernacular and other modes of culture.[5] How this stance of opposition affected the practices of reading and writing and the meanings of "literature," literacy, and authorship is in part what the essays in *Cultures of Print* are about. Yet it is also the case that opposition waxed and waned. One phase of attenuation occurred in the decades after 1700; another, decisive for transmuting Protestantism into Victorianism, occurred in the middle of the nineteenth century when "respectability" became a bridge between moralism and gentility.

The politics I describe in these essays has a second point of departure, the fracturing of culture into the local and the metropolitan. The dispersal of energies away from any putative center is a much-remarked-on aspect of early American history. Vernacular Protestantism abetted this dispersal. At the same time, however, this Protestantism was powerfully consolidated around certain texts, symbols, and story frameworks. No matter how dispersed, Protestants on both sides of the Atlantic shared a constraining awareness of orthodoxy and of common historical experience. As I suggest in the essay that follows on book culture in the Chesapeake, other forms of dependence also weighed upon the colonists—in the domains of statute law, the natural sciences, and the practice of authorship, to name a few. Always, colonial culture was both local and metropolitan. How the people of those

---

5. Two studies that demonstrate in close detail this politics of culture are John N. King, *English Reformation Literature: The Tudor Origins of the Protestant Tradition* (Princeton, N.J., 1982), and Lawrence Buell, *New England Literary Culture from Revolution through Renaissance* (New York, 1986), with its superb analysis of the Connecticut River Valley tradition, epitomized in Harriet Beecher Stowe, and coastal liberalism, epitomized in Nathaniel Hawthorne.

times made their way through these complications is, for me, an essential aspect of the politics of culture in early America.

This politics has a third dimension. High and low, the local and the metropolitan, converged on a middle ground where exchange occurred and where intermediaries flourished. These processes are exemplified in the practices of bookmaking and bookselling, and in the transmission of the lore of wonders. Another example, touched on briefly in "The World of Print," is the resort by ministers like Cotton Mather to sensationalism; a third, which I do not explore in these essays, is witchhunting. The workings of this middle ground lead me away from propositions about elites and the control they may seem to exert; equally, the workings of this middle ground keep me from invoking "the people" as though they had either a single or autonomous culture of their own.

These three realities—the long duration of vernacular Protestantism, the tension between the local and the metropolitan, and the existence of a middle ground where high and low converge—are made forcefully evident through the history of the book. Seeking out the details of printing and bookselling that would demonstrate these processes, I have found myself in the company of the scholars who edit literary texts, prepare bibliographies, and serve as curators of printed books in research libraries. Early on, like everyone who studies the colonial period of American history, I had depended on Charles Evans's indispensable *American Bibliography*. That there was more, much more, to the world of bibliography came home to me during a fellowship in 1981–82 at the American Antiquarian Society, the institution that has done the most to promote the systematic study of American imprints. For the first time, I went through the entire run of *Papers of the Bibliographical Society of America* and similar journals. For the first time, mainly in the context of two conferences held at the Society, I sat down with bibliographers to discuss our common interests. Initially there was an edgy tone to those discussions, for the bibliographers, commanding an unrivaled knowledge of the book trades and of books as artifacts, questioned whether those of us acting as prophets of the history of the book were overly facile in generalizing about "print culture," a phrase no bibliographer cared to use.

Fortunately, these suspicions were tempered by another set of circumstances. Within the field of bibliography itself a fresh wind was blowing as scholars like Donald F. McKenzie argued for reorienting the discipline around the "misreading" of texts.[6] A second, less happy circumstance for bibliographers was that within departments of English and American literature, bibliography had been dethroned by critical theory, a revolution epitomized in the rise of Michel Foucault's "What Is an Author?" to near-canonical importance in the contemporary study of literature. Not quite disfranchised, but certainly displaced from the curriculum, some bibliographers came to welcome the possibility of affiliating with historians. There was every reason for historians to welcome that affiliation, too, for it gave them entry to a vast supply of facts and, on closer familiarity with the field, to certain strategies of research and midrange generalizations. Whenever possible, bibliographers looked at every surviving copy of early printed books. Familiar with the scribal (handwritten) system of production that existed before the invention of movable type in the middle of the fifteenth century, they knew that the formal features of the printed book duplicated the features of handwritten books. Attentive to the actual process of printing, bibliographers thought of books not in their bound form but as sheets of paper folded into different formats. Moreover, they were skeptical of categories dear to most historians, yet in need of criticism. The first and foremost of these was the term "American," as in the phrase "an American book," for bibliographers recognized that most of the books that have figured in our early cultural history originated on the other side of the Atlantic.[7] Another is the term "demand" and its implicit synonym, "the market," for bibliographers knew that printers were poor judges of demand, often engaging in the overproduction of books that no one wanted to buy.

My education at the hands of the bibliographers is ongoing. Early on, I paid the craft homage in an essay, "On Native Ground," that was given as the inaugural James Russell Wiggins Lecture at the American Antiquarian Society. The presence in the audience of Mr. Wiggins, formerly an editor of the *Washington Post*, explains the reference to my

6. D. F. McKenzie, *Bibliography and the Sociology of Texts* (London, 1986). See also Roger Chartier, "Preface: Textes, Formes, Interpretations," to the French translation (Paris, 1991) of McKenzie's work.

7. Bibliographers are also deeply skeptical that the surviving archive, as recorded in imprint lists, adequately captures what was actually produced.

days as a newspaper delivery boy in Alexandria, Virginia, but the presence of bibliographers on the same occasion provided the subtext of
the lecture, the tempered relationship between them and historians. It
is only fair to say that I was eager to play the role of critic myself, as I
did in suggesting some of the ideological limitations of the "history of
printing." Not until I undertook to write the history of the book in the
seventeenth-century Chesapeake did I employ strategies of research
that are commonplace among bibliographers. Embodied in an essay in
this collection, this research presumed that scribal or handwritten production is just as deserving of attention as are the products of the
printing press. In the case of statute laws and other legal or governmen-
tal records, the evidence from Virginia and Maryland speaks for itself.
But because the archives are silent, and because we usually find only
what we look for, let me acknowledge my debt to Harold Love's *Scribal
Publication in Seventeenth-Century England,* a masterpiece of bibliographical scholarship that alerted me to the ongoing importance of this
mode of production.[8]

In another essay that linked cultural history with the history of the
book trades, "The Uses of Literacy in New England, 1600–1850," I
sketched a transition from one mode of production and consumption
to another, contrasting the "scarcity" of the older system with the
"abundance" of the new. My argument remains largely correct. Yet I
have come to realize that Joseph Buckingham and Samuel Goodrich,
whose testimony about the transition I took at face value, were narrat-
ing a deeper story rooted in their own journeys from Calvinist Con-
gregationalism to liberal Unitarianism; in effect, they were enacting a
"reform of popular culture." Hence Goodrich's critique of the *New
England Primer,* and hence the trope of emancipation, which signified
emancipation from the fear of divine judgment. Buckingham and
Goodrich extended this trope to encompass the workings of the commercial market in their own day: implicitly, the abundance of books
and the exhilarating process of choosing items from the "teeming"
shelves of Broadway stores became synonymous with freedom of the
mind and freedom of the will. Looking back on "The Uses of Literacy,"
I wish I had been more alert to the ideological overtones of "abun-

---

8. Harold Love, *Scribal Publication in Seventeenth-Century England* (Oxford, 1993).

dance" and "scarcity." In actual fact, a very large share of book production in the first half of the nineteenth century occurred outside the
commercial market under the sponsorship either of civil governments
(as much printing always has been) or of political parties, church-
related agencies, and voluntary societies, a notable example being the
American Tract Society. Agencies like the Tract Society may have
inadvertently abetted the "market revolution," but their explicit goal
was to strengthen the sway of moral rules, some of which contradicted
the rules of the marketplace. As for the period of supposed scarcity, it
now seems apparent that people in early New England and in the
Chesapeake did well with what they had. Only from the vantage point
of persons participating in the "reform of popular culture" did books (I
should add, the right kind of books) seem scarce.

"The Uses of Literacy" was my initial contribution to yet another
aspect of book history, the practice of reading. Trained in high intellectual history and the close reading of canonical texts, I was well ac-
quainted with scholarship that took seriously the books that were read
by the likes of John Adams, Jefferson, and Emerson. But in the context
of popular culture and popular religion the task was to understand the
"cheap books" that were the stuff of everyday reading and to conceive of
reading as a practice that involved many kinds of interchange. As I have
already indicated in speaking of popular religion, the English booksellers who issued "penny godlies" also issued books that were decid-
edly playful or amusing, and, as I learned from the older literary history
and book trade scholarship, the same writers produced both kinds. The
making of Protestant devotional books thus depended on an alliance of
clergy and booksellers—often as uneasy coalition, but a coalition nonetheless. Was it appropriate to conclude from these circumstances that
readers could find a mixture of meanings in even the most pious of
books? Merely to ask this question was to resist two interpretations that
struck me as distorted, that popular books embodied the thinking of
the people or, on the contrary, were instruments wielded by the upper
or middling classes to promote moral and social control.

This is not to say that writers do not create an "implied reader" and
prescribe how their books should be read. The prefaces in godly books
were explicit in advising a particular mode of reading, a mode I described at length in *Worlds of Wonder* and briefly summarize in the essay

here, "Readers and Reading." Within the New England context, it seemed plausible to link that mode with how children actually learned to read, and in turn to connect this information with the preference, as revealed in probate inventories and in booksellers' stock, for certain kinds of books. Another part of this sequence was the responses people recorded in autobiographical narratives to books they were reading. In the end the point was a simple one, that reading occurred in a cultural field that established the significance and manner of the act. Reading was never an autonomous practice, but embedded in a series of mediations. What book history is about is describing these mediations as they affect not only reading, but also printing, bookselling, book collecting, and authorship.

Because the historian is drawn to examine change over time, book history involves a number of assertions about long-term transitions: in reading, from "intensive" to "extensive" and from partial to near-complete literacy for women as well as for men; in publishing, from a regional or decentralized system to one that by the end of the nineteenth century was consolidated in a few cities and a handful of corporations; in intellectual property and authorship, from a system controlled by booksellers to the emergence of our modern understanding of authorship, copyright, and plagiarism; in printing, from the limitations of the "ancient regime" to the modes of mass production made possible by new technologies of production and distribution and by changing structures of demand; and in the role of the civil state, from a sense of corporate responsibility for the press to permitting unregulated competition. An ongoing task of book history is to clarify the causes and consequences of these transitions while keeping in mind the continuities—the *longues durées*—that complicate any narrative of revolution and democratization. In this respect the essays in *Cultures of Print* record my own second thoughts about the reading revolution that may have spanned the eighteenth and nineteenth centuries.

The history of reading has led me to literary theory at the very moment when many of the scholars who study American literature are reaching out to book history themselves. Like the alliance between historians and bibliographers, this other relationship is not without its complications. I touch on one of these, the priority within literary theory of texts and the representations they contain, in reviewing the history of reading. But let me also affirm that book history must engage with questions arising out of literary and cultural theory—questions about authorship and intellectual property, representations of books and printing, the multivocality of texts, and the modes of "domination," as in forms of patriarchy, that infuse the definition of literature. Only in small ways do the essays in *Cultures of Print* take up these questions. The discussion of authors and censorship in the seventeenth-century Chesapeake must stand for the moment as my contribution to the conversation between cultural and literary historians. Where that conversation has carried us is to the recognition— central to cultural studies in these times—that our categories of analysis are themselves historically constructed. In my own fashion, I have sketched how the category of "literature" existed dialectically with the Protestant vernacular understanding of the written word, how "scarcity" and "abundance" embodied an ideological agenda, and how the history of reading (like much else within culture) is inescapably a matter of long-persisting tropes or forms. But for reasons I have already indicated, I am doubtful about any equating of these forms with "domination" in the many-sided realms of cultural practice.

Summing up current work on popular culture, Chandra Mukerji and Michael Schudson note that scholars come to the field carrying certain baggage depending on their discipline. For this reason, "no single discipline [they argue] has or will ever have a monopoly on the study of popular culture; no discipline represents the 'best' approach. Each sees a different part of the elephant."[9] Book history has the same structure. Written from the perspective of a cultural historian interested in religion, the essays in *Cultures of Print* transpose the social history of literacy and the separate histories of printing, bookselling, reading, and authorship into cultural practices—that is, practices inflected according to the meanings that invested them and the social field in which they occurred. These essays also constitute an enterprise of recovery, in the first instance, of a Protestant vernacular tradition and, in the second, of a middle ground between high and low, the local and the metropolitan.[10] In undertaking to write about the history of the

9. Chandra Mukerji and Michael Schudson, eds., *Rethinking Popular Culture: Contemporary Perspectives in Cultural Studies* (Berkeley, Calif., 1991), 4.
10. An exemplary study in this regard is Joan S. Rubin, *The Making of Middlebrow Culture* (Chapel Hill, N.C., 1992).

book, I have always had in mind the larger goal of a more adequate history of culture in America.

In editing these essays for reprinting, I have made a few changes of wording and have amplified some of the references, in order both to correct mistakes and to indicate more recent scholarship.

One of the great pleasures of traveling the roads I take in these essays is the companionship I have enjoyed along the way. Returning to my native south to work in archives and sources dealing with the seventeenth century, I have benefited greatly from the courtesy and professionalism of librarians and archivists at the Maryland Hall of Records, the Library of Virginia, the Virginia Historical Society, and especially the library and department of historical research of the Colonial Williamsburg Foundation. I am grateful to Lois Green Carr for providing me access to transcripts of inventories for St. Mary's County, Maryland, and to Cary Carson and his staff in the York County Project for access to transcripts of court records and inventories. Darrett and Anita Rutman were similarly generous with materials from Middlesex County, as was Kevin Kelly for Surry County, Virginia; Ann Smart Martin hunted up merchants' inventories and shared unpublished research, and Julie Richter checked certain references. Warren M. Billings provided a thoroughgoing critique of my description of politics and the handling of statute law in Virginia; Thad W. Tate, Brent Tarter, and Calhoun Winton have also provided expert advice. I am indebted as well to J. William Frost and the staff of the Friends Historical Library in Swarthmore, Pennsylvania. Jessica Marshall, Timothy Milford, and John O'Keefe helped further my knowledge of Chesapeake sources.

Three of the essays that follow were written for conferences, and I thank their organizers for inviting me to participate in them. It is a special pleasure to acknowledge friends and colleagues who, over the years, have contributed to my understanding of the history of the book, and who have often been of immediate assistance with these essays: Tom Augst, Ross W. Beales, the late Stephen Botein, Richard D. Brown, Cathy N. Davidson, Norman Fiering, Richard W. Fox, Robert Gross, Carl Kaestle, Marcus McCorison, Meredith McGill, James McLachlan, Elizabeth Reilly, Joan S. Rubin, Barbara Sicherman, Margaret Spufford, Roger Thompson, Michael Warner, Michael Winship, and

Larzer Ziff. Hugh Amory, both a bibliographer and a literary historian by training, has taught me much about the possibilities for linking bibliographical methods with cultural and social history. My other models in this regard have been Robert Darnton and Roger Chartier. It is fitting to enlarge upon a comment I made in a note to "Readers and Reading," that these essays are a payment on the debt I owe to Chartier's wide-ranging scholarship. John Hench has overseen the publication of several of these essays; I thank him for his unstinting care for matters large and small pertaining to the history of the book.

On Native Ground: From the History of Printing to the History of the Book

I AM GRATEFUL for the honor of inaugurating the Wiggins lecture series, and with it, the Program in the History of the Book in American Culture. Out in gold-rush California, Mark Twain used to perform on the lecture circuit of the mining camps. On one occasion he was introduced by a miner who, taking the stage reluctantly, "stood thinking for a moment, then said, 'I don't know anything about this man. At least I know only two things: one is, he hasn't been in the penitentiary, and the other is (a little sadly), I don't know why.'"[1] My credentials as a historian of the book are nearly as precarious as Twain's were that evening. The distinguished bibliographer and librarian Victor Hugo Paltsits once remarked that "anyone can compile a list, many can make a catalogue, but very few can agonize to bring forth a bibliography." Lists I have made, but never shall I experience the rite of passage of the bibliographer. Yet I do bring one credential to this occasion. At the age of eleven I became a newspaper delivery boy in Alexandria, Virginia, for the *Alexandria Gazette*, which in those days, and perhaps still, boasted that it was the oldest continuously published newspaper in

This was presented as the inaugural James Russell Wiggins Lecture in the History of the Book in American Culture given at the American Antiquarian Society in November 1983, and subsequently published in the *Proceedings of the American Antiquarian Society*, n.s., 93 (1983):313–36.

1. *Mark Twain's Autobiography*, ed. Albert Bigelow Paine, 2 vols. (New York, 1924), 1:161.

America. Some months later I moved to higher things as a delivery boy for the *Washington Star,* to which I also contributed a story for the Children's Page about an immense rolltop desk my father had given me. It may not be appropriate for the Wiggins lecturer to stress his connections with the *Star,* now, alas, defunct while its rival the *Post* has reached new heights. In those innocent days of the 1940s it was the *Star* and not the *Post* that reigned supreme in Washington journalism—so supreme, so weighty, that on Sundays I had to endure the humiliation of dragging the gigantic Sunday editions from house to house in a child's wagon. As newspaper delivery boy and one-time journalist, I salute Mr. Wiggins as a fellow laborer in American journalism.

A hundred and seventy-five years ago, in 1808, Isaiah Thomas began to write *The History of Printing in America.* From his day to ours, a coalition of printers, booksellers, collectors, antiquarians, bibliographers, librarians, and historians have pursued the history of printing to the point where we know more about who published what, and where, than do the historians of printing in any other country. We may justly celebrate this scholarship. But as we celebrate there is also reason to reflect and reconsider. The present moment, marked as it is by the founding of the Program in the History of the Book in American Culture, demands critical reflection. What has been our native tradition? What themes, what arguments, what burdens do we inherit from the past? More crucially, what should be the relationship between the history of printing and the history of the book? These are the questions I wish to address this afternoon.

It was the first of April in 1808 when Thomas started on his *History.* His diary entry for that day is unpretentious, though also disconcerting in its juxtaposition of the commonplace and the extraordinary: "Miss Weld left us in Dudgeon. Pleasant for the season. Miss C. returned, and went again to Gov. Lincoln. Began writing a Sketch of the Origin and Progress of Printing. A child fell in a kettle of boiling soap, and died. Its Grandmother going in haste from a neighbouring house to administer relief taken with Asthma, dies instantly."[2] The absence of literary pretension was characteristic of a man who began his career as

2. Charles L. Nichols, ed., "Extracts from the Diaries and Accounts of Isaiah Thomas," *Proceedings of the American Antiquarian Society* 26 (1916):69.

printer, publisher, and bookseller apprenticed to one of Boston's least distinguished printers and who would later publish almost anything and everything, from *Goody Two-Shoes* and the Bible to the pseudo-astrology of *Erra Pater*. Isaiah Thomas was a printer in the days before specialization severed the functions of publisher and bookseller from that of manufacturing books. His pride in an identity as "printer"—late in life he told a correspondent that he preferred this role to any other— spilled over into the *History of Printing in America*.[3] It is the key to his sense of audience, the "professional men" and "professors of the typographic art" for whom he imagined he was writing.[4] The feeling of fraternity with printers past and present led him to insert biographical notices of his fellow craftsmen. His own printer's eye and hand lay behind the notice he took of "neatness and correctness" in certain work, and the description of presses and their technology. From this same identity flowed his interest in the history of journalism, for the printer of his day was especially ambitious to establish a newspaper, regarding it, more so than books, as the crowning glory of his trade.[5] Speaking of his own career, Thomas gave pride of place to publication of the Massachusetts *Spy*, as, before him, Franklin had given pride of place in speaking of his own career to the newspaper and magazine he had founded in Philadelphia.

Isaiah Thomas was a printer, not a learned "scholar" or man of letters. His own schooling had been intermittent at best, and certainly not of the kind to allow him entrance to the world of the scholar—a world still based on the classics. Fortunately for us, Thomas's *un*learnedness made him sympathetic to materials that others would ignore. No man of letters in 1810 would have written a history of printing, and certainly not a history of printing that paid so much attention to newspapers. Nor would a man of letters have *collected* newspapers. All of

---

3. Clifford K. Shipton, *Isaiah Thomas: Printer, Patriot and Philanthropist* (Rochester, N.Y., 1948), 84.

4. Isaiah Thomas, *The History of Printing in America*, ed. Marcus A. McCorison, 2d ed. (New York, 1970), 4, xxi. Thomas hoped that the book would be "amusing to the man of letters, and not altogether uninteresting to the antiquarian."

5. Ibid., 80. Speaking of the "country printer" in the middle of the nineteenth century, William Dean Howells observed, "Their hope was somehow to get hold of a country paper and become editors and publishers" (Howells, "The Country Printer," *Impressions and Experiences* [New York, 1896], 32). See in general Milton W. Hamilton, *The Country Printer New York State, 1785–1830* (New York, 1936).

these activities depended on Thomas's wonderfully undifferentiated sense of himself and on his independence from the hierarchies of traditional literary culture. We catch a glimpse of those hierarchies in a statement of praise for newspapers and their role in modern society that Thomas inserted in the *History*. He borrowed this statement from the Presbyterian clergyman and future Princeton teacher Samuel Miller's *Brief Retrospect of the Eighteenth Century*. Miller was assuredly a learned man. Thomas must have been pleased to dress up, to legitimize, his own commitment to journalism by quoting such an authority. But a statement that began with praise ended by reaffirming the old hierarchies, for Miller complained that in "our country . . . too many of our gazettes are in the hands of persons destitute at once of the urbanity of gentlemen, the information of scholars, and the principles of virtue."[6] For Thomas to admit these words into his *History* was, I suggest, to introduce a tension that would reverberate for another century and a half: the tension between a broad and narrow view of printing, or between the democratic and the genteel view of culture. In the *History*, as in his daily practice, Isaiah Thomas stood for a broad approach; but even in his own day there was a contrary position which he felt it necessary to acknowledge.

Contemporary response to the *History* was modest. No one, not even the American Antiquarian Society, was interested in publishing the revised edition on which Thomas labored for the next twenty years until his death in 1831. After a long pause, the native tradition would resume its development in the 1860s, when Americans set to work again on the tasks of preparing a national imprint bibliography and a more thorough history of printing. Early in the 1860s, Joseph Sabin, a bookseller and antiquarian who arrived at bibliography by way of preparing sales catalogues, started on the first of what would grow into the twenty-nine volumes of the *Bibliotheca Americana*. John Russell Bartlett published the first really significant state bibliography, his *Catalogue of Books Relating to Rhode Island*, following it in 1865 with a *Catalogue of the Library of John Carter Brown*. That same year, Henry Stevens, a Vermonter who had migrated to London, brought out his

---

6. Thomas, *History of Printing*, 18–21. Having allowed these words into his text, Thomas added a note in which he blamed the deficiencies of American journalism on the extreme partisanship of our politics.

Catalogue of the American Books in the Library of the British Museum.[7] Joel Munsell, like Thomas a successful printer and bookseller, complemented his studies of the development of printing and papermaking by editing, together with Bartlett and Samuel Foster Haven, a revised edition of *The History of Printing in America.*[8]

In these years the great collectors of Americana, John Carter Brown, George Brinley, and James Lenox, were making themselves felt. They had allies in booksellers, antiquarians, and the earliest of the professional librarians. The friendships and rivalries among these men are recalled by R. W. G. Vail in his retrospective evocation of Sabin's world in the final volume of the *Bibliotheca Americana:*

> It would have been well worth a winter journey to have heard Sabin pay tribute to Ebeling and Rich and Terneaux-Compans as earlier travellers on his road; to have listened to his comments on Harrisse; to have heard him talk about Henry Stevens . . . to have got his views about George Brinley and John Carter Brown and James Lenox and their libraries; to have known what he thought about Peter Force and Jared Sparks . . . to have watched him compare Samuel G. Drake and William Gowans and Charles B. Norton and Joel Munsell and . . . the other rival booksellers of this day.[9]

Let us pass from this generation, so rich in its accomplishments, to another that accomplished even more. At the turn of the century Charles Evans had begun upon his monumental bibliography of American imprints, to be completed, finally, at the Antiquarian Society in 1970.[10] Clarence Brigham would soon be at work on a bibliography of American newspapers that built upon foundations laid by Thomas.[11] Wilberforce Eames, who as a young Brooklyn bookseller had volun-

7. Joseph Sabin, *Bibliotheca Americana: A Dictionary of Books Relating to America from Its Discovery to the Present Time*, 29 vols. (New York, 1868–1936), begun by Sabin, continued by Wilberforce Eames, and completed by R. W. G. Vail; John Russell Bartlett, *A Catalogue of Books . . . Relating to the State of Rhode Island* (Providence, R. I., 1864), and *Bibliotheca Americana: Catalogue of Books Relating to North and South America in the Library of the late John Carter Brown*, pt. 1 (Providence, R.I., 1865); Henry Stevens, *Catalogue of the American Books in the Library of the British Museum* (London, 1866).

8. Worcester, 1874. Munsell's scholarship is described in David S. Edelstein, "Joel Munsell: Printer and Bibliographer," *Papers of the Bibliographical Society of America* 43 (1946):383–96.

9. Vail, *Bibliotheca Americana*, 29:iv.

10. Charles Evans et al., comps., *American Bibliography*, 18 vols. (Chicago, Worcester, Mass., and Charlottesville, Va., 1903–70).

11. Clarence S. Brigham, *History and Bibliography of American Newspapers, 1690–1820*, 2 vols. (Worcester, Mass., 1947).

teered to assist Joseph Sabin, was now the principal editor of that ever-lengthening series. Underneath the shelter of these great enterprises, hundreds of collectors, antiquarians, librarians, and bibliographers were pursuing the details of local printing in an effort that continues to this day. The quality of these local studies would gradually improve to the point where, by the 1930s, a distinct maturity had been achieved. This maturity is evident in Douglas C. McMurtrie's *History of Printing in the United States*, of which, sadly, only one of a projected four volumes would be published. Yet indirectly and directly, McMurtrie gave direction to and set standards for the history of printing as written according to state boundaries.[12]

The maturing of our native tradition is also evident in another book of the 1930s, Lawrence Wroth's *The Colonial Printer*.[13] To reflect on the strengths and the limitations of *The Colonial Printer* is to reflect on the strengths and limitations of our native way of doing the history of printing. Like so many others before and after him, Wroth had done a local study, following in that regard the tradition that began with Thomas, who had organized the *History* according to geography. Why did geography entrench itself in the history of printing? There was the factor of convenience that the boundaries of a town or state provided. Another reason was surely the sense of place aroused in many Americans, perhaps most among those in the northeast as they experienced the onset of industrialism. Recall, if you will, the great outpouring of town histories in New England that occurred as "olden times" yielded to the "railroad age." Like other landmarks of the past—roads, buildings, families, churches—books seemed somehow different then than now; and the antiquarian reached back across a widening chasm to preserve and record a vanishing past. This sense of jeopardy had waned by the time Wroth came to write *The Colonial Printer*, but the geographical principle, and its corollary, the history of printing told as the rise or spread of printing from one colony or state to the next, remained his vision of the subject.

Wroth would combine localism with a second principle, that of the

12. Douglas C. McMurtrie, *A History of Printing in the United States: The Story of the Introduction of the Press and of Its History and Influence During the Pioneer Period in Each State of the Union* (New York, 1936).

13. Lawrence Wroth, *The Colonial Printer*, 2d ed. (Portland, Maine, 1938).

"fine book." In the last half of the nineteenth century a distinctive understanding and appreciation of the handcrafted book emerged as part of the reaction to industrialism. On both sides of the Atlantic, sensitive persons voiced their dismay at the mediocrity of the mass-produced and mass-consumed artifact. Consider, said Tocqueville in *Democracy in America,* the pocket watch as produced in aristocratic society and as produced in a democracy: the one made slowly and to the highest standards for the aristocratic patron, the other rushed out quickly for patrons who could not tell the difference between the mediocre and the well made.[14] Did this distinction apply also to the book? Reviewing Tocqueville, John Stuart Mill insisted that it did. A fundamental realignment of culture was occurring: "It is the middle class that now rewards even literature and art; the books by which most money is made are the cheap books. . . . Elementary and popular treatises are immensely multiplied, superficial information far more widely diffused; but there are fewer who devote themselves to thought for its own sake, and pursue in retirement those profounder researches, the results of which can only be appreciated by a few. Literary productions are seldom highly finished—they are got up to be read by many, and to be read but once."[15]

From Mill to William Morris and the Kelmscott Press the road is very short. It is a road that led to a new cultural hierarchy: books made by craftsmen using the hand-operated press were superior to books produced by the steam press. More generally, there was something known as "fine" printing, in contrast to mere ordinary varieties. This distinction would increasingly inform the practice of typographic design, the way in which the history of printing was written, and not least, the habits of book collectors.[16] In 1912 the English critic and literary historian Alfred Pollard would advise collectors that "the only good qualities which a book can possess in its own right are those of strength and beauty of form." Age and rarity, he declared, were secondary considerations; the contents were irrelevant. "No collector would value a

---

14. Alexis de Tocqueville, *Democracy in America,* ed. Phillips Bradley, 2 vols. (New York, 1954), 2:50–55.

15. John Stuart Mill, "De Tocqueville on Democracy in America," *Essays on Politics and Society, Collected Works of John Stuart Mill* (Toronto, 1972), 18:195.

16. James M. Wells, "Book Typography in the United States of America," in *Book Typography 1815–1965,* ed. Kenneth Day (London, 1966), 325–70.

dull sermon printed in 1800 any higher than a dull sermon printed in 1900."[17]

On almost every page of Lawrence Wroth's *The Colonial Printer* we sense the impact of this new hierarchy. The wealth of details about the craft of the hand press grew out of a sympathy for the handcrafted book that Wroth made explicit in his preface:

> To love the contents of a book and to know and care nothing about the volume itself . . . is to be only half a lover, deaf to a whole series of notes in the gamut of emotion. The book-lover, more richly endowed, broods over the hand that fashioned the volume he reads, and, like the Tramp Royal, he goes on till he dies observing "the different ways that different things are done," the materials, the processes, the how and what and why of the ancient mysteries of printing, paper making, type founding, ink making, press building, and binding.

Let me call attention to the phrase, "ancient mysteries." It suggests the distance that has intervened between the age of the craftsman and the age of the machine. This expression placed Lawrence Wroth and his readers on one side of a great cultural divide, and even though the span in years was not especially long, a century or less, the distance seemed immense. I take this phrase to imply something else. That which is mysterious and ancient is also, by association, rare and beautiful. Ever since the coming of the book there have been those who wished to elevate, to mystify this artifact, to transpose it from the realm of utility to the realm of the aesthetic or the sacramental. Such an effort, I propose, is suggested by Wroth's evocation of the craft of printing; and his remark a page later that "God save us from the . . . windy fellows who say, 'I had just as lief read an author in a poor edition as a good one.'"[18]

The Colonial Printer is a masterpiece of our native tradition. Wroth's sense of printing as a craft was impeccable; and he was realistic about the utilitarian tasks that early printers undertook to stay in business, the kinds of job printing that seldom were given their due. Nonetheless *The Colonial Printer* was infused with criteria that were foreign to

17. Alfred W. Pollard, *Fine Books* (London, 1912), 9–10.
18. Wroth, *Colonial Printer*, xvii–xviii. Wroth was a principal contributor to Hellmut Lehmann-Haupt, *The Book in America: A History of the Making, the Selling, and the Collecting of Books in the United States* (New York, 1939), another study which in its overall design and themes reflects the ambivalence I am describing.

Isaiah Thomas, printer that he was of many "poor editions" and "dull sermons." In repeating the geographical mode of organization that originated with Thomas's own *History*, Wroth was misleading in a different respect, for the history of printing in America deserved a better framework. Ours was never really a frontier society with culture radically dispersed into local units; the technology in use from one end of the country to the other was derived from a metropolitan tradition, and most of the books being sold and printed had originated in centers such as London, Edinburgh, Boston, or New York. In summing up the strengths of American scholarship, *The Colonial Printer* also indicated some of its limitations.

Similar issues would arise in histories of American literature. A native literary history began to emerge in the early nineteenth century, with Samuel Kettell's *Specimens of American Poetry, with Critical and Biographical Notices* serving as something of a twin to Thomas's *History*.[19] At midcentury the New York critics Evert and George Duyckinck brought out their *Cyclopaedia of American Literature*, an immense anthology-cum-literary history. The *Cyclopaedia* provides a useful benchmark for considering how it was that literary historians would define their subject. What *is* American literature? Each of those words was problematic: the word "American," the word "literature." Well aware of the complications, the Duyckincks chose to solve them in a particular way. "The history of the literature of the country involved in the pages of this work," they declared in a foreword, "is not so much an exhibition of art and invention, of literature in its immediate and philosophical sense, as a record of mental progress and cultivation, of facts and opinions, which derives its main interest from its historical rather than its critical value." Because they preferred a "historical" to a "critical" or aesthetic understanding of literature, the Duyckincks could reach out widely for examples of writing—to the explorer John Smith, for example. And because they did not limit the category "American" to writers born on this soil or identifying themselves with the country, John Smith was doubly welcome to the pages of the *Cyclopaedia*.[20]

19. Samuel Kettell, *Specimens of American Poetry, with Critical and Biographical Notices*, 3 vols. (Boston, 1829).

20. Evert A. and George L. Duyckinck, *Cyclopaedia of American Literature*, 2d ed., 2 vols. (New York, 1866), 1:v.

This same breadth of sympathy would characterize the first academic history of American literature, Moses Coit Tyler's great four-
volume study of colonial and revolutionary period writing. In his pages
on the Revolution, Tyler laid aside as irrelevant the political categories
of Tory and Patriot. Tory writers, he declared, were just as American as
those who labored on the side of independence.[21] Similarly, Tyler set
aside any merely aesthetic conception of literature, recognizing that
"for the purposes of historical interpretation" the "lighter, as well
as the graver, forms of literature" had value. Hence he was willing to
give "full room to the lyrical, the humorous, and the satirical aspects
of our Revolutionary record—its songs, ballads, sarcasm, its literary
facetiae."[22]

Even more remarkable was Tyler's sympathy for the almanac. Admit
the lowly almanac into a history of *literature?* Yes, insisted Tyler: "No
one who would penetrate to the core of early American literature, and
would read in it the secret history of the people in whose minds it took
root and from whose minds it grew, may by any means turn away, in
lofty literary scorn, from the almanac,—most despised, most prolific,
most indispensable of books, which every man uses, and no man
praises, the very quack, clown, pack-horse, and pariah of modern literature, yet the one universal book."[23] These were words to warm the
heart of Isaiah Thomas, who never allowed "lofty literary scorn" to
interfere with his decisions about book publishing. But the very vigor
of Tyler's argument suggested the strength of the alternative he was
rejecting, an alternative but half concealed in the ambiguities of his
own description of the almanac.

In the years ahead, the alternative of an aesthetic understanding of
literature would become increasingly significant. We may trace the
rivalry between broad and narrow understandings of literature through
Barrett Wendell's *Literary History of America,* a notably stingy expression of the genteel tradition, to the *Cambridge History of American
Literature,* the first collaborative, academic history, and one that com-

---

21. Moses Coit Tyler, *A History of American Literature during the Colonial Time,* 2 vols., rev. ed.
(New York, 1897); *The Literary History of the American Revolution,* 2 vols., rev. ed. (New York,
1898).
22. Tyler, *Literary History of the American Revolution,* 1:v–vi.
23. Tyler, *History of American Literature During the Colonial Time,* 1:120.

bined both modes, to the postwar *Literary History of the United States,*[24] where the rivalry is explicit in the juxtaposition of long sections on a handful of "major" writers with others that were broadly historical or cultural in their focus. The sections on major writers reflected the redefinition of literature that was occurring as a consequence of literary modernism. The critical principles of T. S. Eliot, Ezra Pound, and others of their generation amounted to a radical reassertion of aesthetics as the sole basis for understanding literature. The traditional literary hierarchies that Thomas had ignored, and Tyler also, were now reborn. In their wake came the enshrining of Henry James, that most self-conscious and "literary" of our novelists, and the elevation of a modest galaxy of kindred spirits—Poe, Hawthorne, Thoreau, Melville, Whitman, and Twain.[25]

It may seem like something of a paradox that modernist criticism, as practiced by Americans, became intertwined with the search for a "native" literature—but such was the case. Literary critics in the twenties were obsessed with the discovery, and if necessary the creation, of a native literary tradition.[26] Nativism and modernism converged in a study that has exceptional depth and passion, F. O. Matthiessen's *American Renaissance.*[27] It is a book to which, as much as to any other, I owe my own sense of vocation; but in spite of Matthiessen's democratic sympathies, *American Renaissance* stands near one end of a spectrum that stretches from modernist, "aesthetic" criticism to Tyler and the Duyckincks. The fusion of modernism and nativism would have many consequences. The impact on colonial literature has been striking, for the canon of early American poetry gradually shrank to the few, chiefly Anne Bradstreet and Edward Taylor, who bear up under close "liter-

24. Barrett Wendell, *A Literary History of America* (New York, 1900); William P. Trent et al., eds., *The Cambridge History of American Literature,* 3 vols. (New York, 1917–21); Robert E. Spiller et al., eds., *The Literary History of the United States,* 3 vols. (New York, 1947).

25. The transformation of literary criticism may be traced in the anthology assembled by Morton D. Zabel, *Literary Opinion in America,* 2 vols. 3d ed. (New York, 1962).

26. The search for a native literature and its consequences are traced in Richard Ruland, *The Rediscovery of American Literature: Premises of Critical Taste, 1900–1940* (Cambridge, Mass., 1967).

27. F. O. Matthiessen, *American Renaissance: Art and Expression in the Age of Emerson and Whitman* (New York, 1941). To a certain extent Matthiessen believed that great writers absorbed motifs from the wider culture of which they were part, a point of view more forcefully argued in a book that returned to the almanacs for inspiration, Constance Rourke, *American Humor: A Study of the National Character* (New York, 1931).

ary" scrutiny. Yet there were dozens of other poets in the period, as Harold Jantz demonstrated in a remarkable work of literary history in 1943.[28]

But the triumph of modernist criticism placed literary history in the shade, and with it, the concept of "literary culture," that network or community of writers, critics, publishers, and readers that our literary historians had been intent on describing. To our literary historians we owe much, including many studies that have enriched the history of printing. I think of such books as Thomas Goddard Wright's *Literary Culture in Early New England,* based in part on probate inventories; of Louis B. Wright's *First Gentlemen of Virginia,* which made use of similar sources; of its distinguished and more wide-ranging successor, Richard Beale Davis's *Intellectual Life in the Colonial South;* of William Charvat's studies of author-publisher relationships;[29] and not least, of Frank Luther Mott's *History of American Magazines,* the fifth and final volume of which appeared after his death. Mott had earned his Ph.D. degree in English literature at Columbia University. In the preface to the first volume, published in 1930, Mott began by citing the negative opinion that "periodicals have in them little or nothing of reliable information or admirable literature." To the contrary, declared Mott, periodicals "provide a democratic literature which is sometimes of high quality." The remarkable ambivalence of this sentence may have done more to expose a tension than resolve it, but Mott pressed on, offering the prediction that literary history would have to take into account "social, economic, geographical, industrial, and educational factors. . . . The time is happily past when biographical sketches plus criticisms of masterpieces may be accepted as literary history. Much of our literary history must be rewritten from the standpoints of geography and the social sciences. No longer can we consider literature as of the mountain

28. Harold Jantz, "The First Century of New England Verse," *Proceedings of the American Antiquarian Society* 53 (1943):219–508. For a stimulating reappraisal and critique of nativist (and, implicitly, modernist) literary history, see William C. Spengemann, "Discovering the Literature of British America," *Early American Literature* 18 (1983):3–16; Spengemann, *The New World of Words: Redefining Early American Literature* (New Haven, Conn., 1994).

29. Thomas Goddard Wright, *Literary Culture in Early New England, 1620–1730* (New Haven, Conn., 1920); Louis B. Wright, *The First Gentlemen of Virginia: Intellectual Qualities of the Early Colonial Ruling Class* (San Marino, Calif., 1940); Richard Beale Davis, *Intellectual Life in the Colonial South, 1585–1763,* 3 vols. (Knoxville, Tenn., 1978); William Charvat, *Literary Publishing in America* (Philadelphia, 1959).

top, dissociated from social and economic pressures; it has come too close to the people."[30]

A brave prophecy, but for its times a wrong one, if we bear in mind the indifference and even the hostility to economic and social factors that would characterize the dominant school of literary criticism in the postwar years.

I am suggesting that historians of American literature have vacillated between quite different approaches to their subject matter, or even to the question of what their subject matter was. This ambivalence is akin to that we find in Wroth. Is the story one of fine printing or one of books, no matter what their appearance or function? The common issue, the deeper question, concerns hierarchies of value: should the aesthetic merits of a book determine whether it is studied or not, and by what methods? Should historians of printing—of American litera-ture—reserve their efforts for the best that was done, or reach out to the utilitarian, the vernacular, the tawdry? And does place of origin affect the field of study? Does a book conceived and written in America have more value than a book conceived and written somewhere else, though both had readers in this country?

Whatever else the history of the book may be—and I use the term deliberately, to contrast it with the history of printing—it must put to rest this ambivalence. Let me speak directly to the issues. The fact of the matter is that Americans depended on imported books for most of their literary culture in the two centuries and a half of settlement that preceded the Civil War. A history of the book in America is not a history of *American* books. Quite the contrary. Ours was persistently a provincial culture dependent for its modes on a distant cosmopolitan center, be it London or some other central place.[31] We may resonate to Emerson's declaration of cultural independence in "The American Scholar," but the man who defiantly asserted that "books are for the scholar's idle time" was himself a most bookish man, deeply indebted to British and German writers for his romanticism. The American printer and bookseller did not think twice about reprinting or import-

30. Frank L. Mott, *A History of American Magazines,* 5 vols. (Cambridge, Mass., 1930–68), I: 2–4.
31. John Clive and Bernard Bailyn, "England's Cultural Provinces: Scotland and America," *William and Mary Quarterly,* 3d ser., II (1954):200–213.

ing books originating overseas.[32] In our zeal to assert a native tradition, we overlook the contrary example of a Benjamin Franklin; for Franklin repudiated local tradition in favor of the new prose style he encountered in stray copies of the *Spectator* and *Tatler*. His narrative of how he modeled his prose style directly upon theirs bespeaks the powerful appeal of cosmopolitan standards to the aspiring provincial—an appeal that is elsewhere evident in the career of the painter John Singleton Copley, and that colors, I would argue, the entire history of American literature at least until the 1930s.

Ours was not only a provincial culture but also one in which the press was in the service of utilitarian needs. Only incidentally were printers and booksellers responsive to any other patronage than that of the marketplace, or of institutions such as schools, churches, the civil government, and political parties. As time went on, advertising would assume immense importance. In this context, fine books, fine bindings, and first editions do not loom as consequential. Pride of place belongs to more lowly genres—the schoolbook, the almanac, the newspaper, the legal form, the devotional manual. In these utilitarian and provincial functions of the press lie the makings of a history of the book.

Having spoken of the literary historians and historians of printing, let me comment briefly on those who have studied education and ideas, politics and society. The contributions to an understanding of the book in American culture have been many, as in the histories of education that specify which books were used by faculty and students. Samuel Eliot Morison's *Harvard College in the Seventeenth Century* is exemplary in this regard.[33] From the many possibilities in intellectual history, I want to single out Zoltán Haraszti's *John Adams & the Prophets of Progress*, a book originating in a librarian's browsings in a collection he presided over. John Adams responded vigorously to the authors he read, filling margins of his books with pungent marginalia, like the following remark addressed to the philosophe d'Alembert: "Thou Louse, Flea, Tick, Ant, Wasp, or whatever Vermin thou art, was this Stupendous Universe made and adjusted to give you Money, Sleep, or

32. Robert B. Winans, "The Growth of a Novel-Reading Public in Late Eighteenth-Century America," *Early American Literature* 9 (1975):267–75.

33. Samuel Eliot Morison, *Harvard College in the Seventeenth Century*, 2 vols. (Cambridge, Mass., 1936). Many of the relevant studies are listed in the bibliography to Lawrence A. Cremin, *American Education: The Colonial Experience 1607–1783* (New York, 1970), and its sequel, *American Education: The National Experience 1783–1876* (New York, 1980).

Digestion?" Out of all these comments Haraszti wove a stimulating description of Adams's political and moral philosophy.[34] Yet the excellence of these studies was never made the basis for any larger or compelling interpretation of printing or the book in relation to politics, culture, or society. Tocqueville, noting the extraordinary circulation of newspapers in America, had described them as instruments of "association" in a society of individuals.[35] Reflecting on this same proliferation, a modern historian could only ascribe it to the "booster spirit" of Americans.[36] Could the history of printing illuminate the course of American politics? Isaiah Thomas had thought that the rise of independent journalism was a step toward political independence. Arthur Meier Schlesinger pursued the same theme in his study of prerevolutionary journalism, *Prelude to Independence.*[37] Taken as a whole, the history of printing and the history of politics and society achieved tenuous connection through themes like the "rise of the common man," the rise of democracy, or the coming of independence. Apart from their vagueness, these themes did not do justice to the powerful currents of conflict and oppression that existed in the past.

In moving from the history of printing to the history of the book, we must transcend the geographical principle. It is equally imperative that we move beyond nativism, aestheticism, and the instinctive whiggery of themes such as the "rise of democracy." The history of the book in America will be cosmopolitan in its understanding of American culture, democratic in its openness to all forms of print, and alert to the uses of power—a point to which I shall return. Let me close by enumerating four topics or directions the history of the book will undertake.

Lecturing on what pragmatism means, William James described his

34. Zoltán Haraszti, *John Adams & the Prophets of Progress: A Study in the Intellectual and Political History of the Eighteenth Century* (Cambridge, Mass., 1952), 111.

35. Tocqueville, *Democracy in America*, 2:119–22.

36. Daniel Boorstin, *The Americans: The National Experience* (New York, 1965), 124–35.

37. Thomas, *History of Printing in America*, xx; Arthur M. Schlesinger, *Prelude to Independence: The Newspaper War on Britain, 1764–1776* (New York, 1957). There are interesting suggestions about the relations between politics and the press in Leonard L. Richards, *"Gentlemen of Property and Standing": Anti-Abolition Mobs in Jacksonian America* (New York, 1970), 71–73, and in Bernard Bailyn, *The Ideological Origins of the American Revolution* (Cambridge, Mass., 1967), 2–4. See also Bernard Bailyn and John Hench, eds., *The Press & the American Revolution* (Worcester, Mass., 1980); Charles E. Clark, *The Public Prints: The Newspaper in Anglo-American Culture, 1665–1740* (New York, 1994); and for a different angle of vision, A. G. Roeber, *Faithful Magistrates and Republican Lawyers: Creators of Virginia's Legal Culture 1680–1810* (Chapel Hill, N.C., 1981), chaps. 3 and 4.

new philosophy as the very opposite of a "closed system," a dogma or final truth. It is less a "solution," he declared, "than a program for more work. . . . Pragmatism unstiffens all our theories, limbers them up and sets each one at work."[38] In the spirit of William James, we may say that the history of the book is not a system or set of rules, much less a set of a priori truths, but a point of view that unstiffens the heaps, the veritable mountains, of information that have been accumulated by patient research on printers, publishers, booksellers, readers, and the physical book. Consider, for example, the history of bindings. An esoteric subject? Not if we ask the question, Why were some books singled out to receive special attention and others not? for by asking this question we transform the history of bindings into the history of values— that is, of culture. The history of music publishing is extraordinarily revealing of folk values—if we want to use that word in reference to styles of hymnody—in conflict with a more cosmopolitan elite; and, as pianos became household items in the homes of upper middle-class Americans, of shifting modes of gentility.[39] As in these examples, so more widely, the history of the book, like James's pragmatism, will persistently transform isolated and static information into evidence of dynamic social processes.

A second way in which the history of the book departs from the history of printing is via its concern for readers and reading. Readers were scarcely present in the history of printing, and have often proved an embarrassment to bibliographers because of their tolerance for debased versions of popular texts. But the history of reading and of readers is central to the history of the book. In and of itself this statement helps to define the differences between the old history and the new. By reading, I mean the process by which persons responded to a text. It is often said that in early America many persons could not start upon the process of reading because they were illiterate. I wish to cut the Gordian knot that literacy studies pose—what is it they measure, and how accurately?—by asserting that, early and late, the great majority of Americans, men as well as women, could read. When Isaiah

38. William James, *Pragmatism: A New Name for Some Old Ways of Thinking* (New York, 1907), 51–53.
39. Richard Crawford and D. W. Krummel, "Early American Music Printing and Publishing," in *Printing and Society in Early America*, ed. William L. Joyce et al. (Worcester, Mass., 1983), 186–227.

Thomas went to work for Zechariah Fowle at the age of seven, he "knew only the letters, but had never been taught to put them together and spell." Yet literacy came easily to this child, as it did to most Americans: "I was left to teach myself and soon learned by practice to set types, and to read tolerably, and obtained some knowledge of punctuation."[40]

Many persons learned to read by listening to the Bible or some other book as it was read aloud. Samuel Goodrich, the nineteenth-century publisher, writer, and antiquarian, tells a story that bears upon the fusion of oral memory and the culture of print. It concerns a Vermont widow who began each day with family worship. One day she prevailed upon her foreman to lead in family prayers.

> On a bright morning in June . . . the family were all assembled in the parlor, men and maidens, for their devotions. When all was ready, Ward, in a low, troubled voice, began. He had never prayed—or at least not in public—but he had heard many prayers, and possessed a retentive memory. After getting over the first hesitancy, he soon became fluent, and taking passages here and there from the various petitions he had heard—Presbyterian, Methodist, Universalist, and Episcopalian—he went on with great eloquence, gradually elevating his tone and accelerating his delivery. Ere long his voice grew portentous, and some of the men and maids, thinking he was suddenly taken either mad or inspired, stole out on their toes into the kitchen, where, with gaping mouths, they awaited the result. The Widow Bennett bore it all for about half an hour; but at last, as the precious time was passing away, she lost patience, and sprang to her feet. Placing herself directly in front of the speaker, she exclaimed, "Ward, what do you mean?"
>
> As if suddenly relieved from a nightmare, he exclaimed, "Oh dear, ma'am—I'm much obliged to you—for I couldn't contrive to wind off."

In this episode, as in the history of reading in general, access to culture was casual and strangely democratic.[41]

It is certainly the case that some persons achieved greater mastery than others of the books that came their way. A history of reading must

---

40. *Three Autobiographical Fragments by Isaiah Thomas*, ed. Marcus A. McCorison (Worcester, Mass., 1962), 19. My broader assertion requires making a distinction between reading and writing, the latter a skill that many fewer persons possessed. Some of the evidence is reviewed in William T. Gilmore, "Elementary Literacy on the Eve of the Industrial Revolution: Trends in Rural New England, 1760–1830," *Proceedings of the American Antiquarian Society* 92 (1982):87–171.
41. Samuel Goodrich, *Recollections of a Lifetime*, 2 vols. (New York, 1857), 1:158–59.

take account of variations in ability, and of changes in the basic mode of reading over time. The pace could differ, as could the setting in which reading occurred. We read privately and to ourselves, and often own a piece of furniture designed for book storage. These conditions were uncommon before the nineteenth century. The historian of reading must join hands with the historian of material culture in developing our knowledge of physical setting. Probate inventories provide rich information on book ownership; these must be studied systematically, and with attention to key variations. The diaries, autobiographies, letters, and annotated books that survive from the past offer up many kinds of evidence of reading as a style and as an activity. Somewhere and somehow, this complex of evidence and interpretation must include the text itself, for every text offers directions—some of them explicit, as in an author's preface, and others implicit, as in matters of typography—that affect reader response.[42]

A third characteristic of the history of the book is its concern with popular culture. Our literary historians have described certain books that sold extremely well: Michael Wigglesworth's *The Day of Doom*, Susan Warner's *The Wide, Wide World*, Lew Wallace's *Ben Hur.*[43] But the history of popular culture is not synonymous with the history of bestsellers or that of cheap (inexpensive) print; and it is surely not synonymous with the history of literary trash, the books or periodicals that fall below some sort of level. All of these quite common misunderstandings must be set aside in favor of a conception of popular culture that acknowledges its multiple dimensions, and indeed the fluidity of the fundamental boundary between "high" or formal culture and that which we call "popular." Considered as something in and of itself, popular culture was conservative, a place where old values and belief systems lingered on; it was also radical, a place where dominant or official values were resisted and replaced with others; and finally it was playful, a place where truth gave way to fictions, humor, and reversals.

---

42. D. F. McKenzie, "Typography and Meaning: The Case of William Congreve," in *The Book and the Book Trade in Eighteenth-Century Europe*, ed. Giles Barber and Bernard Fabian, Wolfenbütteler Schriften zur Geschichte des Buchwesens, vol. 4 (Hamburg, 1981), 81–125.

43. Relevant studies include Frank L. Mott, *Golden Multitudes* (New York, 1947); James D. Hart, *The Popular Book: A History of America's Literary Taste* (New York, 1950); and the extraordinary bibliography-cum-history, Albert Johannsen, *The House of Adams and Beadle and Its Nickel and Dime Novels*, 2 vols. (Norman, Okla., 1950).

We can detect the conservatism of popular culture in the history of the "steady seller," the book that seemed never to lose its audience even though the learned ceased to acclaim or acknowledge its existence. Certain fairy tales fall into this category, but to an American they are less interesting than the evangelical texts of the seventeenth century that survived into the nineteenth. One such text, originating in the sixteenth century, would continue to be printed in Victorian Britain and America.[44] The conservative and the radical dimensions of popular culture could converge, as they did in the case of enthusiastic religion. The people of seventeenth-century New England lived in an enchanted universe. Ghosts came to people in the night, and trumpets blared, though no one saw from where the sound emerged. Nor could people see the lines of force that made a "long staff dance up and down in the chimney" of William Morse's house. In this enchanted world, the sky on a "clear day" could fill with "many companies of armed men in the air." Voices spoke from heaven, and little children uttered preternatural warnings. Bending over his son Joseph's cradle one evening, an astonished Samuel Sewall heard him say, "The French are coming."[45]

But by the close of the seventeenth century, this openness to visions, prophecy, and "wonder" was coming into disfavor. Witches ceased to work their spells and prophets ceased to testify, at least so far as the official culture was concerned. Where most of these possibilities survived was in a cultural underground well nourished on broadsides and chapbooks, an underground that provided sustenance to many a prophet and visionary of the late eighteenth and nineteenth centuries—a Joseph Smith, a John Humphrey Noyes, a Mary Baker Eddy. The radicalism of popular culture can shade over into playfulness.[46] The almanac was consistently playful in its stance toward truth, inventing weather, inventing remedies for illness, inventing quarrels with a rival publication,

---

44. I refer to the story of Francis Spira, a sixteenth-century Italian apostate from Protestantism. Some seventeenth-century versions of this story are noted in David D. Hall, *Worlds of Wonder, Days of Judgment: Popular Religious Belief in Early New England* (New York, 1989), 132–35.

45. Some of this paragraph is borrowed from my essay, "The World of Wonders: The Mentality of the Supernatural in Seventeenth-Century New England," in *Seventeenth-Century New England*, ed. David Grayson Allen and David D. Hall, Publications of the Colonial Society of Massachusetts, 63 (Boston, 1984), 239–74, where the references are also provided.

46. The line between playfulness or theater and true inversion or revolt is not always easy to discern. An exemplary case study is Peter Burke, "The Virgin of the Carmine and the Revolt of Mesaniello," *Past and Present*, no. 99 (1983):3–21.

inventing its astrology. The humor of the almanacs often involved folk inversions of official culture—the thieving priest, the greedy lawyer, the dishonest politician, the weak husband yielding to his wife. As play, popular culture was available to everyone; it was not the exclusive domain of some particular social group. Yet it always had its enemies, and the history of the book must take account of the antagonisms—the uses of power—that were involved in efforts to exclude and stigmatize.[47]

Yet another task of the history of the book is to incorporate the work of analytical bibliographers and their holy of holies, the text. It may be impossible to arrive at a text that corresponds exactly to the author's intention. Certainly the American printer and the American reader were quite indifferent to this issue, content as they were to publish and to read the most extraordinarily corrupted editions. The very concept of a perfect text is an invention of the twentieth century, and cannot be imposed upon the past. Yet in the details that only bibliographers seem prepared to master lie important evidence of several histories—the history of author-reader relations as seen from the author's point of view, the history of reading as one of quite varied encounters with what passed as the same text, and the history of the physical book itself. I am struck by the personal familiarity with books and their typography that characterized so many of the persons who contributed to the history of printing; Frank Mott had set type for his father's newspaper, while Sabin and Eames had been bookdealers. Inheriting some of their skills and sensitivities, the bibliographer can instructively collaborate with persons trained in other ways.

I have spoken of reading and popular culture, of texts and a general process of "unstiffening." The history of the book is something more than the sum of these four parts. What draws us onward is that glittering phrase, the history of the book as the history of culture and society. The promise of the history of the book is simply this, that it will not tolerate a simplistic or reductionist understanding of the relationship between culture and society. Commonly, we base our understanding of power on how wealth is distributed. But power comes in many other forms than wealth. The history of domination and subordination must take account of gender and age, of demarcations of the sacred, of

47. David H. Hall, "Introduction," in *Understanding Popular Culture*, ed. Steven Kaplan (The Hague, 1984), 5–18.

knowledge and its concentration or diffusion. "Knowledge is power; popularity is power." In the interplay between expertise and popularity, between books restricted to the few and books that circulated widely, lies the making of a different history of American culture. Such a history will proceed as well from the recognition that books embody codes that reflect and act upon the structures of authority.[48] Culture is not synonymous with social class. Any text is too ambivalent, too multiple in its significance, for there to be a one-to-one relationship. Yet we have every reason to regard cultural processes and artifacts—the rituals of a church, the act of reading, the exercise of speech—as bearing on the shape and exercise of power.[49] Deeply sympathetic to this relationship, the history of the book will serve to map with new precision and complexity the axes of conflict and consensus.

I began with Isaiah Thomas in 1808 as he started on his *History of Printing*. Two years later he had finished. I venture to predict that we shall need more time to complete our history of the book. But I fancy him as warmly supportive of our enterprise—of its sweep, its breaking with old hierarchies, its fusion of book, culture, and society. We stand on native ground as we embark on this new program.

48. William Weber, "Learned and General Musical Taste in Eighteenth-Century France," *Past and Present*, no. 89 (1980):58.
49. Rhys Isaac, *The Transformation of Virginia* (Chapel Hill, N.C., 1982), 121–31.

The Uses of Literacy in New England, 1600–1850

JOSEPH BUCKINGHAM and Samuel Goodrich were entrepreneurs of print in nineteenth-century America, the one as editor of Boston's first daily newspaper, the other as a publisher and author. Goodrich was the man behind the pseudonym "Peter Parley," a name attached to children's stories and of such appeal to young readers that unscrupulous publishers stole it for their own ends. Goodrich was not amused by the practice, but his anger was lessened by the sweet smell of success: "I am the author and editor of about one hundred and seventy volumes, and of these seven millions have been sold!"[1]

In that triumphant sentence from his autobiography lies one characteristic of the new world of print that Goodrich helped to create: a vast expansion in the scale of publishing and reading. Goodrich and Buckingham could remember when things were very different. In their respective autobiographies, both published in the 1850s, the two recalled what life was like in the country towns of late eighteenth-century Connecticut. The contrast between then and now was sharp, for in

Written in the aftermath of the conference "Printing and Society in Early America" held at the American Antiquarian Society in October 1980 and published as the introduction to the volume of conference papers: *Printing and Society in Early America*, ed. William L. Joyce, David D. Hall, Richard D. Brown, and John Hench (Worcester, Mass., 1983), 1–47. As reprinted here, references to other papers in the volume have been transferred to the footnotes.

1. Samuel Goodrich, *Recollections of a Lifetime*, 2 vols. (New York, 1857), 2:284.

olden times books were not abundant. Windham farmers owned a mere handful of books: "The Bible and Dr. Watts's Psalms and Hymns were indispensable in every family, and ours was not without them. There were, also, on the 'book shelf,' a volume or two of Sermons, Doddridge's 'Rise and Progress of Religion,' and a very few other books and pamphlets, chiefly of a religious character."

Newspapers were almost as scarce. Buckingham supposed that in the early 1790s, "there were not more than five or six" being published in the entire state. When a printer came to Windham in 1793 and began to publish a weekly paper, the event marked "a memorable epoch in our village history." The sensations Buckingham felt when he bought his first book, a copy of the *New England Primer,* were equally memorable: "no speculator who makes his thousands by a dash of the pen ever felt richer than I did with my purchase."[2]

From scarcity to abundance, from one world of print to another, this was the journey Buckingham and Goodrich would make in the course of their lives. It was a journey most Americans and Europeans were making in the decades between the 1770s and the 1850s, for on both sides of the Atlantic a major transformation of print culture was occurring. Several factors coalesced to bring about this transformation: new printing and paper-making technologies that reduced the price of books, improvements in how books were marketed, a rapid increase in the rate of literacy, and a general speeding up of communication. With abundance came the introduction of new literary genres, like the children's stories Goodrich wrote, and a new relationship between writers and their audience. It may be too extreme to say that print was "democratized." Yet the mass marketing of "Peter Parley" indicates that the age of abundance stood in sharp contrast to the age of scarcity.[3]

Goodrich and Buckingham started out in this older system, and because they experienced its transformation, the contrast between old and new became the major theme of their autobiographies. Goodrich

2. Joseph T. Buckingham, *Personal Memoirs and Recollections of Editorial Life,* 2 vols. (Boston, 1852), 1:15–16, 21, 8.

3. Richard Altick, *The English Common Reader: A Social History of the Mass Reading Public, 1800–1900* (Chicago, 1963), 5. The history of publishing is plagued by mutually inconsistent assertions as to when the transition to a "democratic" system occurred. The root of the problem may be that historians have brought different assumptions to bear upon the issue. It is not obvious that a "mass" reading public is also a "democratic" one.

and Buckingham carry us back into a veritable "world we have lost." In helping us to recover this past, Goodrich and Buckingham provide another service that is of even more importance. Because of their life histories, both men were sensitive to the meaning of the book as a cultural artifact. Enriched by their personal experiences of change, the two were instinctively able to discern some of the connections that run between "the book and society."

These connections are also the concern of the historians and bibliographers who wrote the essays gathered in *Printing and Society in Early America.* Like Buckingham and Goodrich, these historians regard print as a cultural artifact. Like them, they want to tell a story that moves back and forth between this artifact and its broader context. In some of these essays, the context is intellectual and religious history. In others, it is the economics of the marketplace or the system of authority that infused certain books with extraordinary meaning. And in some essays, the context is one of changing patterns of patronage, taste, and cultural organization. In method these essays are equally diverse. Yet there is common ground among them all in two respects: they share the ambition to achieve a new social history of the book, and they owe this ambition to historians of early modern Europe who have made "livre et société" so powerful and compelling a field of study.

In staying this I do not mean to scant the American scholarship on which these essays depend, the achievements of bibliographers and historians during the century and three-quarters since Isaiah Thomas wrote his *History of Printing in America.*[4] Fifty years ago, Samuel Eliot Morison and Perry Miller were making splendid use of probate inventories and book trade records in describing the mental world of the New England colonists.[5] Most of what we know about the economics of the book trade stems from the scholarship of Rollo Silver, William Miller, and the authors of *The Book in America* (1939). In the work of literary historians such as William Charvat lie clues as to how the traditional relationships among authors, publishers, and readers were radically altered in the middle of the nineteenth century.[6]

4. Isaiah Thomas, *The History of Printing in America* (Worcester, Mass., 1810).

5. Samuel Eliot Morison, *The Puritan Pronaos: Studies in the Intellectual Life of New England in the Seventeenth Century* (New York, 1936), chaps. 5 and 6; Perry Miller, *The New England Mind: The Seventeenth Century* (Cambridge, Mass., 1954), 510, 515.

6. Rollo G. Silver, *The American Printer, 1787–1825* (Charlottesville, VA., 1967); G. William Miller, *Benjamin Franklin's Philadelphia Printing 1728–1766* (Philadelphia, 1974); Hellmut

With this work as an intellectual foundation, the 1960s and 1970s were crucial decades in bringing new energies to the history of the book. Those energies originated overseas. They are evident in the two volumes of essays published in 1965 and 1970 under the title *Livre et Société*, in the refounding of the *Revue Française d'histoire du livre* in 1971, and in the rise to fame of the "bibliothèque bleue." The rediscovery of the "bibliothèque bleue" by Robert Mandrou and Geneviève Bollème was especially significant, for it seemed to demonstrate how social history could be integrated with the history of the book.[7] That process of integration was greatly forwarded by Natalie Davis in her essay "Printing and the People" (1975),[8] and by Robert Darnton in a series of contributions culminating in *The Business of Enlightenment* (1979).[9] As the 1970s ended, "livre et société" seemed to come of age.[10]

The essays in *Printing and Society* are hybrids, therefore, owing much to native traditions, but owing even more to the vigor and excitement of a field of study that arose among historians of early modern Europe. Like all hybrids, these essays are selective in how they represent their parents. Some of the methods and assumptions of the European literature fail to reappear. Why is it that no essay deals with the cheapest, most "popular" forms of print in America, or that none em-

Lehmann-Haupt, Ruth Shepard Granniss, and Lawrence Wroth, *The Book in America: A History of the Making, the Selling, and the Collecting of Books in the United States* (New York, 1939); William Charvat, *The Profession of Authorship in America, 1800–1870,* ed. Matthew J. Bruccoli (Columbus, Ohio, 1968). *The Book in America* was first published in Leipzig in 1937 under the title *Das Amerikanische Buchwesen;* a second edition appeared in New York in 1951 with the collaboration of Lehmann-Haupt, Lawrence Wroth, and Rollo G. Silver.

　　7. François Furet et al., eds., *Livre et société dans la France du xviiie siècle,* 2 vols. (Paris, 1965, 1970); Robert Mandrou, *De la culture populaire aux xviie et xviiie siècles: La Bibliothèque bleue de Troyes* (Paris, 1964); Geneviève Bollème, *La Bibliothèque bleue: Littérature populaire en France du xvie au xixe siècles* (Paris, 1971).

　　8. Natalie Zemon Davis, "Printing and the People," in *Society and Culture in Early Modern France* (Stanford, Calif., 1975).

　　9. Robert Darnton, "The High Enlightenment and the Low-Life of Literature in Pre-Revolutionary France," *Past and Present,* no. 51 (May 1971): 81–115; "Trade in the Taboo: The Life of a Clandestine Book Dealer in Prerevolutionary France," in *The Widening Circle: Essays on the Circulation of Literature in Eighteenth-Century Europe,* ed. Paul J. Korshin (Philadelphia, 1976), 11–83; *The Business of Enlightenment: A Publishing History of the "Encyclopédie," 1775–1800* (Cambridge, Mass., 1979); "What Is the History of Books?" *Daedalus* 111 (1982): 65–83, reprint. Darnton, *The Kiss of Lamourette: Reflections in Cultural History* (New York, 1990), 107–35.

　　10. Raymond Birn, "Livre et Société after Ten Years: Formation of a Discipline," *Studies on Voltaire and the Eighteenth Century* 154 (1976): 287–312; G. Thomas Tanselle, "From Bibliography to Histoire Totale: The History of Books as a Field of Study," *Times Literary Supplement,* June 5, 1981, 647–49; John Feather, "Cross Channel Currents: Historical Bibliography and l'Histoire du Livre," *The Library,* 6th ser., 2 (1980): 1–15. Mention should also be made of Lucien Febvre and Henri-Jean Martin, *The Coming of the Book: The Impact of Printing 1450–1800,* trans. David Gerard (1958: London, 1976).

ploys the quantitative, *histoire sérielle* approach so favored by the authors of *Livre et Société?* Generally speaking, these essays are silent on the topic of literacy, as though it were not the problem in America that it is in early modern Europe.[11] But the resemblances are also strong. Historians on both sides of the Atlantic are contending with the same problems: whether "oral" culture was different from and in conflict with the world of print; the relationship between "culture savante" and "culture populaire"; the role of intermediaries; and how diffusion happened.[12] In several of these papers, as in much of the European literature, the relationship of the book to traditional structures of authority—an established church, a social hierarchy, a political elite—is an important issue. Were books subversive or conserving of these systems? Other papers address what may be the most intractable of such questions, the process of reading and what it was that people actually took from the books that came their way.

As these issues were debated at the conference "Printing and Society in Early America," answers to one or two began to emerge. The most explicit of these answers concerned the changing nature of print culture in the century between 1750 and 1850. Several of the papers throw more light on the world that Buckingham and Goodrich recall so richly in their autobiographies. In others, the transformation from old to new was sharply visible from another vantage point, be it the reordering of cultural authority via the lecture system of the 1840s or the emergence of "genteel" songbooks in the 1790s.[13] On the issue of oral culture and the world of print, these papers reflect a rough consensus that these modes were less in conflict than some historians have argued. In this regard, there was a restlessness at the conference with analytical categories that seemed too rigid or that did not bear upon American circumstances. A decade ago, Robert Darnton brought home to historians of

11. François Furet and Jacques Ozouf, eds., *Lire et écrire: l'alphabétisation des français de Calvin à Jules Ferry*, 2 vols. (Paris, 1977); David Cressy, *Literacy and the Social Order: Reading and Writing in Tudor and Stuart England* (Cambridge, 1980).

12. Georges Duby, "The Diffusion of Cultural Patterns in Feudal Society," *Past and Present*, no. 39 (April 1968): 3–10; Henri-Jean Martin, "Culture écrite et culture orale, culture savante et culture populaire dans la France d'Ancien Régime," *Journal des Savants* (July–Sept. 1975; Oct.–Dec. 1975): 225–82.

13. Donald M. Scott, "Print and the Public Lecture System, 1840–1860," in Joyce et al., *Printing and Society in Early America*, 278–99; Richard Crawford and D. W. Krummel, "Early American Music Printing and Publishing," ibid., 186–227.

"livre et société" the limitations of forcing all books of a given period into categories like "religious" or "historical," as though any world view were actually composed of such airtight little units.[14] Do concepts such as oral culture have similar limitations that outweigh their usefulness?

One way of reflecting on such questions is to return to Buckingham, Goodrich, and the uses of literacy in early New England. I want to develop more fully the framework they present. I also want to review the literature on "livre et société," looking again at the major problems in the European historiography and how they bear on the history of the book in America. My purpose is finally to suggest some ways of connecting books and readers. It is the uses of literacy that concern me, the modes of using print that seem predominant in the first two centuries of New England life. To inquire into the uses of literacy is not to ask about the distribution of literacy as a skill, but to explore how reading functioned as a cultural style.[15] In reconstructing that style, we may come closer to a history of the book that is also social history.

∾ I ∾

Of all the kinds of information that bear upon the history of the book, none is more important than descriptive bibliography. As Robert Winans points out in an essay on book trade catalogues and the importation of fiction, bibliography is essential to an understanding of the book trade. His is a precise example of the general thesis, that assertions about reading patterns and their cultural implications must rest on an adequate foundation of bibliography.[16] Given this imperative, historians of the book in early America can regard themselves as extremely fortunate. In Charles Evans's *American Bibliography* and its supplements, they possess a listing of books and other printed matter that grows steadily more complete and accurate. Within the shelter of this great edifice, there have grown up dozens of more specialized

14. Robert Darnton, "Reading, Writing, and Publishing in Eighteenth-Century France: A Case Study in the Sociology of Literature," *Daedalus* 100 (1971): 214–56.
15. I have borrowed the phrase and this meaning for it from Richard Hoggart, *The Uses of Literacy* (London, 1957).
16. Robert B. Winans, "The Growth of a Novel-Reading Public in Late Eighteenth-Century America," *Early American Literature* 9 (1975): 267–75; Winans, "Bibliography and the Cultural Historian: Notes on the Eighteenth-Century Novel," in Joyce et al., *Printing and Society*, 174–85.

bibliographies—listings for colonies, states, and towns, of Bibles, primers, songsters, and children's books, of individual printers and their
shops, to cite but a few.[17] The North American Imprints Program,
underway at the American Antiquarian Society, has produced a thorough revision, in computerized form, of the canon of early American
bibliography begun by Evans and continued by Roger Bristol.

All of these listings invite the curiosity of the historian who wants to
explore themes and problems in the development of American culture.
Merely to glance through Hills's *The English Bible in America* is to
realize that the American book trade in the early nineteenth century
was extraordinarily decentralized; for example, one or more editions of
the Bible or New Testament were printed at twenty-four separate
locations in Massachusetts. In the same source we can trace the rapid
contraction of this network after 1850, until the business of printing
Bibles shrank to only Boston and Cambridge. The mere fact that
Bibles in English were not printed in America until the Revolution
underscores another aspect of the book trade, its provincial relationship to England. Most of the books that Americans bought and read
throughout the early period were imported from London.[18]

Given this provincial dependence, the history of the book in early
America must be understood as part of a larger story. Whether the
setting is eighteenth-century France, seventeenth-century England, or
colonial New England, that story unfolds as a dialectic between certain
fixed, intractable circumstances on the one hand, and flexible, inge-

17. For example: Hazel A. Johnson, *A Checklist of New London, Connecticut, Imprints, 1709–
1800* (Charlottesville, Va., 1978); Marcus A. McCorison, *Vermont Imprints 1778–1820* (Worcester,
Mass., 1963); Charles F. Heartman, *The New-England Primer Issued Prior to 1830* (New York,
1934); Irving Lowens, *A Bibliography of Songsters Printed in America before 1821* (Worcester, Mass.,
1976); d'Alté A. Welch, *A Bibliography of American Children's Books Printed Prior to 1821* (Worcester and Barre, Mass., 1972); Charles L. Nichols, *Isaiah Thomas, Printer, Writer & Collector* (Boston, 1912). In general, see G. Thomas Tanselle, *Guide to the Study of United States Imprints*, 2 vols.
(Cambridge, Mass., 1971).

18. Margaret T. Hills, ed., *The English Bible in America* (New York, 1961). The privilege of
publishing the Bible in English was a legal monopoly of the king's printers in the British empire.
Note in 1996: the "most" in this sentence misstates the situation. The majority of *copies* of books
that were available were printed locally; the majority of *titles*—of which, typically, but a very small
number per title were imported—may have come from overseas. For this correction I am indebted
to the studies of booksellers in Elizabeth C. Reilly, "Common and Learned Readers: Shared and
Separate Spheres in Mid-Eighteenth-Century New England" (Ph.D. diss., Boston University,
1994), and Hugh Amory, "Under the Exchange: The Unprofitable Business of Michael Perry, a
Seventeenth-Century Boston Bookseller," *Proceedings of the American Antiquarian Society*, n.s.,
103 (1993): 31–60, esp. 35.

nious strategies on the other. The essential constraint was a chronic lack of capital in the industry. This shortage of capital was in part a function of printing practices, and in part of limited sales for most types of publications. The pace of book production fluctuated from week to week, a factor that master printers had to reckon with in pricing their services. Robert Darnton's reconstruction of printing office practices confirms the picture of a fluctuating rhythm of production.[19] Entrepreneurs in the book trade, like Darnton's Parisians who were out to market the *Encyclopédie,* were always on the hustle seeking to finance press runs larger than the normal size. Printing houses could not afford to tie up capital in paper, the most expensive of the ingredients in bookmaking. In any case, the market could not ordinarily absorb large quantities of most forms of print. Books cost too much to be items of frequent purchase by any but professionals and the affluent.[20]

Hence the search for ways around these limitations. For some book sellers, the answer lay in patronage, though this had ceased to be significant by 1640.[21] For others, and especially in the eighteenth century, the ways to finance a book and to build an audience for it included publishing in parts and advertising for subscriptions. Publishing by subscription was how Daniel Henchman and Benjamin Eliot dared to print Samuel Willard's *The Compleat Body of Divinity* in 1726, the first book in folio to be published in New England.[22] Another way of saving

19. Donald McKenzie, "Printers of the Mind: Some Notes on Bibliographical Theories and Printing-House Practices," *Studies in Bibliography* 22 (1969): 1–75; Darnton, *The Business of Enlightenment,* chap. 5.

20. On price, see McKenzie, "Printers of the Mind"; F. R. Johnson, "Notes on English Retail Book-Prices, 1550–1640," *The Library,* 5th ser., 5 (1950): 83–112; Edwin H. Miller, *The Professional Writer in Elizabethan England* (Cambridge, Mass., 1959), 41; Altick, *The English Common Reader,* 21–23, 51–53; and the references and information in Stephen Botein, "The Anglo-American Book Trade before 1776: Personnel and Strategies," in Joyce et al., *Printing and Society,* 48–82; Cynthia Z. and Gregory A. Stiverson, "The Colonial Retail Book Trade: Availability and Affordability of Reading Material in Mid-Eighteenth-Century Virginia," ibid., 132–73. On the size of editions, see H. S. Bennett, *English Books and Readers, 1475 to 1557* (London, 1952), 228, and the relevant sections of succeeding volumes in this series: *English Books and Readers, 1558 to 1603* (Cambridge, 1965) and *English Books and Readers, 1603 to 1650* (Cambridge, 1970).

21. Bennett, *English Books and Readers, 1558 to 1603,* chap. 2; Miller, *The Professional Writer,* 129.

22. My statement in 1983 that "no comprehensive study of publishing by subscription in early America has been undertaken, to the best of my knowledge," should be altered to take account of Donald Farren, "Subscription: A Study of the Eighteenth-Century American Book Trade" (D.L.S., Columbia University, 1982). Individual lists of subscribers invite analysis as evidence of readership and diffusion patterns. See the references in note 29, below, and Samuel G. Drake, *Some Memoirs of the Life and Writings of the Rev. Thomas Prince* (Boston, 1851), for the interesting subscribers' list to Prince's *Chronological History of New England* (1728). The format of folio had been used before Willard's *Compleat Body* for collections of statute laws.

money was to not pay the author. The usual practice was for authors to receive their "pay" in copies, the rule of thumb being 10 percent of an edition. Among themselves, moreover, booksellers made exchanges on the basis not of cash but of copies. If someone wished to carry the books of a competitor in his store, the way of doing so was to swap one set of books for another. The undercapitalization of the *American* book trade is also evident in Robert Winans's discovery that American printers chose to republish only that British fiction which was short. The two or three volumes of a *Pamela*, or even the complete text of a *Robinson Crusoe*, were usually beyond their resources.[23]

In the nineteenth century the book trade became transformed in its capital structure. For Americans and the French, the change came after 1830.[24] Change was already well underway in Britain, where the structure of the book trade was shifting after 1780 "from a series of independent but cooperative bookselling firms into a group of large corporate enterprises. . . . The extent of this transformation is indicated by the number of booksellers that went out of business during these years [1780 to 1820]."[25] The golden age of local publishing in America came between 1800 and 1840, when almost anyone could set up shop. Alexis de Tocqueville's astonishment at the quantity of newspapers Americans could absorb—the highest per capita in the world—was related to the ease with which an Anthony Haswell and a William Lloyd Garrison could publish.[26] Carey, Lea in Philadelphia and the Harpers in New York were of a different order of magnitude, and their emergence by the 1830s signaled a process of consolidation. This process, with all of the advantages accruing to publishers who seized a metropolitan location, was essentially complete by the Civil War, when the village printer-bookseller was rapidly becoming a figure of the past.[27] Gone were the days when the many each produced a few for a limited audience; now a few produced great quantities for an audience that numbered in the millions.

23. Winans, "Growth of a Novel-Reading Public."
24. Roger Chartier, "L'ancien régime typographique: reflexions sur quelques travaux recents," *Annales E.S.C.* 36 (1981): 191–209, esp. 201ff.
25. Leslie Chard, "Bookseller to Publisher: Joseph Johnson and the English Book Trade, 1760 to 1810," *The Library*, 5th ser., 32 (1977): 138, 150.
26. Alexis de Tocqueville, *Democracy in America*, ed. Phillips Bradley, 2 vols. (New York, 1954), 1:193.
27. The story may be followed in Milton W. Hamilton, *The Country Printer: New York State, 1785–1830* (New York, 1936).

This analysis of the book trade depends on the work of bibliographers. They have less to say, however, about the interaction between books and readers. Here, alas, the evidence for saying *anything* is much more elusive and fragmentary. Every source has its limitations. Probate inventories are incomplete—characteristically they lump most books together in a single category, or do not mention them at all—and offer no means of distinguishing between books that were merely owned and books that mattered.[28] Bibliographers can tell us that certain books went through many editions, but not the reasons for this popularity. Subscription lists can serve to link books and readers,[29] as do the records of circulating libraries.[30] Among French historians of the book, a common method is to assign the books in inventories or a national bibliography to certain categories—"religious," "historical," and the like—and to argue that changes over time in the relative size of these categories inform us of shifting preferences among their readers. But as Darnton has pointed out, this method has its limitations.[31]

How then do we proceed with a history of the book that extends to culture and society? Any such history must confront certain fundamental problems. Two of these are illiteracy and the role of oral culture. In early modern Europe, the relationship between books and readers was powerfully affected by illiteracy. The half or two-thirds of the population that could not read were presumably excluded from the book trade. In this context, it is easy to overstate the impact of the book. But it is just as easy to swing to the other extreme of denying that print ever penetrated the oral culture of the peasantry. If the impact of printing

28. The absence of books in so many inventories is open to conflicting interpretation. Margaret Spufford argues that certain books had so little value that no one bothered listing them; Peter Clark argues against ownership at all. Margaret Spufford, *Small Books and Pleasant Histories: Popular Fiction and Its Readership in Seventeenth-Century England* (Athens, Ga., 1982), 48; Peter Clark, "The Ownership of Books in England, 1560–1640: The Example of Some Kentish Town Folk," in *Schooling and Society*, ed. Lawrence Stone (Baltimore, 1976), 95–111. Spufford and Clark agree that chapbooks and their ilk were easily destroyed and thus are not likely to turn up in inventories.

29. Sarah L. C. Clapp, "The Beginnings of Subscription Publication in the Seventeenth Century," *Modern Philology* 29 (1931–32): 199–224. See also Peter J. Wallis and Francis J. G. Robinson, "The Potential Uses of Book Subscription Lists," in *The Art of the Librarian*, ed. A. Jeffreys (Newcastle, England, 1973); F.J.G. Robinson and P. J. Wallis, *Book Subscription Lists: A Revised Guide* (Newcastle, England, 1975).

30. Paul Kaufman, "The Eighteenth-Century Forerunner of the London Library," *Papers of the Bibliographical Society of America* 53–54 (1955–56): 89–100, reprinted with many other studies in Kaufman, *Libraries and Their Users* (London, 1969).

31. See the essays in Furet et al., *Livre et société*, vol. 1; and Darnton, "Reading, Writing, and Publishing."

must not be overstated, so too the role of oral culture must yield to a common-sense recognition of its limits.[32] One of the weaknesses of the concept is its holistic implications, as though the mental world of the peasantry were thoroughly self-contained. It is also weakened by the evident fact that Europe had been a literate culture for a millennium. David Buchan has proposed a useful distinction between "oral," referring to "the tradition of non-literate societies," and "verbal," referring to "the word of mouth tradition of a literate culture."[33] Early modern Europe would seem to fall into the second of these categories, where oral knowledge is always touched by print. The situation in early modern Europe was one in which apparent barriers were constantly breached by intermediaries—the peddlers with their *littérature du colportage,* the village curés who knew a little Latin, the fathers who read aloud in households.[34]

Certain forms of print most certainly were intermediaries. Geneviève Bollème has suggested that French almanacs of the sixteenth and seventeenth centuries were available to the illiterate because they were composed in a system of "signs" meaningful to everyone.[35] The "bibliothèque bleue," the classic *littérature du colportage,* was another intermediary. This literature was the dust bin of Western culture, its myths and commonplaces reduced to almost incoherent rubbish. But when French peasants came in touch with this debris, something stuck. Like it or not, they were in contact with the culture of the learned. Altogether, there seems reason to believe that the distance between print and oral culture has been overemphasized.

Leaving these categories aside for the moment, we can turn in their absence to intellectual history as a means of connecting books and readers. Each of the great movements of thought that swept across Europe and America in the sixteenth and seventeenth centuries became embodied in print. Historians of the book have done notable work in describing the diffusion of these movements. To cite an Amer-

---

32. Elizabeth Eisenstein, *The Printing Press as an Agent of Change,* 2 vols. (Cambridge, 1979), 130; Cressy, *Literacy and the Social Order,* 14; Ian Watt, *The Rise of the Novel* (Berkeley and Los Angeles, 1957), 196; François Furet and Jacques Ozouf, "Trois siècles de métissage culturel," *Annales E. S. C.* 32 (1977): 488–502.

33. David Buchan, *The Ballad and the Folk* (London, 1972), 1–2.

34. Peter Burke, *Popular Culture in Early Modern Europe* (New York, 1978), chap. 4 and p. 257.

35. Geneviève Bollème, *Les Almanachs populaires aux xviie et xviiie siècles* (Paris, 1969), 7–15.

ican example, we know that Princeton undergraduates in the 1770s drew on the classics for the pseudonyms which were used in the rituals of debate. As reconstructed by James McLachlan, this little world of books and readers becomes a microcosm of the impact and penetration of the Whig mentality that was so crucial for Americans in the Revolutionary period.[36] In another American example, Elizabeth Reilly suggests that the business of the Boston bookseller Jeremiah Condy may have flourished because of intellectual affinities between him and his customers. Condy and his customers were more advanced in their thinking than the majority of colonists.[37] It may well be that in the specific circumstances of learned cultures, we can more readily connect books and their readers.

Most historians prefer to work with books that are popular. The scholarship on popular literature has often remained at a very general level.[38] More recently, historians have been focusing on particular genres or types of literature: the almanac or chapbook, or products like the "bibliothèque bleue de Troyes," the little paperbound books that were churned out on a veritable assembly line and peddled across the countryside. Seventeenth- and eighteenth-century printers could produce astonishing quantities of single-sheet books. In a good year, the London publishers of almanacs in the latter decades of the seventeenth century turned out 400,000 copies, and perhaps as many ballads. Meanwhile the partnerships devoted to the publishing of chapbooks were printing these inexpensive items at a rapid pace.[39]

In a study of English chapbooks, Margaret Spufford demonstrates

36. James McLachlan, "Classical Names, American Identities: Some Notes on College Students and Classical Tradition in the 1770s," in *Classical Traditions in Early America*, ed. John W. Eadie (Ann Arbor, Mich., 1976), 81–98. See also David Lundberg and Henry F. May, "The Enlightened Reader in America," *American Quarterly* 28 (1976):262–93.

37. Elizabeth Reilly, "The Wages of Piety: The Boston Book Trade of Jeremy Condy," in Joyce et al., *Printing and Society*, 83–131.

38. James D. Hart, *The Popular Book: A History of America's Literary Taste* (New York, 1950); Frank Luther Mott, *Golden Multitudes* (New York, 1947); Russel B. Nye, *The Unembarrassed Muse: The Popular Arts in America* (New York, 1970).

39. Cyprian Blagdon, "The Distribution of Almanacks in the Second Half of the Seventeenth Century," *Studies in Bibliography* 11 (1958): 107–16; Blagdon, "Notes on the Ballad Market in the Second Half of the Seventeenth Century," ibid. 6 (1954):161–80; Spufford, *Small Books and Pleasant Histories*, chap. 4. For earlier decades, Tessa Watt, *Cheap Print and Popular Piety, 1550–1640* (Cambridge, 1991), is a remarkable demonstration of how much of the archive of cheap print can be recovered. An informal general history is Leslie Shepard, *The History of Street Literature* (Newton Abbot, England, 1973). See also Victor E. Neuburg, *The Popular Press Companion to Popular Literature* (Bowling Green, Ohio, 1983).

that they were printed in remarkable quantities—at his death, one publisher had enough copies in his warehouse to supply one out of every fifteen families in England—and that the methods of distribution were surprisingly efficient. She moves to a thematic analysis of the chapbooks, and especially those on religious subjects, on the assumption that books which were so widely bought and read inform us of beliefs among the general population. In support of this argument, she has collected stories of people's reading and book ownership—as of the two books that John Bunyan's wife included in her dowry—that bespeak the significance of easily available books. Here as with Bollème and Mandrou, we sense that we are on the verge of uncovering the mental categories of a world view that would otherwise lie largely hidden from our sight.[40]

The question can still be asked of chapbooks, almanacs, and their kin: is this a literature "of" or "for" the people? By the end of the seventeenth century, a recognizable group of writers and booksellers in Britain were earning their livelihoods producing books and ballads for the people. John Shirley cranked out bastardized versions of traditional stories at the rate of two or three a year.[41] Richard Sault invented the story of *The Second Spira*, which tells of an atheist who suffered the most extraordinary pangs of conscience as he was dying.[42] Professional writers were delighted to feed a public taste for sensationalism by providing "one-signature tracts on earthquakes, macabre events, or some new freak with two heads recently born in a remote shire of England."[43] Reports of apparitions and wonders, as of the Devil appearing in the guise of a bear or wheat pouring from the sky, were nearly always fictional.[44]

This is certainly a literature *for* the people, but in what sense is it *of* them? The answer to this question may be as simple as observing that

40. Spufford, *Small Books and Pleasant Histories;* John Bunyan, *Grace Abounding to the Chief of Sinners,* ed. Roger Sharrock (Oxford, 1962), 8. The two books were *The Plain Mans Pathway to Heaven* and *The Practice of Piety.*
41. Barbara L. Magaw, "The Work of John Shirley, an Early Hack Writer," *Papers of the Bibliographical Society of America* 56 (1962):332–45.
42. [Richard Sault], *The Second Spira,* 6th ed. (Boston, 1715, from the 1692 London ed.). See note 96, below.
43. Miller, *The Professional Writer,* 54–55.
44. Hyder E. Rollins, ed., *The Pack of Autolycus: or, Strange and Terrible News of Ghosts, Apparitions, Monstrous Births, Showers of Wheat* (Cambridge, Mass., 1927), 36, 40, 219. For a fuller consideration of the inventiveness of the writers and booksellers of this literature of "wonders," see David D. Hall, *Worlds of Wonder, Days of Judgment: Popular Religious Belief in Early New England* (New York, 1989), chap. 2.

the "people" had nowhere else to go for reading matter than to the London market. Willy-nilly, the mentality of artisans and husbandmen was shaped by the booksellers who assembled the ballads, broadsides, almanacs, and chapbooks that sold so widely. The booksellers' social identity was ambiguous, and the cultural message of their products fluctuated within a wide range. A good many chapbooks were mildly pornographic.[45] This circumstance, together with the persistence of sensationalism as a motif of street literature, suggests that the producers of these items were attuned to the reading tastes of the barely literate.[46] Yet the chapbook editions of Richard Baxter's *Call to the Unconverted* also seem to indicate that some printers were intermediaries between evangelicalism and the culture we want to call popular.[47]

Those who served as go-betweens in the making of popular books must have been conscious of not one, but several reading publics for their wares. Historians of the book could profit from thinking along these lines themselves. As it is, the category "popular" is stretched this way and that to fit quite different groups. Many of the books that John Sommerville describes as "popular" religious reading in Restoration England were written by ordained ministers, most of whom were Anglicans.[48] In seventeenth-century Britain the readers of this devotional literature—undoubtedly quite numerous—were probably different from the readers of ballads and the more traditional chapbooks. The distance between these groups could be large, as the following account of "peasant" reading in early eighteenth-century England may suggest: "The peasant father of the poet John Clare, though barely able to read, doted on such penny treasures as Nixon's Prophesies, Mother Bunches Fairy Tales, and Mother Shipton's Legacy, and late in the century Clare himself learned to read from chapbooks like Cinderella, Little Red Riding Hood, and Jack and the Beanstalk."[49]

A literary historian has divided seventeenth-century fiction and its

45. Roger Thompson, ed., *Pepys' Penny Merriments* (London, 1976); Thompson, "Popular Reading and Humour in Restoration England," *Journal of Popular Culture* 9 (1975): 653–71.

46. Margaret Spufford argues, and I feel convincingly, that all social groups or classes in seventeenth-century England relished "bawdy" humor. The same point has been made in studies of Shakespeare's "bawdy." Spufford, *Small Books and Pleasant Histories*, chap. 7. On sensationalism, see Martha Vicinus, *The Industrial Muse: A Study of Nineteenth Century British Working-Class Literature* (New York, 1974), chap. 1.

47. Spufford, *Small Books and Pleasant Histories*, chap. 8.

48. C. John Sommerville, *Popular Religion in Restoration England*. University of Florida Social Science Monographs, No. 59 (Gainesville, Fla., 1977).

49. Altick, *The English Common Reader*, 38.

readers into two categories. In one of these, the books were "sturdily old-fashioned, presenting both in appearance and content antiquated, indeed anachronistically retarded, tastes . . . [they] continue [their] popularity right through the century with no regard for fashion in literary style or material; [their] appeal is exotic, dealing as [they do] in wondrous feats of arms, strange locales and descriptions of lushly opulent displays, and enchantments, prophecies and spells." The other type consisted of the "fashionable" literature of the day: the "secret histories" translated from the French, the duodecimos of "exotic amorous adventures."[50] Presumably the first of these categories was relegated to readers lower down in the social scale while the other was consumed by a metropolitan audience that had more advanced tastes and consciousness.

In late seventeenth- and early eighteenth-century Wales, an evangelical literature of devotion was widely read and much republished. Many of the classics of the Puritan tradition—*Pilgrim's Progress,* Baxter's *Call,* Joseph Alleine's *Alarm*—were translated into Welsh and went through innumerable editions. But, as in the case of other genres, literacy, education, and wealth were factors that intervened to shape the distribution of these books: "Of those below the level of the gentry, only professional men, substantial farmers, merchants and tradesmen, skilled artisans and craftsmen were consistently able to afford elementary education for their children. Subscription lists and probate material confirm that these were the groups that bought books, created a demand for more books, and set a high premium on literacy." In Wales as elsewhere, the popular literature of devotion circulated in specific milieus.[51]

These bits and pieces of description point toward two or three broad groupings within the general rubric of the popular book: readers of devotional literature, whether Anglican or evangelical; readers of "fashionable" books, especially fiction; and readers of traditional prophecies, fairy tales, and romances. I do not mean to insist on these groups. In real life they must have overlapped, and certain books must have circu-

50. Charles C. Mish, "Best Sellers in Seventeenth-Century Fiction," *Papers of the Bibliographical Society of America* 47 (1953): 356–73, esp. 370–72.
51. Geraint H. Jenkins, *Literature, Religion and Society in Wales, 1660–1730* (Cardiff, Wales, 1978), 300 and chap. 10.

lated among them all. But distinctions of this kind are in order lest we stretch the term "popular" to cover every kind of circumstance.[52] Certainly the seventeenth-century reader was aware of distinctions. The learned and the fashionable mocked the tastes of the "vulgar." Moralists decried "bad" books, enjoining readers young and old to restrict themselves to books that qualified as "good." "When thou canst read," Thomas White cautioned in 1702, "read no Ballads and foolish Books, but the Bible." In a chapbook of the same period, the author warned, "Let not your Children read these vain Books, profane Ballads, and filthy songs. Throw away all fond and amorous Romances, and fabulous Histories of Giants, the bombast Achievements of Knight Errantry, and the like; for these fill the Heads of Children with vain, silly and idle imaginations."[53] Here the anger seems to focus especially on the motifs and forms of print—ballads, chapbooks, and broadsides—favored by or most accessible to readers in the lowest social groups, like John Clare and his father.

Anger means conflict. If the history of the book and the history of society are ever to converge, the most fruitful bond between them may be their common interest in the conflicts that reverberate through early modern history. Print may have worked in several different ways in regard to conflict. It could have served as an agent of control, extending and enhancing the legitimacy of an established, hierarchical system. But in a fluid, multilayered marketplace, the book could also have been a means of asserting cultural independence. In certain situations the book became the vehicle of far-reaching dissent.

Protestantism provides the perfect example of this latter process in sixteenth- and seventeenth-century Europe. Protestantism owed its rapid growth to the book. Martin Luther turned at once to the vernacular as a means of spreading his new faith. By 1523 he had mated the Protestant critique of Rome to the chapbook genre of remarkable prodigies and portents.[54] In England, Margaret Spufford has docu-

52. Robert Mandrou, "Cultures Populaires et Savante: Rapports et Contacts," in *The Wolf and the Lamb: Popular Culture in France, from the Old Regime to the Twentieth Century*, ed. Jacques Beauroy, Marc Bertrand, and Edward T. Gargan (Saratoga, Calif., 1977), 17–38, urges that we speak in terms of several "cultures populaires."
53. Thomas White, *A Little Book for Little Children* (Boston, 1702), 19; Victor Neuburg, *The Penny Histories: A Study of Chapbooks for Young Readers over Two Centuries* (New York, 1969), 20.
54. Eisenstein, *The Printing Press*, chap. 4; L. H. Buell, "Elizabethan Portents: Superstition or Doctrine," in *Essays Critical and Historical Dedicated to Lily B. Campbell* (Berkeley and Los

mented the importance of vernacular Bibles that drifted into the hands of Cambridgeshire farmers.[55] A church trial of the 1530s turned up striking evidence of how such books—illegal though they were—were welcomed and transmitted. A fifteen-year-old boy caught owning a primer and New Testament described how "divers poor men in the town of Chelmsford . . . bought the new testament of Jesus Christ and on sundays did sit reading [aloud] in lower end of church, and many would flock about them to hear their reading then I came among the said readers to hear them . . . then thought I will learn to read english, and then I will have the new testament and read thereon myself." Such scenes must have been multiplied a thousand times over in early modern Europe, even down to the detail of hiding the illegal book in the "bedstraw."[56] The rise of Protestantism was closely tied to the diffusion of such books, all written in the vernacular and all aimed at lay readers.

So too in seventeenth-century England, evangelical Protestants who had been defeated in their ecclesiastical ambitions turned to the press, creating a devotional literature that was rapidly absorbed by pious householders. As this process unfolded in late seventeenth-century Wales, it involved not only translating into Welsh the classic texts of the evangelical tradition, but also exploiting the popularity of certain vernacular literary genres: "Many Welsh religious reformers . . . realized that the easiest and most natural way of instilling Reformation truths was by casting scripture, private devotion and moral codes into popular verse-form. Among semi-literate folk in particular, verse had the mnemonic advantages of rhythm and rhyme. That is why so many authors chose to turn the catechism, the decalogue, the Lord's Prayer, and even parts of devotional books into verse."[57]

The same process of mating devotional themes with verse and other popular genres was at work in England and New England. Benjamin Harris, a zealous Protestant and a London bookseller who lived briefly in Boston, published and probably wrote a history of the Bible in verse.

Angeles, 1950), 27–41. See also R. W. Scribner, *For the Sake of Simple Folk: Popular Propaganda for the German Reformation* (Cambridge, 1981).

55. Margaret Spufford, *Contrasting Communities: English Villagers in the Sixteenth and Seventeenth Centuries* (Cambridge, 1974), chap. 8 and p. 247. In more recent work, Spufford and her fellow researchers have painstakingly examined aspects of literacy and religious affiliation in local settings. Spufford, ed., *The World of Rural Dissenters: 1520–1725* (Cambridge, 1995).

56. Charles C. Butterfield, *The English Primer, 1529–1545* (Philadelphia, 1953), 202.

57. Jenkins, *Literature, Religion and Society*, esp. 52.

It was also Harris who assembled the *New England Primer*, which blended piety with anti-Catholic propaganda.[58]

Like evangelical Protestantism with its primers, chapbooks, and versified devotion, every social movement had a literary arsenal. The conflict between Royalists and Parliamentarians was mirrored in competing versions of astrological and portent literature of the Civil War period.[59] At Douai on the continent, and at secret presses scattered about England, recusants created a vernacular literature of martyrology and devotion to sustain a beleaguered community of English Catholics.[60] Rhys Isaac has argued that certain books in eighteenth-century Virginia functioned as symbolic tokens of social and ecclesiastical authority.[61] Few, if any, books were neutral in the early modern period. Instead they were caught up in tangled webs of controversy, be it Catholic versus Protestant, evangelical versus standpatter, Royalist versus Parliamentarian; or, at a deeper level yet, the world of "magic" that Keith Thomas has so magisterially described versus the rationalist mentality of the bourgeoisie.[62]

The history of the book thus leads readily to issues that engage the historian of culture and society: the ways in which a social order can maintain itself or be subverted; the distribution of popular belief; the rise of Protestantism or rationality. These issues are common to Europe and America, though the differences are also interesting to consider. The New England colonists, for example, were very largely literate, and because they were two or three generations removed from the coming of a vernacular religious literature, they were comfortably accustomed to a fusion of identity, print, and religion that the Welsh would not experience until the very end of the seventeenth century. It is difficult to believe, moreover, that a full-blown "peasant" culture made its way across the Atlantic, though enough "bad" books did to worry

58. Charles L. Nichols, "The Holy Bible in Verse," *Proceedings of the American Antiquarian Society* 36 (1926):71–82; Worthington C. Ford, "Benjamin Harris, Printer and Bookseller," *Proceedings of the Massachusetts Historical Society* 57 (1924):34–68.

59. The rival astrological predictions of William Lilly and John Gadbury are a case in point; and see Bernard Capp, *English Almanacs 1500–1800* (Ithaca, N.Y., 1979), 47–50, 79, 86.

60. John Bossy, *The English Catholic Community, 1570–1850* (London, 1975), 170–71 and chap. 15.

61. Rhys Isaac, "Books and the Social Authority of Learning: The Case of Mid-Eighteenth-Century Virginia," in Joyce et al., *Printing and Society*, 228–49.

62. Keith Thomas, *Religion and the Decline of Magic* (London, 1971).

the authorities.[63] As in eighteenth-century Virginia, the book in colonial New England was closely tied to certain structures of authority.
We would not expect otherwise in a society that proclaimed itself to be
a single, covenanted whole. But in time there was opposition, and with
opposition came a pluralistic culture of the book.

ɷ 2 ɷ

In *Recollections of a Lifetime*, Goodrich remembered the Ridgefield of
1790 as a self-contained, self-sufficient community. People lived simply,
making their own clothes and raising most of what they ate. Access to
books and printing was limited, for in this as in other modes of material
life the town kept to itself. As if in compensation for the limits on
supply, people read with care the texts that came to hand. The reading
style of olden times was deliberate and reverential.

> The amusements were then much the same as at present—though some
> striking differences may be noted. Books and newspapers—which are
> now diffused even among the country towns, so as to be in the hands of
> all, young and old—were then scarce, and were read respectfully, and as if
> they were grave matters, demanding thought and attention. They were
> not toys and pastimes, taken up every day, and by everybody, in the short
> intervals of labor, and then hastily dismissed, like waste paper. The aged
> sat down when they read, and drew forth their spectacles, and put them
> deliberately and reverently upon the nose. These instruments were not as
> now, little tortoise-shell hooks, attached to a ribbon and put off and on
> with a jerk; but they were of silver or steel substantially made, and calcu-
> lated to hold on with a firm and steady grasp, showing the gravity of the
> uses to which they were devoted. Even the young approached a book
> with reverence, and a newspaper with awe. How the world has changed!

63. No fully adequate study of literacy exists for New England. Kenneth Lockridge has used
the method of signature counts in *Literacy in Colonial New England: An Inquiry into the Social
Context of Literacy in the Early Modern West* (New York, 1974), where he measures the distribution
of the skill of writing. But as Margaret Spufford and others have argued (*Contrasting Communities*, chaps. 7 and 8), many persons, and especially women, could read but not write. This point is
crucial to my description of traditional literacy, below. For an argument that Lockridge's figures
for the eighteenth century should be adjusted upwards, see Ross W. Beales, Jr., "Studying
Literacy at the Community Level: A Research Note," *Journal of Interdisciplinary History* 9 (1978):
93–102; see also the references in "Readers and Reading in America: Historical and Critical
Perspectives," below. When I say that peasant culture did not become transplanted to New
England, I have in mind the ideal type that Robert Muchembled describes in *Culture populaire et
culture des elites dans la France moderne* (Paris, 1978). Many attitudes among the colonists—those
toward property, gender roles, sexuality, and health, for example—were of course rooted in
tradition.

The very gestures that Goodrich describes for us—sitting down to read, or putting glasses on "deliberately"—bespeak a distinctive relationship to print.[64]

Another characteristic of the relationship between books and readers was that people read aloud. Often this happened in the context of religious devotion. "In her devotional exercises," Buckingham recalled, "my mother often introduced passages from Watts and Doddridge. One of them now recurs to me, as having been so often repeated as to become almost a part of her daily devotion." Where he lived as a servant, Buckingham spent every Saturday evening reciting the Westminster Catechism and "such Psalms or Hymns as I might have committed to memory in the course of the week. There was a time when I could recite Watts's version of the Psalms from beginning to end, together with many of his Hymns and Lyric Poems." In that same household it was his duty to read aloud from the Bible.

> For a number of years . . . I read every day, [in the presence of his master and mistress] at least one chapter, and often two or three chapters in the Bible. . . . I have no doubt that I read the Bible through in *course* at least a dozen times before I was sixteen years old, with no other omissions than the jaw-breaking chapters of the Chronicles. The historical parts I had read much oftener, and the incidents and the language became almost as familiar as the grace . . . said before and after meals,—neither of which ever varied a word during . . . nine years.

As for the Goodrich household, every morning after breakfast Samuel, senior, read a chapter. "In our family Bible it is recorded that he thus read that holy book through, in course, thirteen times, in the space of about five and twenty years."[65]

In recalling this practice of reading aloud, Goodrich and Buckingham also alert us to its consequences. People came to know certain texts by heart, sometimes because the religious customs of the day demanded it—Goodrich and Buckingham both had to memorize the Westminster Catechism—but more often through the force of repetition. This was especially true of Scripture, parts of which became the basis of everyday conversation. Looking back upon his own immersion in this text, Goodrich realized that he could not write without invoking

64. Goodrich, *Recollections of a Lifetime*, 1:71–72, 75, 86.
65. Buckingham, *Personal Memoirs*, 1:11, 16, 19; Goodrich, *Recollections of a Lifetime*, 1:157.

in some manner the key motifs and narrative style of the Bible. His imagination was founded on a language he had learned almost unconsciously.[66] Because Buckingham had absorbed this same language from the earliest moments of his life, he was able as a very young child to *read* the Bible, and this without the benefit of any formal instruction. Literacy flowed directly from his household experiences. "I have no recollection of any time when I could not read. . . . In December, 1784, the month in which I was five years old, I went to a master's school, and, on being asked if I could read, I said I could read in the Bible. The master placed me on his chair and presented a Bible opened at the fifth chapter of Acts. I read the story of Ananias and Sapphira falling down dead for telling a lie. He patted me on the head and commended my reading."[67] Goodrich learned to read at school, though for him as for Buckingham organized schooling was intermittent. But in telling us that he learned a little Latin by overhearing the lessons of an older brother and piecing out the words in a battered Corderius, he provides a parallel example of how reading aloud became the route to literacy.[68]

To trace out all the consequences of reading aloud is eventually to arrive back at Goodrich's description of the relationship between books and readers. People approached print with "reverence," he reports, because books were scarce. But the stories that he and Buckingham tell of their experiences with print make it clear that reverence was also a response to the religious context in which reading seems to have begun. The books that figured in devotional practice and that were also the stuff of elementary reading—descriptions of the spiritual life, like Doddridge's *Rise and Progress of Religion in the Soul,* catechisms, psalmbooks, and religious verse—had an aura of the sacred. People returned to such texts many times over, whether in public ceremonies or in reading silently. This repetition of a few books made it easy for children to memorize and eventually to become readers of these texts themselves. All of these factors—the religious context, the scarcity of print, the habit of repetition—were cumulatively involved in the pace and quality of reading as a style. Reading in early New England was an

66. Goodrich, *Recollections of a Lifetime,* 1:157–58.
67. Buckingham, *Personal Memoirs,* 1:8–9.
68. Goodrich, *Recollections of a Lifetime,* 1:152–53.

act that took place slowly and with unusual intensity, in contrast to the faster pace and casualness of mid-nineteenth-century reading.

Let me refer to the older style as "traditional literacy."[69] Traditional literacy prevailed on both sides of the Atlantic in the seventeenth and eighteenth centuries; it is another of the fundamental continuities between European and American history in the early modern period. Generalizing from what I have already noted of its nature, we can identify traditional literacy in terms of four characteristics:

1. People valued learning to read over learning to write; and the first was taught prior to the other as a skill, often in the household or else at "dame schools."

2. Children learned to read by memorizing certain texts, most of which also had a role in church services and devotional practice. Memorizing occurred in situations where reading aloud was practiced, and where children were expected to recite from memory.

3. People came in contact with a limited number of books. Most persons had the use of, or owned, a Bible, psalmbook, primer, and catechism. Almanacs were widely available. Otherwise, the factors of cost and distribution were barriers to extensive reading.

4. Certain books nonetheless circulated widely, and had an extremely long life among the reading public. Such "steady sellers" were staple reading in the culture of traditional literacy.

What Buckingham and Goodrich have to say about this system, and especially about the coherence of its parts, can scarcely be improved upon. Each came to literacy by the road of recitation and reading aloud; each began to read in a context of devotional practice. The books that circulated in their households were true examples of the steady seller— Watts and Doddridge, the *New England Primer*, and most important, the Bible. Other than these books and the almanac, they had little access to print.

All of their description is borne out in other sources. For example,

---

69. What I mean by this term is not quite the same as what François Furet and Jacques Ozouf mean by "restricted literacy," a term they borrow from Jack Goody. See Furet and Ozouf, "Trois siècles de métissage culturel," 491–92. Some historians speak of certain social groups in early modern Europe as "semiliterate." Carlo Ginzburg's portrait of Menocchio is a brilliant reconstruction of a curiously naive style of literacy: *The Cheese and the Worms: The Cosmos of a Sixteenth-Century Miller,* trans. John and Anne Tedeschi (New York, 1982).

Goodrich and Buckingham imply that children learned to read before they learned to write. There is frequent evidence that the two skills were kept separate, with reading ranked first in order of priority. Town records distinguish between "woman schools" that taught reading, and "Masters Schools" where children learned to write. Many children went off to school already knowing how to read. When the Reverend Peter Thatcher took on a new student in 1680, he noted in his journal that "I was to perfect him in reading, and to teach him to write."[70] In his autobiography, Samuel Johnson of Connecticut tells of a typical experience—typical in that he learned to read at home by a process of listening and memorizing: "This Samuel was early taught to read by the care of his grandfather, who was very fond of him, and being apt to learn, he taught him many things by heart, beginning with the Lord's Prayer and Creed, and as he delighted to read the Scriptures, he got many passages of them by heart, which his grandfather, carrying him about with him to visit the ancient people, his contemporaries, made him recite *memoriter,* in which he much delighted." As for learning to write, Johnson indicates that it happened "after" the death of his grandfather.[71]

In this statement Johnson touches on two other aspects of learning to read, the household context and the role of recitation. Most New England autobiographies report that it was the mother who taught reading to her children; and though there are exceptions, it was the father who taught his children to write. "I lived in my Fathers Family 12 years," Increase Mather remembered, "I learned to read of my mother. I learned to write of Father." In 1704, Deacon John Paine wrote of his mother's cares to have him educated: "carefull mother eke She was / unto her children all / in teaching them gods word to read / when as they were but Small."[72] In such households, the act of learning to read was inextricably linked with the practice of reading aloud. Fathers often played a major role as readers. The husband of Sarah Goodhue

70. "Extracts from Salem School Committee Records," *Essex Institute Historical Collections* 91 (1955): 53; Peter Thacher, Journal, MS, p. 644, Massachusetts Historical Society, Boston. I am grateful to Ross W. Beales, Jr., for these references and also for those in note 72.

71. Herbert and Carol Schneider, eds., *Samuel Johnson, President of King's College, His Career and Writings,* 4 vols. (New York, 1929), 1:3–4.

72. "The Autobiography of Increase Mather," ed. Michael G. Hall, *Proceedings of the American Antiquarian Society* 71 (1961):278; "Deacon John Paine's Journal," *Mayflower Descendants* 8 (1906):230.

"read aloud" each Sunday from his transcriptions of the minister's sermons. Samuel Sewall read the Bible aloud "in course" to his children, and as they grew older each had to join in the exercise.[73] For children who were just beginning to encounter print, reading aloud, reciting, and memorizing were acts that fused together. Samuel Johnson's is a key statement: he began by learning "things by heart"— the Lord's Prayer, the Apostles' Creed—and by an almost intangible progression found himself able to read, meanwhile continuing to memorize from Scripture. All this he accomplished when he was but four or five years old. Johnson was probably using a *New England Primer* or something like it, for such books ordinarily added the Lord's Prayer, the Apostles' Creed, a catechism, and selections from the Bible to an alphabet and lists of words. From cover to cover, the material in the *Primer* was designed to be memorized. At home as in school, the children chanted aloud, sounding out words and memorizing texts before they could actually read.

In early New England, school books like the primer were among the most widely owned and distributed kinds of books, rivaled only by catechisms, psalmbooks, and the Bible. All of these books owed their wide distribution partly to official regulations, which themselves grew out of the Puritan supposition that reading was a "great help" to "salvation."[74] From time to time the Massachusetts government would order house-to-house inspections to see if every family owned a Bible; and there were similar inspections of children's knowledge of the catechism.

Other than the Bible and its kin, books were scarce, as Buckingham and Goodrich both suggest. The situation in England and New England was one of small press runs and limited circulation for most items. Press runs for quartos and octavos could dip as low as 300 or 400 copies, and rarely went above a maximum of 1,500. The economics of publishing—the shortage of capital, the inefficiencies of distribution—made larger editions unusual. Taking these figures into account, David Cressy has calculated that the entire production of London printers in 1640 could have been absorbed by the households of the gentry, the clergy, and professionals. On the eve of the English Revolution, the London

73. Thomas Waters, *Ipswich in the Massachusetts Bay Colony*, 2 vols. (Ipswich, Mass., 1905), 1:523; *The Diary of Samuel Sewall*, ed. M. Halsey Thomas, 2 vols. (New York, 1973), 1:115, 384, 404.
74. Waters, *Ipswich*, 1:277; Israel Loring, *The Duty and Interest of Young Persons* (Boston, 1718), 21–22.

book trade may have scarcely touched the artisans and yeomanry of the countryside save for occasional chapbooks and broadsides.[75] No one has made similar calculations for New England, where in any case the substantial business in importations makes local figures of less use. But here as in England, press runs were small, prices high, and distribution a matter of catch-as-catch-can.[76] As Edward Taylor headed west to become the first minister of a new Connecticut River Valley town, he carried with him a precious hoard of manuscript copies he had personally made of books in Cambridge and Boston. Ministers were exceptional in building up substantial libraries, though we may know more about the large collections than the small. In most probate inventories, however, books fail to appear.[77]

If the situation in New England was not quite as bright as it is often painted, the situation in mid-eighteenth-century Virginia was one of real limits on the circulation of print. The publisher of the *Virginia Almanac* managed an annual press run of 5,000 copies, at a time when New Englanders were buying up to 60,000 copies a year of a single almanac, and sustaining several others. Gregory and Cynthia Stiverson have calculated that the most active bookseller in mid-eighteenth-

75. Cressy, *Literacy and the Social Order*, 47. "Though it is pleasant to envision the Elizabethan cottage with its faded and tattered ballads on the wall, and the cottager crouching over the feeble fire spelling out the words of a chapbook . . . , it would be a mistake to imagine that reading had any but the most incidental place in the life of the masses" (Altick, *The English Common Reader*, 29). The paradox is nonetheless that (as Margaret Spufford and others argue) certain inexpensive forms of print were remarkably abundant.

76. Rollo G. Silver, "Financing the Publication of Early New England Sermons," *Studies in Bibliography* 11 (1958):163–78; Silver, "Publishing in Boston, 1726–1757: The Accounts of Daniel Henchman," *Proceedings of the American Antiquarian Society* 66 (1956):17–36; Silver, "Government Printing in Massachusetts, 1751–1801," *Studies in Bibliography* 16 (1963): 161–200; Marcus A. McCorison, ed., "A Daybook from the Office of the *Rutland Herald* Kept by Samuel Williams, 1798–1802," *Proceedings of the American Antiquarian Society* 76 (1966): 293–395.

77. Norman Grabo, *Edward Taylor* (New Haven, Conn., 1961), 25. Thomas Goddard Wright, *Literary Culture in Early New England, 1620–1730* (New Haven, Conn., 1920), reprints a number of ministers' library inventories; for others, see the references in Miller, *The New England Mind*, 509–11. Comprehensive studies of book holdings in a particular community tend to indicate that between half and two-thirds of surviving inventories do not include books. See, for example, Harriet S. Tapley, *Salem Imprints* (Salem, Mass., 1927), 164; Minor Myers, Jr., "Letters, Learning, and Politics in Lyme: 1760–1800," in *A Lyme Miscellany 1776–1976*, ed. George Willauer, Jr. (Middletown, Conn., 1977), 48–80; Christopher M. Jedrey, *The World of John Cleaveland: Family and Community in Eighteenth-Century New England* (New York, 1979), 103 (the figure here is 13 percent). Hart, *The Popular Book in America*, has a figure of 60 percent for Middlesex County, Massachusetts, in the seventeenth century. *Note in 1996:* my own case study of probate inventories from Middlesex County bears Hart out. Hall, "A Note on Book Ownership in Seventeenth-Century New England," *Worlds of Wonder*, 247–49; and for comparative figures on the Chesapeake in this same century, see the essay on the Chesapeake in this collection.

century Virginia sold books to perhaps no more than 250 customers a year. And not very many books at that: a total of 2,028, excluding almanacs, for a white population that exceeded 130,000 persons.[78]

The celebrated autobiography of Devereux Jarratt adds to the gloom of these figures, for Jarratt remembered provincial Virginia as a veritable desert in regard to books. Wanting to know something of "philosophy, rhetoric, and logic," he discovered that "there were no books on such subjects among us." In order to learn arithmetic he "borrowed a plain book, in manuscript." The very "first sermon book I ever had seen, or, perhaps, heard of," had been "left, by some one," at a neighbor's. When he had been spiritually awakened and became curious to understand the meaning of the Bible, he found that "I had not a single book in the world, nor was I able to buy any books, had I known of any for sale. But, by some means, I got hold of a little old book, in a smoky condition, which I found to be Russel's seven sermons. I borrowed the book, and read the sermons again and again." Later on, by word of mouth, "I was told of a very large book, belonging to a gentleman, about five or six miles distant across the river, which explained all the New Testament. I resolved to get the reading of that book, if possible." Only when he came into contact with a Presbyterian minister—from whom he heard his first sermon—did Jarratt finally have access to "a number of very excellent books, written by men of the greatest eminence for learning and piety, such as Baxter, Watts, Doddridge, Young, etc."[79]

Through the story of this search for books runs another motif of traditional literacy, the importance of certain "steady sellers" in the reading done by ordinary people. Steady sellers were books that remained in print for several decades. Some of these books showed an astonishing longevity, circulating among a popular audience for at least 200 years. Nowhere is there evidence of total sales for any of these titles. Once or twice we hear of press runs—Joseph Alleine's *Alarm for the Unconverted* was published, we are told, in "one Impression" of 30,000 copies, and altogether 70,000 were sold in the space of a few

78. Stiverson and Stiverson, "The Colonial Retail Book Trade."
79. Devereux Jarratt, *The Life of the Reverend Devereux Jarratt . . . Written by Himself* (Baltimore, 1806), 24–26. In "Books and the Social Authority of Learning," Rhys Isaac offers a somewhat different interpretation of this journal.

years.[80] But for the most part the evidence that these books were popular, and *that they were also readily available,* lies half-obscured in bibliographies, booksellers' catalogues, probate inventories, and memoirs such as those by Goodrich, Buckingham, and Jarratt. Steady sellers were never available in the same quantities as psalmbooks, primers, catechisms, and the Bible. But they turn up so many times and in so many places that they must be seen as cultural artifacts of a special kind. No less than the Bible and the catechism, steady sellers stand at the very center of traditional literacy.[81]

The identity of some of these books is revealed in occasional recommendations of "good" reading. In one of these statements, an English clergyman in 1702 advised young people to "read the Bible, and get the *Plain Mans Pathway to Heaven,* a very plain holy book for you, get the *Practice of Piety,* Mr. Baxters *Call to the Unconverted,* Mead's *Almost Christian,* Vincents *Advice to Young Men,* and read the Histories of the Martyrs that died for Christ, and in the *Book of Martyrs."*[82] In another, a young widower of Bennington, Vermont, in the early nineteenth century urged women to spend their days "diligently reading the Scriptures through in course every year, in selecting and committing to memory several hundred of the most striking passages of scripture, which may appear of the highest doctrinal and practical importance, in reading the writings of Baxter, Flavel, Bunyan, Berkitt, Henry, Saurin, Mason, Watts, Guyse, Doddridge, J. Edwards, Davies, Hopkins, John Newton . . . Young's Night Thoughts, and a few of the best histories."[83] Even though this nineteenth-century list has all of the eighteenth to draw upon, the similarities of title and of type are striking.

Steady sellers also figured significantly in the production of country

80. These figures are cited on the inside back cover of the 1767 Boston edition of *Alarm to the Unconverted.*

81. In the late seventeenth century, Boston booksellers repeatedly ordered certain titles from London; most of these were or became steady sellers. A guide to these books is Worthington C. Ford, *The Boston Book Market, 1679–1700* (Boston, 1917). Steady sellers were a phenomenon of the book trade in seventeenth- and eighteenth-century Germany, Netherlands, and France; in these countries, as in Britain and America, books of devotion and their kin were frequently reprinted and widely owned. Albert Ward, *Book Production, Fiction and the German Reading Public 1740–1800* (Oxford, 1974); 4; Julien Brancolini and Marie-Thérèse Bouyssy, "La vie provinciale du livre à la fin de l'Ancien Régime," in Furet et al., *Livre et société,* 2:3–37. Ministers in late seventeenth-century Wales were translating the same familiar titles into the vernacular; see Jenkins, *Literature, Religion and Society,* 133.

82. White, *A Little Book for Little Children,* 19. Two of these titles were in Bunyan's dowry.

83. *The Religious Experience of Mrs. Emerson* (Bennington, Vt., 1809), 53 n.

printers in New England. These books originated in the metropolitan book trade of London and Boston, but in the course of their existence became increasingly the business of the country or provincial printer. As printing offices sprang up outside Boston in ever increasing numbers during the eighteenth and early nineteenth centuries, each new entrepreneur looked around him for items he was sure of selling. The local writer and the local patron provided some work in the form of funeral, ordination, and election sermons, and perhaps an almanac. But to get more work, every country printer turned eventually to the titles that were known to everyone, and that always seemed to sell.

Consider E. Merriam, & Co., founded in the Worcester County town of Brookfield, Massachusetts, in 1798. The Merriams were more ambitious than most country printers. Their list included a few novels, two songbooks, a dictionary, and some spellers, all sandwiched in among the usual funeral sermons and orations. But much of their business for the first twenty years lay in printing steady sellers: four editions of Isaac Watts and two of Doddridge's *Rise and Progress of Religion*, together with single editions of Baxter's *Call to the Unconverted* and *The Saints Everlasting Rest*, Thomas Shearman's *Divine Breathings*, captivity narratives by Mary Rowlandson and John Williams, and Young's *Night Thoughts*. The steadiest of the "steady sellers" on the Merriam list was Robert Russel's *Seven Sermons*, published by them in 1818, but originally appearing before 1700. This was the "little old book, in a smoky condition" that Jarratt came across in Virginia, a stray from one of the *forty-three* printings this book had in America between 1701 and 1820, when it finally ceased being published.[84]

Early and late, printers in New England relied on steady sellers for their business. The pattern holds for nearly everyone who entered the book trade, be it James Franklin in his Newport days, the Greens in Hartford and New London, Isaiah Thomas in Boston and Worcester (though Thomas had wider interests), or Anthony Haswell in Bennington. In search of printers and their consciousness of steady sellers, we can return to the seventeenth century and the two men who ran the Cambridge press in the 1660s and 1670s. Marmaduke Johnson and Samuel Green kept a sharp eye on the London book market for titles

84. Printed in England by 1699, though whether this represents the initial edition is unclear. An edition *was* published after 1820 in Mountain Valley, Virginia (1853).

that would sell in New England. One or two of their reprints were sensations of the moment, like a nobleman's account of Mount Aetna in eruption. But most were books that already qualified as steady sellers, or would soon become so: *Old Mr. Dod's Sayings;* William Dyer's *Christs Famous Titles;* Thomas Vincent's *Gods Terrible Voice,* a powerful sermon on the great plague and London fire (still of interest to a printer in Windham, Connecticut, in 1795); Thomas Wilcox's *A Choice Drop of Honey* (at least fifty English editions, and reprinted in Boston as late as 1807); and books by two of the colonists, in one case printed originally abroad, Shepard's *The Sincere Convert* and Wigglesworth's *The Day of Doom.*

The world of steady sellers is revealed to us, finally, in the stories people tell of their reading. From these stories we learn something else of equal importance: these books were read in a special manner that befit their religious or devotional contents. Samuel Goodrich has already told us of the "awe" and "reverence" with which people came to books. His words are borne out in advice on how to read, and in the simple and naive statements people left behind of their experience as readers.

A motif of all such statements is intensity. Here is Thomas White telling readers how to use a book: "As you read (if the Books be your own) Mark in the margin, or by underlining the places you find most relish in, and take most special notice of, that that doth most concern thee, that you may easily, and more quickly find them again."[85] And here is the anonymous author of *The Life and Writings of Miss Eliza Waite* (1813) on why it is worthwhile to read the journals of pious young ladies: "The end of reading is not attained by getting through the book, but by receiving those serious and deep impressions, which will have a practical influence upon the future life."[86]

In line with this advice, people read with care, returning again and again to the same text to ensure they got its meaning. Robert Keayne of

85. White, *A Little Book for Little Children,* 19. He continues: "I would have you learn some Sentences out of the Scripture by heart; of which you may have constant use."

86. *Life and Writings of Miss Eliza Waite* (Hallowell, Maine, 1819), 246. There is no shortage of instructions on how to read. "Be diligent in reading the scriptures: First, you must every morning and evening, read a chapter in your Bible, or else some part of a godly sermon; and when you read, you must not run it over, and then leave it, you had as good do nothing as do so; but when you read, you take especial heed, what you be reading of; and when you have done, look back a little upon what you have read" (Robert Russel, *Seven Interesting Sermons* [Boston, 1767], 127).

Boston, the man who left so long and famous a will, bequeathed to his son, "As my special gift to him my little written book in my closet upon I Cor. II, 27, 28, which is a treatise of the sacrament of the Lord's Supper. . . . [It is] a little thin pocket book bound in leather, all written with my own hand, which I esteem more precious than gold, and which I have read over I think 100 and 100 times. . . . I desire him and hope that he will never part with it as long as he lives."[87]

As in Keayne's "100 and 100 times," people read slowly—so slowly, and so repeatedly, that parts of these texts became embodied in their memories. Let me offer some examples. Sarah Osborn went to nurse her eldest son:

> He was given over by the doctors and all friends, who lamented him, and did the best for him in their power, as to the body. But alas! my great concern was for that precious jewel, his immortal soul. I endeavoured to improve every opportunity to discourse with him, and read to him such portions of scripture as I thought suitable, with passages out of Mr. Allein's Alarm.[88]

Like Goodrich, Buckingham, and so many others, a young man was especially responsive to Isaac Watts:

> For about twenty four hours before he died [he] seemed to be in an extasy of joy, and so remained till he could speak no longer; and when he was speechless he by signs desir'd the Company to sing praises to God; and when they seem'd backward, he was the more earnest, and took Dr. Watts' hymns and turned them to the third hymn of the second book of Spiritual Songs, and by signs urged them to sing, which they did; and he endeavoured to join them as well as he could; and then with Eyes and Hands lift up, fell asleep.[89]

A minister recalled the time when, temporarily out of school, he

> read over all the vollums of Foxes Acts and Monuments, which I much delighted in, and how much of espetially the two last vollums, which I read over diverse times, where, in my young years, I showd a tendr heart, yet could not forbare melting into tears, when I read of the cruelty showd against the Masters and blessed servants of Jesus Christ.[90]

87. *The Apologia of Robert Keayne*, ed. Bernard Bailyn (New York, 1965), 28–29.
88. Samuel Hopkins, *Memoirs of the Life of Mrs. Sarah Osborn* (Worcester, Mass., 1799), 66.
89. *The Christian History, Containing Accounts of the Revival and Propagation of Religion in Great-Britain & America for the Year 1744* (Boston, 1745), 112.
90. Lilley B. Eaton, *Genealogical History of the Town of Reading, Mass.* (Boston, 1874), 53.

The mother of Carteret Rede remembered that when

> I came up into her Chamber, I found her reading Mr. *John Janeway's* Life
> and Death; she was all in Tears, she said to me, Oh! that I were such a
> Worm as this was! that God would give me Repentance unto Life! Oh!
> that I were in the Bosom of Jesus! Oh! that my Sorrow might be true
> Sorrow![91]

Or consider the fusion of world view, reading, and emotion in the
life of Joseph Croswell. Born in 1712 in Charlestown, Croswell was
converted during the Great Awakening and became a lay itinerant
preacher. His "favorite" authors, an anonymous biographer informs us,
"were those of the Calvinistic description, such as Flavel, Erskine,
Bolton, Edwards, & c." The statement is borne out by the journal in
which he recorded his reading and the impact that it had upon him.
Often as he read he experienced "quickenings." Thus,

> In the evening realized some quickenings in reading the believer's
> journey to the heavenly Canaan, by Mr. Erskine.
> Experienced quickening influences of the Divine Spirit whilst reading
> an account of the joyful deaths of young people at Haverhill about 22
> years past, which was occasioned by the throat-distemper.

But Croswell's most passionate responses as a reader were to Scripture,
the steadiest of all the steady sellers: "I know not when I have experienced greater consolation in reading the word of God. Blessed be its
glorious and gracious Author. Sweetly regaled in the afternoon by the
heavenly south breezes of the divine Spirit, whilst repeating scripture
passages." And having memorized one part of the Bible—"I have this
day repeated the whole book of Canticles by heart"—he returned to the
exercise again and again: "Some enlivening about noon while passing
through woods and repeating the last three chapters in the Canticles. . . . Refreshed in repeating passages from the Canticles."[92]
    Traditional literacy culminates in the intense relationship between
book and reader recounted in these episodes. To understand the reasons why, we need to look beyond the cultural process of becoming
literate to consider the contents of the steady sellers. All of them were

91. [Mrs. Sarah Rede], *A Token for Youth* (Boston, 1729), 12.
92. *Sketches of the Life, and Extracts from the Journals, and other Writings, of the Late Joseph Croswell* (Boston, 1809), 8, 14–40.

concerned with religion as a mode of living and a mode of dying.[93] As they define it, the religious life encompassed four great crises or rites of passage. The conversion process in all of its amplitude was the dominating event in the steady sellers; many of them were specifically about the process, and each assumed that it was fundamental. Other steady sellers focused on the imperative for self-scrutiny when coming to the Lord's Table to receive communion.[94] Still others dramatized the experience of "remarkable" afflictions. A final group taught the art of dying well, of turning the terror of death into the joy of eternal life with Christ.[95]

The steady sellers told stories of specific people and their ways of dealing with these crises. Children underwent conversion and died in bliss in James Janeway's *A Token for Children*. Martyrs suffered the most terrible punishments, but withstood them because of God's assistance. In one of Robert Russel's *Seven Sermons*, Devereux Jarratt came across the history of Francis Spira, and was "deeply impresst" by this vivid narrative of the agonies of conscience suffered by an apostate from Protestantism. "Spira" was a commonplace of diaries and the sermon literature, so widely known that people used this single word to convey a wealth of meaning.[96] The people who read or listened to such stories came to feel that their structure coincided with the very "plot" of human life: the pilgrimage from sin to grace, from bondage to salvation. The distance between books and life was very short, if any real distance existed in the first place. The hymns of Watts that Buck-

93. I am indebted to Charles Hambrick-Stowe's splendid study of Puritan devotional practice, *The Practice of Piety* (Chapel Hill, N.C., 1982), for this argument concerning the relationship between reading and the structure of the religious life; Hambrick-Stowe also called my attention to the passage about reading in Keayne's will.

94. Two examples that were widely read in New England were Thomas Doolittle, *A Treatise Concerning the Lords Supper* (London, 1665, and many subsequent editions), and Jabez Earle, *Sacramental Exercises* (London, 1707), which Samuel Sewall was reading in 1715. *The Diary of Samuel Sewall*, 2:790.

95. The longest-lived of these was doubtless Charles Drelincourt, *The Christian's Defence against the Fears of Death* (Boston, 1744), which was originally published in France in the middle of the seventeenth century. Flora Thompson, in *Lark Rise to Candleford* (London, 1954), 110, remembers *Drelincourt on Death* as a staple of cottager reading in north Oxfordshire in the 1880s.

96. Leonard Hoar, *The Sting of Death and Death Unstung* (Boston, 1680), 9; Andrew Jones, *The Black Book of Conscience* (Hartford, 1767), 14; *Thomas Shepard's Confessions*, ed. George Selement and Bruce C. Woolley, *Publications of the Colonial Society of Massachusetts* 58 (Boston, 1981):168. I am grateful to Patricia Caldwell for this last reference. John Bunyan "did hit upon that dreadful story of that miserable mortal, Francis Spira; A book that was to my troubled spirit as salt, when rubbed into a fresh wound" (*Grace Abounding*, 49).

ingham learned from his mother, and could still quote after half a century, were reality to people who lived within the boundaries of traditional literacy.

Let us suppose, therefore, that traditional literacy evokes a world view. This world view was embodied not only in the steady sellers but also in much of the street literature of Anglo-American print culture, the broadsides, chapbooks, and almanacs that were dispersed quite widely. Some of this street literature was devoted to "amazing" portents and prodigies that were God's warning voice to man. Some of it recounted the behavior of criminals awaiting execution, who in their final words always warned the young to avoid their sad fate.[97] The almanacs catered to a Protestant self-awareness with their talk of "popery." "Penny godlies" taught the difference between right and wrong ways of dying.[98] Broadside elegies described the saint in flight to heaven.[99] Altogether the most "popular" forms of print in England and New England shared much in common with the steady sellers.

By one route or another, the world view of these texts became the world view of most New Englanders. The social boundaries of this world view were broad, encompassing both the highly educated and the barely literate.[100] In seventeenth-century England, the reformation of manners was visibly incomplete, and the process of replacing traditional rural culture with evangelical Christianity involved open conflict between the social orders. Perhaps because the colonists had undergone this process before migrating, conflict in New England is less evident than consensus. Here, the ministry spoke the same language as the farmers and artisans who paid their salaries. Here too, the Baptists and Quakers who opposed the "New England Way" of organizing churches continued at more basic levels to share the mentality of those in the majority.[101] Even the curse that ordinary people exchanged so

97. Increase Mather, *A Sermon Occasioned by the Execution* (Boston, 1686), 27ff.

98. Spufford, *Small Books and Pleasant Histories,* chap. 8; and see Hyder E. Rollins, *Old English Ballads, 1553–1625, Chiefly from Manuscripts* (Cambridge, 1920), ix–xvi.

99. Ola E. Winslow, ed., *American Broadside Verse* (New Haven, Conn., 1930).

100. The intellectual world of the "learned" in New England embraced a wider range of reading than the steady sellers. Some of this reading, or its possibilities, is indicated in Norman S. Fiering, "The Transatlantic Republic of Letters: A Note on the Circulation of Learned Periodicals to Early Eighteenth-Century America," *William and Mary Quarterly,* 3d ser., 33 (1976):642–60.

101. [Thomas Maule], *New-Englands Persecutors Mauld with Their Own Weapons* ([New York, 1697]), sig. A2 recto, 9, 19, 32.

often in the street—"the devil take you"—owed its being to a common set of ideas.[102]

The alternatives to this traditional mental world were unsystematic and intermittent in seventeenth- and early eighteenth-century New England. Two such divergences can be distinguished. To give one a more elaborate name than it deserves, we can speak of the culture of the alehouse. Like ordinary people everywhere, the colonists gathered at the local tavern to down their rum or beer. Winter evenings, they told stories of thieving lawyers and cuckolded husbands. They sang "wicked" ballads and swapped copies of dirty books, including most likely that illicit steady seller, *Aristotle's Master Piece*. Certainly, they laughed. Guilt and fear were the province of the meetinghouse; release and humor the province of the tavern.[103]

Occasionally the almanacs play up to this world. In Tully's almanac for 1688 the sober plainness of the almanac tradition in New England was challenged by a closing "prognostication" in verse:

> January's Observations.
> The best defence against the Cold,
> Which our Fore-Fathers good did hold,
> Was early a full Pot of Ale,
> Neither too mild nor yet too stale.

Under February, young men

> Do present their Loves
> With Scarfs . . .
> And to show manners not forgot all,
> Give them a lick under the 'Snot-gall.'

The prognostication for February concludes in kind: "The Nights are still cold and long, which may cause great Conjunction betwixt the

---

102. [Cotton Mather], *The Young Mans Preservative* (Boston, 1701), 64; *Records and Files of the Quarterly Courts of Essex County*, 9 vols. (Salem, Mass., 1911–75), 1:134.

103. Peter Clark, "The Ale-house and the Alternative Society," in *Puritans and Revolutionaries: Essays Presented to Christopher Hill*, ed. D. Pennington and K. Thomas (Oxford, 1978), 47–72; Benjamin Wadsworth, *An Essay to Do Good. Being a Disswasive from Tavern-haunting, and Excessive Drinking* (Boston, 1710); John Barnard, *The Nature and Danger of Sinful Mirth, Exhibited in a Plain Discourse* (Boston, 1728); Otho T. Beale, "Aristotle's Master-Piece in America: A Landmark in the Folklore of Medicine," *William and Mary Quarterly*, 3d ser., 20 (1963):207–22. I am grateful to Roger Thompson for this reference. He informs me that this and other dirty books are frequently mentioned in cases involving sexual offenses in the Middlesex County (Mass.) Court records for the seventeenth century. See also Thompson, "The Puritans and Prurience: Aspects of the Restoration Book Trade," in *Contrast and Connection*, ed. H. C. Allen and Roger Thompson (London, 1976), 36–64.

Male and Female Planets of our sublunary Orb, the effects wherof may be seen about nine months after, and portend great charges of Midwife, Nurse, and Naming the Bantling."[104]

Lest these verses be misinterpreted as tokens of an anti-Puritan mentality—an overdue revolt of the long-repressed masses—the peculiar history of Tully's almanacs must be taken into account. In 1688 Tully inserted Anglican saints' days and secular holidays into his calendar, while referring in his chronology to "blessed Charles martyr" and "Oliver the tyrant." This vigorous trampling on New England sensibilities grows out of a single circumstance: Tully had chosen to write for the tiny community of Anglicans and Royalists then in command of civil government in New England, a community that constituted the other alternative. When the Revolution of 1689 swept this group from office, Tully changed directions, stripping his almanacs of all saints' days and licentious verse, and reverting to the New England norm. His almanac for 1688 is nonetheless a straw in the wind. Puritan culture in New England had been breached by cosmopolitanism. As the decades passed, the influence of this alternative would gradually increase. Thanks to this tendency, a century later Boston had a professional theater, dancing schools, and subscription libraries concentrating on fiction. But to look this far ahead brings us back to Goodrich and Buckingham and the transformation of print culture in which they had taken part.

∾ 3 ∾

To Goodrich and Buckingham the first half of the nineteenth century was a time of rapid progress out of "barbarism." The upward "march of civilization" was as evident in print as in the temperance movement. Goodrich could remember when "a half-pint of [rum] was given as a matter of course to every day-laborer" who worked on a Connecticut farm. But no longer: the standards of morality had changed, leaving demon rum behind. The improvements in communications and material comforts were equally marked. At the turn of the century Ridgefield was breaking out of its isolation. As local farmers abandoned

104. John Tully, *An Almanack* (Boston, 1687), 15–16.

native wares in favor of the latest styles in furniture, the "homely" picture of "half a century ago" shifted to one of "Kidderminster carpets—
made at Enfield or Lowell—mahogany bureaus, gilt looking-glasses,
and a small well-filled mahogany bookcase."[105]

The same improvements in technology that opened up Ridgefield to
the world were carrying books and newspapers into such towns at a
faster rate. Goodrich knew that his mid-nineteenth-century readers
would be struck by the scarcity of books in the Ridgefield of memory.
He made this point repeatedly in terms of children's literature, jux-
taposing his own excitement as a child at owning two or three precious books to the abundance of opportunities children of the new age
enjoyed.

> It is difficult now, in this era of literary affluence, almost amounting to
> surfeit, to conceive of the poverty of books suited to children in the days
> of which I write. Except the New England Primer . . . I remember none
> that were in general use among my companions. When I was about ten
> years old, my father brought from Hartford, Gaffer Ginger, Goody Two
> Shoes, and some of the rhymes and jingles, now collected under the
> name of Mother Goose,—with perhaps a few other toy books of that day.
> These were a revelation.
>
> In casting my mind backward over the last thirty years—and compar-
> ing the past with the present, duly noting the amazing advances made in
> every thing which belongs to the comfort, the intelligence, the luxury of
> society—there is no point in which these are more striking than in the
> books for children and youth. Let any one who wishes to comprehend
> this matter, go to such a juvenile bookstore as that of C. S. Francis, in
> Broadway, New York, and behold the teeming shelves—comprising al-
> most every topic . . .—and let him remember that nineteen twentieths of
> these works have come into existence within the last thirty years.[106]

Somewhere in his consciousness, Goodrich must have realized that
books in such abundance were no longer "revelations" to their readers,
and that he as Peter Parley was expendable. But any ambivalence he
might have felt about the age of abundance was minimized in his rush
to extol the progress of children's literature.

105. Goodrich, *Recollections of a Lieftime*, 1:69, 82.
106. Ibid., 165–66, 174. Books of this sort were being advertised as "Little Books for the
Instruction and Amusement of Children, adorn'd with a Variety of Cuts and bound in Gilt
Paper," in *A Catalogue of A Very Large Assortment of the Most Esteemed Books* (Boston, [1772]).
Isaiah Thomas would make a specialty of such items, most of them copied from the publications
of John Newbery.

This motif applied as much to the moral contents of children's literature as to its availability. The Mother Goose rhymes his father gave
him had in retrospect been "painful" reading:

> I recollect, while the impression was fresh in my mind, that on going to
> bed, I felt a creeping horror come over me, as the story [Little Red
> Riding Hood] recurred to my imagination. As I dwelt upon it, I soon
> seemed to see the hideous jaws of a wolf coming out of the bedclothes,
> and approaching as if to devour me. . . . at last I became so excited, that
> my mother was obliged to tell me that the story was a mere fiction.
> 'It is not true, then,?' said I.
> 'No,' said my mother, 'it is not true.'
> 'Why do they tell such falsehoods, then,?' I replied.

"False" is but the mildest of the epithets he uses for the stories of his
childhood. Jack the Giant Killer teaches readers "to forgive, nay, to love
and approve, wickedness,—lying, deception, and murder." Puss in
Boots teaches its readers to "cheat, lie, and steal,"—in effect, "to hate
virtue itself." Such tales inculcate "the love of the horrible, the monstrous, the grotesque." Their moral standard is "debased" and "coarse."
They have, concludes Goodrich, no place in the Christian home.[107]

This reaction has little to do with how Mother Goose stories were
perceived in the eighteenth century, but much to do with Goodrich in
his adult identity as Peter Parley. As a writer he proposed to enter the
marketplace and drive out all wicked stories, replacing them with "nur-
sery books . . . [that] consist of beauty instead of deformity, goodness
instead of wickedness, decency instead of vulgarity." The models for
the stories he would write were the moral tales of Hannah More, an
English Evangelical who preached the virtues of poverty and strict
temperance to English workers.[108] Hannah More and Samuel Goodrich shared in common a ferocious antipathy to the uses of literacy they
had known as children. In *The Fortune Teller*, Hannah More derides
the mentality of a farm girl who delights "in dream books," buys "very
wicked ballads" from an old woman peddler, and takes all kinds of
portents seriously. Sally Evans, the antiheroine of the tale, is betrayed
by her world view into abandoning an honest lover for a man who has

---

107. Goodrich, *Recollections of a Lifetime*, 1:166–70.
108. Ibid., 172. Harry B. Weiss, *Hannah More's Cheap Repository Tracts in America* (New York, 1946).

no morals. Sally dies, and the old woman fortune teller who has led her astray is declared a criminal and transported.[109]

Goodrich is less specific but no less hostile in the Peter Parley stories. The children who move through these stories are gentle, loving, and full of heart. The natural world which they encounter is personified as smiling and benevolent. Implicit in these settings is a theology at odds with the theology of the *New England Primer;* the God of Samuel Goodrich was as smiling and benevolent as the sunshine, flowers, animals, and children of his stories. Contrary to the *Primer,* and contrary to the practices of his own youth, Goodrich believed that children must be educated with special care:

> Children are simple, living, true—
> 'Tis God that made them so;
> And would you teach them?—be so, too,
> And stoop to what they know. . . .
> Begin with simple lessons, things
> On which they love to look;
> Flowers, pebbles, insects, birds on wings—
> These are God's spelling-book!

That Goodrich was aiming to reverse a traditional consciousness is directly suggested in a story that ends with an analysis of thunder and lightning. He is at pains to demonstrate the purely natural origins of the phenomena, for in the rational world of Peter Parley an older mentality, with its fearful awareness of the supernatural, was to be discarded.[110]

Something seems at work in these stories that can only be described as a fundamental shift of sensibility. Goodrich and Buckingham indicate another aspect of the changes taking place in their mature reflections upon Scripture. In hindsight, Buckingham regretted his absorption in the Bible. Using language akin to Goodrich's, he remembered being terrified by what he read, and especially by the apocalyptic chapters:

> What agonies have I not felt, after reading the description of the opening of the seals, the pouring out of the seven vials, with the sounding of the

109. Hannah More, *The Fortune Teller* (Philadelphia, [1807]), 8, 11–12, 25.
110. [Samuel Goodrich], *Peter Parley's Juvenile Tales* (Boston, 1830); [Samuel Goodrich], *One of Peter Parley's Winter Evening Stories* (Boston, 1830), 7, 16.

trumpets!—when, if alone, in the evening I dared not turn my eyes to
look behind me, lest I should see the pale horse with death, and hell
following, or the dragon vomiting a flood to drown the woman clothed
with the sun. . . . The passages referred to, and indeed almost every
chapter of the book, is adapted to fill the mind of a child with terror,
and it is, in my humble judgement, a piece of gratuitous and unprofitable cruelty . . . to place before him any thing to inspire terror or produce affright. Why should children be made to read what they cannot
comprehend?[111]

Goodrich had a parallel reaction to the *New England Primer.* His
contempt for this book seeps through the description he provides
for readers who had never seen it: "The New England Primer—the
main contents of which were the Westminster Catechism—and some
rhymes, embellished with hideous cuts of Adam's Fall, in which 'we
sinned all;' the apostle and a cock crowing at his side, to show that
'Peter denied his Lord and cries;' Nebuchadnezzar crawling about like
a hog, the bristles sticking out of his back, and the like." By association,
the *New England Primer* lay on the wrong side of the line that separated vulgarity from moral truth, barbarism from civilization.[112]

In the context of this reaction, we can begin to understand why so
many of the steady sellers limped into the nineteenth century and
expired. Some were kept alive by tract societies, but we can regard these
printings as artificial in comparison to the dozens of locally produced
editions that had once made such titles plentiful. With one or two exceptions the steady sellers of the seventeenth and eighteenth centuries
reached their end by 1830. Several of the genres of print that had been
companions of the steady sellers also vanished, like broadside elegies
and the literature on portents and prodigies. The almanac lost much of
its importance. The *New England Primer,* after passing through 450
editions by 1830, was rapidly displaced by more secularized and cosmopolitan school books. The old style of "lining out" in church music
also vanished, though not without much conflict.[113]

A broader unsettling of authority seems to have occurred in the years

    111. Buckingham, *Personal Memoirs,* 1:17. Nor could he abide Michael Wigglesworth's *The Day of Doom.*
    112. Goodrich, *Recollections of a Lifetime,* 1:165.
    113. Winslow, *American Broadside Verse,* xxv; Neuburg, *The Penny Histories,* 47. On conflict and change in music, see David P. McKay and Richard Crawford, *William Billings of Boston* (Prince-ton, N.J., 1975).

on either side of 1800, as the old moral and social order came under attack. Radical democrats wanted to tear down all hierarchies of wealth and privilege. As Nathan Hatch has argued, these democrats made effective use of journalism, turning its expansion to political advantage. In ironic counterpoint to democratization, the new publishers of secular sheet music were catering to the urban rich, who may have stood apart from the great evangelical revival. These diverging tendencies could have pulled American society asunder had other forces not been at work to create some kind of center. Amid the discordant sounds of conflict, the voices that spoke for an emerging civil religion—the American version of Victorianism—grew stronger all the time, as did the vehicles of print that echoed this synthesis.

The vehicles of print that created and embody this synthesis were fiction, journalism, and children's literature. Fiction had existed in the seventeenth and eighteenth centuries, but was barred from wide distribution by factors of cost and of cultural hostility. The second of these barriers had begun to weaken by the middle of the eighteenth century. Thereafter, in Europe and America, fiction steadily gained on religious and devotional literature as a percentage of total book production. The transition to an age of fiction was complete by the 1850s.[114] The progress of journalism was equally rapid, culminating in the emergence of the "penny press" in the 1830s and 1840s. Children's literature was slower to emerge. The annus mirabilis was 1745, when the Englishman John Newbery began to publish attractive, inexpensive editions of children's stories, some old, some new. But many children continued to read "adult" books like the Bible well into the next century.

These new genres were both cause and consequence of changes in the book trade. Fiction was costly. Unlike the steady sellers, it was also expendable, in that patrons craved fresh reading. Circulating and subscription libraries, which came into being in the middle of the eighteenth century, were a means of spreading the cost while offering variety. In America, subscription libraries first appeared in the 1760s. Their number slowly rose until the 1790s, when it abruptly doubled.[115] As

---

114. Ward, *Book Production*, chap. 2; Ilsedore Rarisch, *Industrialisierung und Literatur: Buchproduktion, Verlagswesen und Buchhandel in Deutschland im 19. Jahrhundert* (Berlin, 1976); Altick, *The English Common Reader*, chap. 13.

115. Winans, "The Growth of a Novel-Reading Public"; Winans, *A Descriptive Checklist of Book Catalogues Separately Printed in America 1693–1800* (Worcester, Mass., 1981), xvii.

book prices began to fall in the nineteenth century, publishers were also introducing serialized fiction into magazines. The combination of these several techniques made the genre increasingly accessible. The very scale of the reading public for fiction, together with the possibilities for distribution that the railroad opened up, pushed the book trade toward consolidation. As the country printer vanished, his place was taken by firms like Harper's, armed with steam presses and a railroad to distribute cheap products—mainly fiction—all across America.

According to Goodrich and Buckingham, the very style of literacy changed to one more in keeping with the new genres. A shift in rhythm was already evident in 1713, when Richard Steele complained of the "unsettled way of reading" and its "transient satisfactions."[116] Describing the older style, Goodrich had emphasized the stateliness and "reverence" of the act of reading. In the new age of fiction and daily journalism, people moved "hastily" from one day's paper to the next, and from one novel to another. No book, not even the Bible, retained the aura that certain texts had once possessed. Bit by bit, the structure of traditional literacy unraveled as print became abundant, school books were secularized, and the steady sellers vanished.

These changes betoken the decay of one mentality and the emergence of another. This is not to say that traditional literacy and its world view disappeared overnight. Aspects of it lingered on in nineteenth-century evangelicalism. Tract societies and denominational publishers continued to reprint Baxter, Wilcox, and Alleine. In Lyman Beecher's household, little Harriet still had to memorize some chapters from the Bible.[117] Certain works of fiction were transitional. *Clarissa* has a section on death which Richardson regarded as in keeping with conduct manuals on how to die. But the "rise of the novel" can also be linked with fundamental shifts in the value system of the middle class. The old awareness of time as an eternal present gave way to an understanding of time as merely chronological. Fiction catered in its social ethos to individualism, or, as in Peter Parley's stories, to sentimentalism. Goodrich himself had become a Unitarian. Like so many other religious liberals, he transmuted his new faith into children's stories,

---

116. Watt, *Rise of the Novel,* 48. It is tempting to speculate that, with novels, the practice of reading aloud slackened.
117. Charles Edward Stowe, *Life of Harriet Beecher Stowe* (Boston, 1889), 8.

school books, and fiction, the themes of which were utterly opposed to evangelical Calvinism.[118] The social correlations of literacy were also changing in the eighteenth and early nineteenth centuries. In the culture of traditional literacy, the distinction between elite and popular belief had not been consequential, at least in New England. With relatively few exceptions, the colonists in 1650 or 1700 were all engaged with the same forms of reading, the same popular culture. Buy by the 1740s certain groups were beginning to withdraw from this common world into a new gentility. The coming of gentlemen's libraries, together with dancing assemblies, the tea ceremony, and the theater, were steps in the making of a cosmopolitan alternative to the culture of traditional literacy.[119] Not surprisingly, the taste of those who used the Redwood Library, founded at Newport in 1741, was for other reading matter than the steady sellers, not one of which was purchased for the collection.[120] The withdrawal of urban merchants and their allies from the older culture is also evident in their discomfort with "enthusiasm," their scorn for "superstitions," like taking comets as portentous,[121] and in the vogue of *Mrs. Chapone's Letters to Her Niece*, an English conduct book. Like Goodrich and Buckingham, Mrs. Chapone urged her readers not to begin upon the Bible until they were mature enough to cope with its language. According to her calculations, young ladies should wait until they were fifteen. Even then, she urged them to skip the prophetic books. Mrs. Chapone regarded skill in dancing and French as essential "accomplishments." She would not exclude fiction (of a moral nature) from her pupils' reading.[122]

Yet by the 1850s the old hostility between the genteel and the evan-

---

118. Watt, *Rise of the Novel*, 22–24 and chap. 3; Ann Douglas, *The Feminization of American Culture* (New York, 1977); David S. Reynolds, *Faith in Fiction: The Emergence of Religious Literature in America* (Cambridge, Mass., 1981).

119. Rodris Roth, "Tea Drinking in 18th-Century America: Its Etiquette and Equipage," *Contributions from the Museum of History and Technology, United States National Museum Bulletin* 225, paper no. 14 (Washington, D.C., 1969), 61–91. See also Laurel T. Ulrich, *Good Wives: Image and Reality in the Lives of Women in Northern New England 1650–1750* (New York, 1982), 115–16; "Extracts from a Journal of a Gentleman Visiting Boston in 1792," *Proceedings of the Massachusetts Historical Society* 12 (1871–73):60–66.

120. Marcus A. McCorison, ed., *The 1764 Catalogue of the Redwood Library Company at Newport, Rhode Island* (New Haven, Conn., 1965).

121. Andrew Oliver, Jr., *An Essay on Comets* (Salem, Mass., 1772), 3.

122. [Hester Chapone], *Letters on the Improvement of the Mind* (Boston, 1783), 19, 26–28, 49, 190, 205.

gelical was waning. Fiction brought these groups together in the culture we call Victorianism. Writing in the 1850s of the transformation they had witnessed, Goodrich and Buckingham remind us often of its benefits. What they could not see so clearly were the drawbacks. The story papers and the dime novels that were also making their appearance in the 1850s catered to a reading public that lay beyond the reach of liberal moralists.[123] Once or twice Buckingham and Goodrich acknowledged that all was not well—that the daily press had grown "licentious," and that publishers no longer treated authors with due respect.[124] But the faults and failures of the new age were less apparent than its differences from the eighteenth-century world in which Goodrich and Buckingham had begun. Their autobiographies are crucial testimony of the journey they and many others made from scarcity to abundance.

123. Q. D. Leavis, *Fiction and the Reading Public* (New York, 1979), chap. 7; David D. Hall, "The Victorian Connection," *American Quarterly* 27 (1975):561–74.
124. Buckingham, *Personal Memoirs*, 2:37; Goodrich, *Recollections of a Lifetime*, 2:253–60.

The World of Print
and Collective Mentality
in Seventeenth-Century New England

A TWELVE-YEAR-OLD BOY, precociously alert to the literary marketplace, writes a ballad (in "Grubstreet" style) on the drowning of a lighthouse keeper. Printed as a broadside, the poem is hawked in the streets of Boston and sells "wonderfully." An old man retells a family legend of how, in the persecuting times of "Bloody Mary" more than two centuries earlier, his ancestors hid their Protestant Bible in a stool. A young minister, ambitious as a writer, dreams of hiring a peddler who will carry cheap religious tracts from town to town.[1]

These are gestures that draw us into the world of print as it was experienced by Americans in the seventeenth century. I begin with this world because it is a useful starting point for rethinking the limitations and possibilities of intellectual history. A starting point, but not the means of answering every question, because the world of print is an imperfect mirror of intellectual experience, a partial reflection of all that is thought and believed. My evidence is taken from the seventeenth century, but I mean to contribute to a more general debate. This

Prepared for a conference on "New Directions in American Intellectual History" organized by Paul Conkin and John Higham and held at Wingspread in Racine, Wisconsin, in October 1977. Published in *New Directions in American Intellectual History,* edited by John Higham and Paul Conkin (Baltimore, 1979), 166–80.

1. *The Autobiography of Benjamin Franklin* (New Haven, Conn., 1964), 50, 59–60; *The Diary of Cotton Mather,* ed. W. C. Ford, 2 vols. (1911–12; reprint., New York, [n.d.]), 1:65.

is the debate between social and intellectual historians about the distance that exists between elites or intellectuals and other groups; between "high" culture and that which is usually described as "popular"; between books and collective belief.

If we feel uneasy with the intellectual history of seventeenth-century New England, the explanation is our renewed sense of distance in any or all of these forms. It is the felt distance of the ministers from the rest of society that limits them to being spokesmen for an elite. It is the distance between the ministers, who live in the world of print, and the mass of the people, who retain "peasant" ways of thinking.[2] This last distinction has been enormously reinforced by the work of Keith Thomas, which shows that in seventeenth-century England formal systems of religious belief competed with alternative, more "primitive" beliefs, and, more generally, by the work of French historians of *mentalité*, which uncovers for early modern France a mental world of superstition and folk belief apparently quite separate from the mental world of the literate.[3] In effect, the discovery of collective mentality is being used as a weapon against intellectual history, a means of restricting it within narrow boundaries.

In taking up the world of the book, I mean to explore the possibilities for extending these boundaries. There are many limitations to what can be accomplished by the history of the book, one of which is intrinsic in the complexity of any verbal statement: how much or what parts of that complexity is transmitted to any reader?[4] Many assumptions must be made, the chief one being that those books which sold in largest quantity reflect collective ways of thinking. Nonetheless, I want to use the history of print as a means for reappraising the relationship between the ministers and society as a whole in seventeenth-century

2. Kenneth Lockridge, *Literacy in Colonial New England: An Inquiry into the Social Context of Literacy in the Early Modern West* (New York, 1974). Important arguments correcting Lockridge appear in Lawrence Cremin, "Reading, Writing and Literacy," *Review of Education* 1 (November 1975): 517–21.

3. Keith Thomas, *Religion and the Decline of Magic* (London, 1971); Robert Mandrou, *De la culture populaire aux xvii and xviii siècles: La Bibliothèque bleue de Troyes* (Paris, 1964).

4. "Mais à propos de chaque image et de chaque theme reste posée la question pour qui étaient-ils comprehensibles?" George Duby, "Historie des mentalités," in *L'Histoire et ses méthodes*, ed. Charles Samaran (Paris, 1961), 923. *Note in 1996: mentalité* has waned as a descriptive and analytical category, in part because of reasons sketched in Dominick LaCapra, "Is Everyone a *Mentalité* Case? Transference and the 'Culture' Concept"; see also the companion essay, "*The Cheese and the Worms:* The Cosmos of a Twentieth-Century Historian," both in LaCapra, *History & Criticism* (Ithaca, N.Y., 1985).

New England, and in so doing, to point the way toward a broader understanding of intellectual history.

The world of print in seventeenth-century New England was broadly continuous with that of Europe. Shortly after the discovery of printing, the book in Europe assumed the form it would have for centuries to come, even as techniques for the book trade also became standardized. In the early years, and especially in England for much of the sixteenth century, individual patrons played an important role in deciding what was published. Early and late, the state attempted to control the world of print by restrictive licensing and censorship. But every effort at restraint was undercut by the lure of the marketplace. Printers produced whatever readers would buy. One-third of the books published in sixteenth-century England were not entered in the Stationers' Register, and in France, taking into account both what was printed within its borders and what was made available from outside, the actual world of print was far larger than any official version.[5] The entrepreneur reigned. What Robert Darnton says of publishers in Paris on the eve of the French Revolution, though colored by legal conditions, reflects the situation everywhere:

> "Innovation" came through the underground. Down there, no legalities constrained productivity, and books were turned out by a kind of rampant capitalism. . . . foreign publishers did a wild and wooly business in pirating [books officially licensed in France]. . . . They were tough businessmen and produced anything that would sell. They took risks, broke traditions, and maximized profits by quantity instead of quality production.

Almost as soon as printing began, printer-publishers were reaching out for the widest possible audience.[6]

The printing technology of the day was amazingly responsive to

---

5. H. S. Bennett, *English Books & Readers, 1475 to 1557* (London, 1952); idem, *English Books & Readers, 1558 to 1603* (Cambridge, 1965), referred to hereafter as Bennett, *English Books & Readers,* 1, and Bennett, *English Books & Readers,* 2. The importance of patronage is argued in Bennett, *English Books & Readers,* 2, chap. 2, and the figure concerning the Stationers' Register is given in Bennett, *English Books & Readers,* 2, 60. The situation in eighteenth-century France is described in the essays brought together in François Furet et al., *Livre et société dans la France du xviiie siècle,* 2 vols. (Paris, 1965, 1970).

6. Robert Darnton, "Reading, Writing, and Publishing in Eighteenth-Century France: A Case Study in the Sociology of Literature," in *Historical Studies Today,* ed. Felix Gilbert (New York, 1972), 261–62.

demands for quantity and speed.[7] But speed and innovation were not the only rhythms of the marketplace. For every Nathanael Butter (a London printer of the early seventeenth century who specialized in domestic intelligence, murders, cases of treason, and adventure stories, all requiring rapid publication before they fell out of date),[8] there was a printer who catered to needs that seemed unchanging, a printer who marketed the same product year in and year out. Provincial booksellers in eighteenth-century France published catechisms, liturgical hand-books, books of devotion, and similar steady sellers in far greater quantity than anything else; these were books, moreover, for which the copyrights had lapsed.[9] Their lack of glamour should not betray us into ignoring the significance of such steady sellers and the audience they served. In effect two major rhythms crisscrossed in the marketplace: one of change, the other of repetition. A constant recycling of tried and true literary products accompanied the publication of new styles and genres.

These rhythms offer clues to the relationship between modes of print and modes of thinking. But before pursuing them further, we must turn to evidence about literacy and book ownership in order to gain a clearer understanding of the marketplace. Figures on literacy vary from country to country and within each country by region. National averages can conceal the crucial difference in France between the North (literate) and the South (illiterate). What seems true of early modern Europe is that each country had its "dark corners of the land," regions in which the book was rare, few printers set up shop, and illiteracy (at least in the national language) was high. These were regions, moreover, where cosmopolitan travelers could barely make themselves

7. Bennett, *English Books & Readers*, 2, 244.

8. Butter's career is described in Leone Rostenberg, *Literary, Political, Scientific, Religious & Legal Publishing, Printing & Bookselling in England, 1551–1700* (New York, 1965), chap. 3.

9. Julien Brancolini and Marie-Thérèse Bouyssy, "La vie provinciale du livre à la fin de l'Ancien Régime," in Furet et al., *Livre et société*, 2:3–37. *Note in 1996:* my citation of this essay should be corrected in light of Robert Darnton's observation that the data cited by Brancolini and Bouyssy omit "probably the most important component in the stock of provincial bookdealers: books acquired by purchases or, more often, by exchanges." Darnton goes on to remark that "the *permissions simples* [the source of Brancolini and Bouyssy's data] covered primarily a specialized and unrepresentative segment of the provincial book trade: the relatively stable market for school-books and religious works" (Darnton, "The Social History of Ideas," in *The Kiss of Lamourette: Reflections in Cultural History* [New York, 1990], 244–45).

understood.[10] In more integrated communities, literacy and book ownership varied with social and economic rank. By the early seventeenth
century, professionals (clergy, lawyers) in England were completely
literate, the aristocracy nearly so, with the rate descending to approximately 50 percent for yeomen and small tradesmen. Thereafter the
decline is rapid, to a low of a few percent for laborers.[11] As for book
ownership in England, a careful study of probate inventories in three
towns in Kent has shown that by the early seventeenth century, between 40 and 50 percent of males owned books. This figure conceals
immense variances: no laborer owned any books, but close to all professionals did.[12]

These estimates for literacy and book distribution are perplexing. It
is possible to interpret them as meaning that a chasm separated the
culture of the elite, who lived in the world of print, from that of the
poor, who did not. Since the printed book was something new in
European culture, historians have also argued that a "traditional oral"
culture remained intact among "peasants" even as the world of print
came into being in urban areas and among the upper classes.[13] But the

10. Thomas, *Religion and the Decline of Magic*, 165; Eugen Weber, *Peasants into Frenchmen: The Modernization of Rural France, 1870–1914* (Stanford, Calif., 1976), pt. 1, especially chaps. 1 and 6 (on language).

11. John Cressy, "Literacy in Seventeenth-Century England: More Evidence," *Journal of Inter-disciplinary History* 8 (Summer 1977):141–50; Lawrence Stone, "Literacy and Education in En-gland, 1640–1900," *Past and Present*, no. 42 (February 1969): 69–139. The methodological limita-tions in reckoning literacy on the basis of signatures are underscored in Cremin's review of Lockridge, "Reading, Writing and Literacy," and in Margaret Spufford, *Contrasting Commu-nities: English Villagers in the Sixteenth and Seventeenth Centuries* (Cambridge, 1974). Spufford demonstrates that persons who signed their wills with an x had written out their names on other documents (chap. 7).

12. Peter Clark, "The Ownership of Books in England, 1560–1640: The Example of Some Kentish Townsfolk," in *Schooling and Society*, ed. Lawrence Stone (Baltimore, 1976), 95–111. The situation in sixteenth-century France is touched on in Natalie Zemon Davis, *Society and Culture in Early Modern France* (Stanford, Calif., 1975), 195–97. Probate inventories record holdings at the time of death, not the flow of experience with print over time. Since books get used up and discarded, the inventories are at best a partial record of encounters with the world of print. That no copies survive of the first edition of *The Day of Doom* or of any of the *New England Primer* published before 1729 are cases in point of books that were widely owned and used but that do not often turn up in inventories simply because they perished from so much use.

13. Davis, *Society and Culture*, chap. 7. Davis (and also Kenneth Lockridge) invokes the work of the anthropologist Jack Goody in drawing a sharp line between oral and literate experience. I question the usefulness of this distinction when applied to European culture two millennia after the emergence of writing. Goody's point of view is presented in *Literacy in Traditional Societies* (Cambridge, 1968). But see the review by Daniel McCall, "Literacy and Social Structure," *History of Education Quarterly* 11 (Spring 1971):85–92.

evidence about literacy and reading may really indicate that these categories of elite and non-elite are too limiting. Every social group contained a certain percentage of persons who could read, even if their
doing so defies our expectations. To us there is a mystery about the
ways and means by which a French peasant in the sixteenth century
taught himself to read the Bible he had acquired. Yet it happened.[14] In
the sixteenth- and seventeenth century Cambridgeshire towns Margaret Spufford has studied, books were read with extraordinary care by
persons of every description, including many women. Her evidence,
which goes beyond quantitative estimates of literacy to consider how
print was put to use, indicates that social, economic, and sexual boundaries all yielded to the book.[15] As for "oral" culture, it too was entwined
with the world of print. The culture of the European peasant may be
likened to a river full of debris. That debris had various origins and
qualities. Some of it arose from communal experience and was therefore "folk" in nature. But much of the rest of it is easily recognized as
bits and pieces of literary culture extending from Christianity as far
back as classical civilization. By the early seventeenth century this
accumulation of materials effectively meant that there was nothing
immaculate about "oral" culture. We must speak instead of a con-
tinuum between print and oral modes.[16]

That the boundaries of print were fluid and overlapping is apparent
from books themselves. The reach of some books in the early modern
period was extended visually by the woodcuts that embellished broadsides, primers, almanacs, emblem books, and the like. Collectively
these pictures transmitted ideas beyond the reach of print. Iconography
carried ideas downward into social milieux where the book may not
have widely penetrated. It also seems true that certain kinds of books
circulated in ways that touched even the apparently illiterate—the
Bible, naturally, but also the cheapest of pamphlet literature, such as
the "many old smokie paperbacks" on astrology complained of by a
late–sixteenth-century English writer, and the equally inexpensive

14. Davis, *Society and Culture*, 203.
15. Spufford, *Contrasting Communities*, pt. 2, chap. 8; pt. 3.
16. The most substantial demonstration of this point is Peter Burke, *Popular Culture in Early Modern Europe* (New York, 1978). The "oral" culture of the French peasants who proved impervi-
ous to Protestantism was rich in Catholic ideas and images; see Davis, *Society and Culture*, 203–8.

"Bibliothèque Bleue" of Troyes, a series of books designed to be read aloud.[17] We must also bear in mind that the illiterate participated in communal gatherings (fairs, festivals, church services) that functioned as occasions for the exchange of knowledge among different social groups. For all of these reasons it should be "obvious that illiteracy does not mean stupidity or mental blankness." The illiterate in early modern France, Pierre Goubert has observed, "are Christians, if unaware of the controversies over the nature of grace; . . . all of them receive an oral culture and even a bookish culture, by way of a reader or story-teller, since there is a whole printed literature designed especially for them." In England the same fluidity prevailed. There as elsewhere, illiteracy cannot be equated with a "peasant" mentality cut off from the world of print.[18]

To be sure, some boundaries do cut through the world of print. Most of the literate could not read Latin, but a large (though after 1600, a steadily decreasing) percentage of books were published in that language. In some sense books in Latin bespoke a separate culture. But as translations multiplied in the late sixteenth century,[19] and as the classics were redacted in popular formats, Latin lost most of its significance as a carrier of ideas or as a cultural code. Meanwhile printer-entrepreneurs were responding to the needs of professional groups, publishing law books and manuals of church practice that had little circulation beyond their immediate audience.

But over all such categories of books stand others that, to judge from the number of editions and the quantities produced, reached a general audience. That such books bear witness to shared beliefs and common ways of thinking seems apparent from two kinds of evidence. One is the marketplace rhythm of long duration, the continuous production of certain literary genres and formulas over centuries. The other is evidence about quantity: the sheer number of books that were printed.

17. Bennett, *English Books & Readers*, 2, 204; Mandrou, *De la culture populaire*.
18. Pierre Goubert, *The Ancien Régime* (New York, 1974), 263, generalizing from Mandrou, *De la culture populaire*. "If it is true that the parish meeting did not yet involve the kind of collective guidance of the community's spiritual life which it became at the end of the seventeenth century, the parish was nevertheless alive in the form of the Sunday gathering for mass, when for a long time the priest . . . communed with his flock." Robert Mandrou, *Introduction to Modern France, 1500–1640: An Essay in Historical Psychology* (New York, 1976), 91.
19. Bennett, *English Books & Readers*, 2, chap. 4.

Together, these types of evidence point to three major categories as dominant in the marketplace.[20] Let me consider each in turn.

Religious books outnumber all other kinds. This fact, like others in the history of print, may perplex historians who think of religion solely as a system of doctrine. H. S. Bennett, describing the situation in pre-Reformation England, brings us closer to actuality:

> The religious houses required works of spiritual instruction and consolation in the vernacular. . . . The reader of pious legends, such as those contained in that vast compilation, *The Golden Legend,* or in smaller collections, . . . was catered for. Volumes of pious stories; handbooks of practical help in church worship; books of systematized religious instruction; volumes of sermons and homilies; allegorical and lyric poems. . . .

Still closer is the anecdote repeated by Keith Thomas of an "old woman who told a visitor that she would have gone distracted after the loss of her husband but for the *Sayings* of the Puritan pastor John Dod, which hung in her house." Similarly, the wife of John Bunyan thought so much of Arthur Dent's *The Plaine Mans Pathway to Heaven,* a book that went through twenty-five editions between 1601 and 1640, that she included it in her dower, together with Lewis Bayly's *Practice of Piety.* Such devotional manuals flourished beneath the level of doctrinal controversy. Medieval *fabula* reappeared in Protestant guise, just as emblems were freely exchanged between Catholic and Protestant moralizing tales. Given this intermingling, it comes as less of a surprise that in 1667 a printer in Cambridge, Massachusetts, proposed to publish an edition of Thomas a Kempis's *Imitation of Christ.*[21]

Romances—fairy stories, chivalric poems, light fiction—tell of " 'Superman': the Paladin who splits Saracen skulls with a single blow; the crusader knight on his way to liberate Jerusalem and pausing to do the same for 'Babylon'; . . . the good giant Gargantua, coolly removing the bells of Notre-Dame; the artful righters of wrongs, straight or comic, Lancelot or Scaramouche; the invincible good enchanters and powerful fairies whose miracles almost outshine the saints." A recurring the-

20. There are tables quantifying production by types in Furet et al., *Livre et société,* 1:14–26. Less precise information is in Bennett, *English Books & Readers,* 1 and 2.

21. Bennett, *English Books & Readers,* 1, 8; Thomas, *Religion and the Decline of Magic,* 82; Spufford, *Contrasting Communities,* 210.

matic structure of danger and rescue can be said to have appealed to the wish to escape. In the "Bibliothèque Bleue," a paradigm of the literature of escapism, there is nothing of everyday reality, no poor people, no artisans, merely the sensation of entering, however briefly, a glittering world of miracle and magic. Allied to these romances were those kinds of print, especially broadsides, which played upon spectacular events such as murders and acts of treason. In Protestant England and Catholic France the genre was identical. The London printer Nathanael Butter printed news sheets and broadsides catering to "the public's innate curiosity in the strange, the supernatural, the gruesome, the intrepid and the splendid." Meanwhile in France the news sheets were telling of "juicy crimes sung in interminable lays, one *sou* per sheet, incendiarism, maned stars, weird, contagious ailments," all perhaps serving, as one historian has suggested, to provide "useful employment for the bemused minds of the . . . poor."[22]

Books of history range from travel narratives that verge on being sensational to the most ponderous of chronicles. Little of what passed as history was critical, in the sense of detaching legend from fact. Rather, legend was the stuff of historical writing. Most of these legends had to do with the history of the Christian church or the Christian community. The great example in English is Foxe's *Book of Martyrs*. Its structure as myth, providing a sacred interpretation of community origins and community destiny, together with its symbolism of light (the saints) warring against dark (the devil), were characteristic of popular history as a whole, though in any particular example the symbolism was adapted to partisan purposes.[23]

Books of history, romance, and religion as I have described them constituted a special kind of literary culture. The rhythms of this culture were slow, for what sold in the marketplace were formulas that did not need changing. Equally slow was the pace of reading, as the same books were read and reread. This practice may be designated "inten-

22. Goubert, *Ancien Régime*, 267–68, relying on Mandrou, *De la culture populaire*; Geneviève Bollème, "Litterature populaire et litterature de colportage au xviiie siècle," in Furet et al., *Livre et société*, 1:61–92; Rostenberg, *Literary . . . Publishing, Printing & Bookselling*, 78. *Note in 1996:* rereading these statements about popular literature, I find myself uncomfortable with the implication that this literature embodies an escapism.
23. William Haller, *Foxe's Book of Martyrs and the Elect Nation* (London, 1963).

sive," in contrast to the "extensive" style of persons wanting novelty and change.[24] Some readers in early modern Europe wanted new ideas from books or regarded them as objects of fashion, valuable for a season but then falling out of style. Not so the booksellers and their patrons in provincial France who sought books that had long since passed out of copyright. Not so the Franklin family or John Bunyan's wife, for whom Scripture and books of devotion gained in meaning as time went by. Such examples suggest the power of a world of print in which certain formulas had enduring significance.

Let me call this the "traditional" world of print. By doing so, I mean to emphasize the continuities between oral and print modes of culture, and among social groups. Class is certainly a factor in the making of the world of print, but the literary formulas that comprised "traditional" culture had appeal across class lines. I find it interesting that many of the stories in the "Bibliothèque Bleue" of Troyes, a true peddlers' literature, were derived from classical authors, or from "high culture" authors of a century earlier. Motifs, both literary and iconographic, seem to circulate among milieux and levels, some starting "high" and descending, others starting "low" and moving upward. What this means I do not know, but it surely suggests that all readers in early modern Europe, and many of the illiterate, participated in a common culture.[25]

Keith Thomas and Robert Mandrou argue differently. In *Religion and the Decline of Magic*, Thomas says that the reach of Protestantism extended only so far in post-Reformation England, leaving untouched an area of culture that included belief in magic, astrology, and witchcraft in ways that were contrary to orthodox religion. Adapting the view of Christopher Hill, Thomas suggests that this clash of cultures links up with the hostility between the middle class and social groups placed beneath it. An aggressively Protestant middle class preferred

---

24. This distinction between types of reading was drawn to my attention by Norman Fiering. The original sources is Rolf Engelsing, *Der Bürger als Leser: Le sergeschichte in Deutschland 1500–1800* (Stuttgart, 1974). It is Fiering's view that the experience of reading romances and other fiction was not like the experience of reading devotional manuals, the difference being the novelty of successive works of fiction.

25. Duby, "Histoire des mentalités," 923. I am sympathetic to Alan Gowans's argument that "no consistent pattern of styles related to social class can be ascertained; in every one of these popular arts [in nineteenth- and twentieth-century America] every sort of form can be found, from the most abstract to the most photographically literal" (Gowans, *The Unchanging Arts* [Philadelphia, 1970], 53).

rationality, while groups lower in the social scale, suffering from dis-
possession and never in control of things, turned to magic and astrology for their world view. This world view is a survival from earlier
times; it is "traditional" in the sense of having been around for ages, and
also in not depending on books (though manifesting itself in the world
of print) for transmittal. A kindred argument is made by Robert Mandrou, who believes that "French popular culture of the ancient regime
constituted a separate category of culture, characterized by a literature of colportage portraying an unchanging wonderland of magic and
miracles."[26]

These efforts to describe the mental world of the lower classes may
help to correct the distortions inherent in labels like the "Age of Reason," and they teach us to take seriously the most casual of literary
productions. But in the case of French popular culture an alternative
interpretation is easily available, as I have already indicated.[27] And in
the case of Thomas's "traditional" culture, the argument depends upon
a sociology of religion (that marginal groups, or groups hard pressed by
the environment, turn to "magic" for relief), or on assumptions about
"ritual" (meaning a more "primitive" form of religion, appealing to
lower classes) that cannot be borne out. Nor does the concept of a
"rational" middle class take adequate account of the sloppy reading
tastes of the literate, at once serious and sentimental, realistic and
escapist. The case for separate and segregated cultures is yet to be
made.[28]

The exception may be the milieu of the urban avant-garde. Here,
two worlds of print coexist: the world of slow and repetitious rhythms,
and that concerned with the new and critical. In ways we perhaps know
little of, this latter had its own formulas and rituals bound up with
distinctive cultural agencies (the literary salon, the Royal Society)
and distinctive modes of communication (the *Journal des Savants*, the

---

26. Thomas, *Religion and the Decline of Magic*, 76, 111–12, 145, and passim; Robert Mandrou, "Cultures ou niveaux culturels dan les societes d'Ancien Régime," *Revue des études Sud-Est européenes* 10, no. 3 (1972):415–22, as summarized in Traian Stoianovich, *French Historical Method* (Ithaca, N.Y., 1976), 170n.
    27. See the work of Geneviève Bollème on the "Bibliothèque Bleue" in "Litterature populaire."
    28. Hildred Geertz, "An Anthropology of Religion and Magic, I," *Journal of Interdisciplinary History* 6 (Summer 1975): 71–89; Mary Douglas, *Natural Symbols* (New York, 1973), chap. 1. The most impressive demonstration of the circulation of motifs and the wholeness of popular culture (meaning without class boundaries) is Burke, *Popular Culture in Early Modern Europe.*

Proceedings of the Royal Society).[29] Yet the line between readers of these journals and readers of "traditional" books cannot be drawn too sharply. There was always an intermediary group interpreting the one to the other. And there came moments when the need for reassurance could only be satisfied by returning to the formulas that never changed.

In the storybook version of New England history, every one in Puritan times could read, the ministers wrote and spoke for a general audience, and the founding of a press at Cambridge in 1639 helped make books abundant.[30] The alternative, argued most strenuously by Kenneth Lockridge, is that illiteracy shackled half of the adult males and three-fourths of the women, with consequences for the whole of culture.[31] Any of these statistics is suspect. More to the point, they do not really define the relationship between the colonists and the world of print. In thinking about that broader problem, it is important to recognize that the "dark corners of the land" that figure in the European landscape failed to reappear in New England. A considerable number of seventeenth-century Europeans had to contend with three languages: Latin, a formalized version of the vernacular, and a local dialect. In New England these distinctions became insignificant. While allowing for minor variations, we can say that a common language linked all social groups. We can also say that the colonists lived easily in the world of print. In part this was owing to Puritanism, a religion—and here I repeat a cliché—of the book. In part this sense of ease was merely a consequence of the times, for by the mid-seventeenth century the book had lost its novelty. Whatever the reasons, the marketplace of print in New England was remarkably complex and mature.

Throughout the seventeenth century the colonists depended upon imports for the bulk of their reading. In buying from abroad, these

29. See Jean Ehrard and Jacques Roger, "Deux périodiques français du xviii siècle: 'le Journal des Savants' et 'des Memoires de Trevoux,' Essai d'une étude quantitative," in Furet et al., *Livre et société*, 1:33–59.

30. As found in Samuel Eliot Morison, *The Intellectual Life of Colonial New England* (New York, 1956).

31. Lockridge, *Literacy in Colonial New England*. Apart from its methodological limitations, Lockridge's argument proceeds in complete disdain of what was printed and read in New England, and his opposing of "traditional" or "peasant" modes of thinking to others, which are denoted "modern," can only be regarded as a case of being trapped in abstract categories. For further comments, see my "Education and the Social Order in Colonial America," *Reviews in American History* 3 (1975): 178–83.

Puritans acted much like the typical patron of print in early modern Europe. Religious books dominated, forming nearly half of the imports of Hezekiah Usher, a Boston bookseller, in the 1680s. Schoolbooks, the staple of many a bookseller then and now, ranked second. Aside from books in law, medicine, and navigation, all of which catered to professional needs, the next largest category was belles-lettres—romances, light fiction, modern poetry.[32]

Already, then, we know from Hezekiah Usher's records that two of the three basic types that made up the "traditional" world of print recurred in New England. And once printer-entrepreneurs began to publish locally, their imprints round out a picture of remarkable continuity between old world and new. In its early years the Cambridge press was responsive to state patronage, publishing books for the Indians, law codes, and public documents. But by the 1660s the imprint list was reflecting the entrepreneurial instincts of printers and booksellers. Almanacs and catechisms (all written locally) made their appearance.[33] History became important, as did a closely related literature of disasters. *The Day of Doom* struck a popular nerve, an edition of 1,800 copies selling out within a year.[34] Other popular books followed, like Mary Rowlandson's captivity narrative and Cotton Mather's execution sermon for the pirate Morgan. That the American marketplace was like the European in catering to "intensive" readers and the rhythm of long duration is stunningly suggested by the reprinting in 1673 of John Dod's *Old Mr. Dod's Sayings; or, a posie out of Mr. Dod's Garden.* Here too it must have become a family household object as, sixty years before, it had been in England.

The Cambridge press did not publish any romances, but almost from the outset included works of history in responding to colonial needs. A familiar structure reappears in the history published locally. All of these books taught either a generalized version of the Protestant myth or a version tied more closely to the founding of the colonies.

---

32. Worthington C. Ford, *The Boston Book Market, 1679–1700* (Boston, 1917); books are analyzed according to subject categories in James D. Hart, *The Popular Book: A History of America's Literary Taste* (New York, 1950), 8.

33. The early almanacs were commissioned by the first Boston bookseller, Hezekiah Usher.

34. *Note in 1996:* according to Hugh Amory, it is highly doubtful that this many copies of any printed book would have been sold in New England. See in general Amory, *First Impressions: Printing in Cambridge 1639–1989* (Cambridge, Mass., 1989).

Some of this literature dealt with the millennium and the Last Judgment (for example, Samuel Whiting's *Discourse of the Last Judgment*);
some of it was about enemies of the saints, not only Catholics, but also
those Protestant groups who wandered from the truth.[35] Local publications, chiefly election- and fast-day sermons, drew the colonists
themselves into the drama of a chosen people warring against their
enemies.

Judging by the quantities of what sold and the interaction of the
local press with the marketplace, the world of print in seventeenth-
century New England bespeaks collective mentality. As in Europe, the
"traditional" literary culture reached out to and engaged every social
group. There is other evidence as well of how certain ways of thinking
extended across the levels of society. The case is clearest, perhaps,
with anti-Catholicism, always a "popular" form of belief, and one that
found expression in the iconography and rites of street festivals such as
the celebration of Guy Fawkes Day.[36] The iconography of gravestones
is something of a parallel case, for various of the symbols circulated
from emblem books through poetry to carvings done by untrained
artists.[37] The extraordinary publishing history of *The Day of Doom*
grows out of the fact that all the basic themes of the "traditional"
marketplace converged in a single text, a text that also borrowed its
literary form from the ballad by which current events ("sensations")
were announced to a popular audience. The event itself is sensational,
the return of Christ to earth amid thunder and convulsions of the
natural world. And in Wigglesworth's vivid pictures of heaven and hell
his readers could find the excitement of adventure and assurance that
the faithful would triumph over pain, disorder, and their enemies. All
these forms of sustenance recur in Mary Rowlandson's captivity narrative. The book as artifact, the literary marketplace, the "intensive"
reader, and collective ways of thinking all are joined in the history and
substance of such texts.

What, then, of the ministers and their relationship to collective mentality? It is worth noting that no New England minister ever com-

35. For example, a translation of a French history of the Anabaptists, published in 1668 as the
Baptists in Boston were challenging the orthodoxy.
36. "Samuel Checkley's Diary," *Publications of the Colonial Society of Massachusetts* 12 (1908–9):
288–90.
37. As demonstrated in Allan Ludwig, *Graven Images* (Middletown, Conn., 1966).

plained of having parishioners who could not understand his diction. The "dark corners of the land" in England and France were alien territory to persons speaking the English or French of the city. By comparison, the whole of New England constituted a reasonably uniform language field, a circumstance that helps us understand how deeply the culture was bound up with print as a medium of communication.[38]

We err greatly in thinking of the ministers as intellectuals, if by that we mean they formed a coterie, dealt in abstractions, and were interested in new ideas or criticism. Leaving aside all the other ways in which the ministers mingled with a general audience, their relationship to the literary marketplace would alone disprove this view. The ministers who entered the marketplace as writers offered a wide range of fare, from almanacs and poetry to works of history and popular divinity. They published in every size and format, from the cheapest broadside to the folio. Some of their publications sold well, others poorly. In nearly all, the contents were conventional, as were their intentions. The author in seventeenth-century New England did his writing in harmony with the modes of collective mentality. A "traditional" relationship, one ensuring the widest possible audience, existed between the ministers and the world of the book.

Two brief examples must do as illustrations of this argument: Cotton Mather and the Antinomian controversy.

Mather, like Franklin, seems to have arrived in the world with a full-blown awareness of the literary marketplace. The intensity of his life as reader and writer is obvious from the extraordinary number of books he owned, and equally from the number he wrote. The *Diary* makes it clear that this intensity flowed in traditional channels.[39] The marketplace in Mather's Boston was competitive (nineteen booksellers and seven printers were at work by 1700), pluralistic, and patterned to meet certain kinds of cultural needs. When Mather began his career as a minister, each week preaching sermons to an audience in Second Church, he simultaneously launched himself as a writer who with each book felt his way toward a popular audience. The two roles of minister and writer were really one. As minister-writer he spoke to and for

38. Lucien Febvre and Henri-Jean Martin, "Printing and Language," in *The Coming of the Book: The Impact of Printing 1450–1800*, trans. David Gerard (1958; London, 1976), 319–32.

39. It is also true that Mather and his father were attracted to, and tried to create in New England, an urban avant-garde culture, their model being the Royal Society.

collective needs, appropriating in his turn the formulas and genres of the traditional marketplace. Like the precocious Franklin, a youthful Mather took advantage of the formulas of "sensation" literature in his first publication, *The Call of the Gospel,* a sermon preached "to a vast Concourse of People" prior to the execution of the criminal James Morgan in 1686. Here is Mather speaking for himself about his literary endeavors and the marketplace: "Now it pleased God, that the people, throughout the Country, very greedily desired the Publication of my poor Sermon. . . . The Book sold exceedingly; and I hope did a World of Good . . . There has been since, a second Edition of the Book, with a Copy of my Discourse with the poor Malefactor walking to his Execution, added at the End." That is, Mather told the world the conversation he had had with Morgan as the criminal walked to the scaffold. This mating of morality with sensation, one that endures into our own day, was thereafter a formula Mather used frequently. The literature of remarkable providences and the literature of captivity narratives are related formulas, which he and his father produced in abundance and with excellent success in the marketplace. Cotton Mather was a popular writer alertly responsive to audience needs and audience tastes.[40]

At a certain point every student of the Antinomian controversy comes to appreciate John Winthrop's rueful remark that no one at the time could understand what separated the parties in terms of doctrine. Winthrop's point is really that the controversy had become rhetorical, a controversy that revolved around popular catchwords more than issues of Christian doctrine. Although the controversy included both, my purpose is to suggest why it expanded outside the circle of ministers to engage the anger and interests of all the colonists. The explanation lies in the rhetoric of the controversy. It is a rhetoric built around simple contrasts that invoke the symbolism of collective identity. On the part of the Antinomians, the basic pairing is that of light (Christ, the gospel, free grace, freedom) against dark (Adam, the law, bondage, captivity), a pairing that John Wheelwright, in a fast-day sermon that is a remarkable example of popular speech, applied to the nature of history: the ultimate struggle between the children of light and the children of darkness is occurring right here and now in New England. The "legal"

40. *The Diary of Cotton Mather,* 1:54, 65, 106, 122–23.

preachers, Wheelwright made clear, were threatening figures, not because they misinterpreted the exact position of faith in the order of
salvation, but because they represented, they were agents of, a gigantic
conspiracy against the saints. The "legal" preachers were equally rhetorical in linking Anne Hutchinson with the Familists, a shadowy but
monstrous group, as though "free love" were really at issue in 1637. But
the ministers themselves on either side of the controversy could conceive of the situation in no other terms. Their rhetoric was not a matter
of expediency, but was intrinsic to a collective mentality they shared
with ordinary people. The Antinomian controversy had its roots in and
drew energy from ways of thinking that united ministers and laity.[41]

I do not mean to simplify the position of the ministers. University
educated and at ease in the world of Latin, they stood apart from the
general population. As writers and readers they participated in a wider
range of literary culture than most of their parishioners, moving from
formulas and proverbs that are very nearly "folk" in character to more
esoteric prose, and back again. The contradictions in Cotton Mather's
character exaggerate but also accurately reflect the complexity of roles:
at once a pedant and a popularizer, Mather was also a man who eagerly
read new books while continuing to publish in old forms. After this
complexity is acknowledged, however, the fact remains that Mather
was primarily engaged with the formulas of popular religion, and with
the forms of print most suited to them.[42]

Leaving aside the ministers and their relationship to the "traditional" world of print, I want again to warn against the presumption
that ordinary people think in different ways, or possess a separate
culture, from the modes of an "elite." It does us little good to divide up
the intellectual world of seventeenth-century New England on the
basis of social class, or even, for that matter, of literacy. Rather, we can
move from the world of print, with its fluid boundaries and rhythms of
long duration, to an understanding of intellectual history as itself having wider boundaries than many social historians seem willing to recognize. How precisely to describe the formulas, the assumptions, that
comprise collective mentality in seventeenth-century New England is

41. David D. Hall, ed., *The Antinomian Controversy: A Documentary History* (Middletown,
Conn., 1968).
42. Burke, *Popular Culture in Early Modern Europe*, 133–36.

a task that lies ahead. Another task is to locate the breakdown of "traditional" literary culture, a process that may well have been underway in Mather's time, and that was certainly occurring in the eighteenth century as upper-class groups began to detach themselves from popular culture.[43] But change came slowly. It is really the continuities that impress. In taking them seriously, we free ourselves from distinctions that seem to have restricted the scope and significance of intellectual history.

43. Ibid., chaps. 8 and 9.

The Chesapeake in the Seventeenth Century

THE ENGLISH came late as colonists to the new world. A century after the Spanish embarked on the conquest and colonization of the Americas, the Virginia Company of London, chartered in 1606, dispatched a group of colonists in 1607 to the coast of Virginia. Early on, the chances of success at Jamestown seemed little greater than they had been for the "lost colony" of Roanoake, attempted in the 1580s in Albemarle Sound. An adverse disease environment, the hostility of local Indians, and shortages of food caused near-catastrophic rates of sickness and death, and failures of leadership made matters worse. Even so, the stockholders in the Virginia Company continued to finance shipments of people and supplies in the hope of carrying out an expansive economic program directed at the production of silk, glass, wine and iron. Individual entrepreneurs, using dividends of land grants from the Company, turned instead to raising tobacco. The high price it brought in Europe ensured that the economy became oriented around an export, "staple" crop. To the north, a separate political jurisdiction was created in 1632 when Charles I awarded Cecil Calvert, Lord Baltimore, a former royal bureaucrat, the territory that Calvert named Maryland. Here too, tobacco became the basis of the economy. Immi-

Written for volume one of *The History of the Book in America*, to be published by Cambridge University Press.

grants continued to arrive, many of them as indentured servants. In 1660 Maryland had a population of about 8,000 and Virginia, of 25,000; at the end of the century, Virginians of European origin numbered some 65,000 and in 1704, the total for Maryland was 36,000. During the final two decades of the seventeenth century, the slave trade brought an ever-increasing number of Africans to the Chesapeake and to the newer colonies under way in the Carolinas. As of 1700, the slave population of the Chesapeake had reached approximately 10,000.[1]

At first glance, the history of printing, publishing, writing, and reading in the seventeenth-century Chesapeake is a history of absences and censorship. Not until the 1680s was a printing office opened in Maryland after being transferred from Virginia, where the authorities closed it down before William Nuthead, the printer, had issued a single book. Books were an insignificant element in the trade that brought scores of ships to the Chesapeake each year to exchange European goods for tobacco. No merchant in these two colonies specialized in bookselling, and few stores carried more than a minuscule supply of printed books. The institutions that in England served as patrons of learnedness, and therefore as patrons of printing and bookselling, did not exist or, as in the case of the colonial version of the Church of England, were too short of clergy and funds to really matter. A minister-naturalist who arrived in Virginia in the 1680s underscored these differences when he observed to a friend in England that the colony had "few Schollars" and suffered from a "want of bookes." Other contemporaries lamented the extraordinary dispersal of settlement that made it almost impossible to create the semblance of towns. Not until the very end of the century did this situation begin to change in Virginia with the founding of Williamsburg and the College of William and Mary.[2]

Was the absence of a printing press intentional, the doing of a civil state bent on domination and well aware of how, in England, printers always seemed to elude regulation? This possibility is suggested by

1. Edmund S. Morgan, *American Slavery, American Freedom: The Ordeal of Colonial Virginia* (New York, 1975), 404, 423–24; Russell Menard, "Five Maryland Censuses, 1700–1712: A Note on the Quality of the Quantities," *William & Mary Quarterly*, 3d ser., 37 (1986):620.

2. *The Reverend John Clayton: A Parson with a Scientific Mind*, ed. Edmund and Dorothy Berkeley (Charlottesville, Va., 1965), 4; Henry Hartwell, James Blair, and Edward Chilton, *The Present State of Virginia, and the College*, ed. Hunter Dickinson Farish (Williamsburg, Va., 1940), 4–5, 12; Robert Beverley, *The History and Present State of Virginia*, ed. with an introduction by Louis B. Wright (Chapel Hill, N.C., 1947), 57–58.

William Berkeley's critique of printers and schools. Answering queries from the English government in 1671, Berkeley, the long-term governor of Virginia, linked the stability of church and state to the absence of printers and free (Latin) schools:

> But I thank God, there are no free schools nor printing, and I hope we shall not have these [for a] hundred years; for learning has brought disobedience, and heresy, and sects into the world, and printing has divulged them, and libels against the best government. God keep us from both![3]

The reference in this passage to "sects" suggests that Berkeley was thinking of the recent turmoil in England when a hitherto national church had splintered into a variety of competing groups, some of them heterodox on certain points of doctrine. He may also have been thinking of the Licensing Act of 1662, which reestablished a system of state control over printers and booksellers. When, with a different governor in office, the Virginia government thwarted the attempt in 1683 to found a printing office, its action flowed from the assumption, not unique to Berkeley but a commonplace in the seventeenth century, that the corporate state and the national church were empowered to limit the uses of printing to those that served the purposes of constituted authority, both civil and ecclesiastical.

Yet Berkeley and his political allies were not hostile to printing, per se. At one moment in his governorship he encouraged a London printer to issue an edition of the Virginia statutes, a practice he intended to continue.[4] Depending on the circumstances, therefore, the assumption that civil government was entitled to supervise the press could result in more, not less, production. Indeed it was the patronage of the civil government in Maryland that enabled William Nuthead's press to survive, and William Bladen counted on the same patronage when he set up another press in Maryland in 1700. A better explanation for the absence of a printing office in the Chesapeake is an economic one. There was little work for printers in any of the colonies to do, a

---

3. William Waller Hening, *The Statutes at Large; Being A Collection of all the Laws of Virginia,* 2d ed., 13 vols. (New York, 1819–1823), 2:517.
4. Petition to the Council for Foreign Plantations, [21 July 1662], Colonial Office 1/16 at folio 18, Public Record Office, London (reference supplied by Warren Billings; to appear in *The Papers of Sir William Berkeley,* ed. Warren Billings [Richmond, Va., forthcoming]). Hereafter cited as CO.

situation exacerbated in the Chesapeake by the dispersal of settlement, the effectiveness of scribal publication, and the absence of literary patrons.

For reasons unrelated to the presence or absence of a press, the expectation of political and cultural order that Berkeley voiced in 1671 is not what came to pass in the Chesapeake. A near-endemic restlessness with political authority is apparent in the abundance of oppositional texts, some of them scribally published in the two colonies and others ushered into print in London. This restlessness had much to do with the tug-of-war between periphery and center, colonies and empire. Another source of opposition was the very sectarianism that Berkeley feared. No group in the colonies controlled the interpretation of the vernacular Bible, which many of the colonists owned. Nor was any government able to monopolize inkhorns and paper. Within sectarian communities, people who might ordinarily have remained on the periphery of cultural production became writers and readers in spite of efforts by the civil state to limit their freedom. Hence it happened that the history of the book in the Chesapeake involved different and sometimes openly contested versions of authority in religion and civil government.

The story of scarcity is, like Berkeley's vision of civic and cultural order, also but a half-truth. Even without a local printing office, much was produced and published in the Chesapeake by the means of scribal production, as when the civil state issued handwritten "books" containing the sessions laws enacted by the assemblies in each of the colonies. County and provincial courts used the same means to satisfy the demand for legal documents, and the technology worked equally well for the publication of other kinds of texts—histories, religious tracts and manifestos, and scientific reports, to name a few. Texts were also "published" by the age-old method of being read aloud. Indeed the colonists used the word "publish" mainly to signify this mode of communication. Once we broaden our definition of book, scarcity becomes relative, for "paper" (handwritten) books and legal documents were abundant.

Remarking on the pairing of scribal and oral production, the Maryland Assembly characterized the situation in the late seventeenth-century Chesapeake as akin to the situation in England "afore there was printing."[5] This statement may be interpreted to mean that the colonists acknowledged the superiority of printing to older technologies of communication and regretted being *retardataire*. But we must not translate this feeling—to the extent it may have existed—into a teleology that represents printing as the inevitable and necessary successor to scribal and oral modes of publication. Nor should we simply adopt the perspective of metropolitan culture in evaluating the role of books and printing in the Chesapeake. The hegemony of the metropolis was real, for in most respects the colonists aspired to resume in the new world cultural practices familiar to them in the old. Yet the continuities were imperfect and the lines of authority too multiple and improvised—in a word, too fractured—for this to constitute the entire story.[6]

∾ I ∾

Governments in the seventeenth century depended on information being written down. So did people with property. Living on the nearer side of the transition "from memory to written record" that was under way in England by the twelfth century,[7] and recognizing, as the Virginia government declared in 1664, that "in all Countryes the well or ill keeping of the Records, is of the highest Consequence, as being the only means to preserve the Rights and Properties of all the Inhabitants of the same," the colonists began at once to create an archive of documents.[8] The setting in which many of these documents accumulated was the civil court system, especially the county courts. To these courts came hundreds of men and women seeking to secure their claim to property—to land, to pigs and cattle, to indentured servants, to a share

5. *Archives of Maryland,* ed. William Hand Browne et al., 72 vols. (Baltimore, 1883–   ), 2:55. Hereafter cited as *Md.Arch.*
6. See, in general, Darrett and Anita Rutman, *A Place in Time: Middlesex County, Virginia, 1650–1750* (New York, 1984), esp. 20–21, 59–60.
7. M. T. Clanchy, *From Memory to Written Record: England, 1066–1207* (Cambridge, Mass., 1979).
8. *A Complete Collection of all the Laws of Virginia now in Force* (London, [1684?]), 128. Excellent historical reviews of record keeping in Maryland may be found in the essays in Elisabeth Hartsook and Gust Skordas, *Land Office and Prerogative Court Records of Colonial Maryland,* Publications of the Hall of Records Commission No. 4 [State of Maryland], (1946; reprint., Baltimore, 1968).

of someone's estate. To these same courts came creditors wanting to enforce a contract or bargain. All of this business generated a stream of deeds, inventories, warrants, indentures, accounts, bonds, writs, receipts, patents, surveys, bills of sale, subpoenas, depositions, actions, executions, attachments, and petitions, each and every one of them scribally produced.[9] Other documents emerged from the governors and assemblies that ruled in each of the colonies—in particular, orders, commissions, statute laws, and proclamations. Agencies in England imposed various forms of record-keeping or reportage on local officials who themselves required lesser bodies—county sheriffs, parish ministers, church vestries—to enumerate "tithables" and preserve vital statistics.[10]

This archive was complemented by oral knowledge. In the early years, much was not put on paper—a dying man's instructions on how to dispose of his property, an exchange of services or goods, an agreement between master and servant over a term of indenture, the ages of children who became orphans. Illiteracy, and especially the inability to write, ensured the continuing presence of oral knowledge even after the civil courts indicated their preference that things be written down. That preference became a matter of statute law—for example, in 1663 when the Maryland legislature ordered that indentures and land transfers be in writing.[11] Ordinary people also liked it this way. On his deathbed Benjamin Gill of Maryland craved a written instrument to convey his property. But he had to settle for second best; "there being nobody then there lyung that could write, he requested this deponent to bear [oral] witness."[12] Early on, many must have had to make the same compromise.

9. See, e.g., *Md.Arch.* 41: deeds (4), bill (4), inventory (5), warrant (18), indenture (19), accounts (19), bond (28), writ (38), receipt (41), patent (51), survey (52), bill of sale (75). Wesley Frank Craven describes the recording of land titles in *The Southern Colonies in the Seventeenth Century, 1607–1689* (Baton Rouge, 1949), 277–80.

10. The scope of this archive at the level of a colony secretary is indicated in a Maryland document of 1673, "A list of Records belonging to the Secretaryes Office." *Md.Arch.* 15:32–34.

11. *Md.Arch.* 1:488 (1663). In 1639 the Maryland government had ordered each court to "keep a book of Record" for land titles (*Md.Arch.* 1:61–62), although it called for the written record to be supplemented with oral publication, ordering the registrar of deeds to "proclaime and publish the said Claime . . . and such proclamation shall be Continued and renewed in open Court once at least in every year for three years." On the preservation of property boundaries through collective memory rather than through written deed, see Rutman and Rutman, *Place in Time*, 122. The time-honored method of claiming land via turf and twig was also employed in the colonies: *Md.Arch.* 49:xii.

12. *Md.Arch.* 41:197.

That so much was written down reflects the expectation that written instruments made economic transactions more secure and civil government more legitimate. Yet the materiality of scribal production could undercut this expectation. It was common knowledge that handwritten texts could easily be altered by the simple insertion or deletion of words. Moreover, errors inevitably occurred as a consequence of the process of making copies. Thus it was that civil courts had to inquire into whether a document was "authentic" or a "true copy" and to seek corroborating testimony for the attribution of a text to someone on the basis of handwriting. Scrutinizing the materiality of an "instrument in writing" presented to it in 1661, the Virginia Assembly discovered that the text was "rased and obliterated in many parts" and promptly declared it "void in law."[13] At the highest level of government, the proprietor of Maryland confronted the fluidity of scribal texts when he challenged the wording of a commission Parliament had issued in 1652 authorizing certain agents to act on its behalf in Virginia and Maryland. Lord Baltimore charged that, contrary to the intentions of Parliament, the word "Maryland" had been inserted into the text by a faction hoping to usurp his authority.[14] At the lowest level of society things were no better, for indentured servants sometimes turned up in county courts complaining that their masters had altered the term of years in an indenture.[15] Of necessity, therefore, local courts took on the task of adjudicating the authenticity of documents. Certain rules and processes worked to the same end, as when the assemblies in Maryland and Virginia prescribed various methods of comparing copies to originals. To signify the finality of certain documents, governments stamped them with a seal and had them "engrossed" on the more permanent medium of parchment. The very quality of the handwriting, as when a document was "fairly" or "legibly" written, could also abet the authenticating of a text.[16]

13. Hening, *Statutes,* 2: 280; H. R. McIlwaine, ed., *Journals of the House of Burgesses of Virginia 1659/60–1693* (Richmond, Va., 1914), 18; *Md.Arch.* 54:568.

14. Clayton Colman Hall, ed., *Narratives of Early Maryland 1633–1684* (New York, 1910), 167–68, 303. The commissioners admitted that the original had been lost in a shipwreck. But the Parliamentarian forces also questioned the authenticity of the documents on which William Stone, the proprietary governor, rested his authority. *Md.Arch.* 3:31.

15. *Md.Arch.* 60:492–93; the Virginia government had to order that clerks not issue sealed indentures with names and dates omitted. Hening, *Statutes,* 2:488.

16. *Md.Arch.* 2:133; 13:448; Hening, *Statutes,* 2:147.

Notwithstanding the uncertain authority of scribal texts, everyone in the Chesapeake accepted the premise that written or printed documents embodied political legitimacy. Assertions of sovereignty sometimes involved the performance of such texts in a public setting. So too, some of the challenges by outsiders involved the production and display of alternative texts and the questioning of others as inauthentic. At the outset of colonization, the single most important category of document was the royal charter and its equivalent, a commission from a proprietor or chartered company, declaring the sovereignty of the king's representatives and affirming their rights to land. The performance of these texts in open-air ceremonies was a distinctive feature of colonization. Thus the proprietor of Maryland, knowing in advance that his patent had been encroached upon and that the Virginia government was opposed to the new colony, gave careful instructions to the first group of colonists on how they should deploy the documents on which his authority rested, to the point of outlining the scenario for the moment when the colonists first reached Maryland:

> That [his agents] . . . do assemble all the people together in a fitt and decent manner and then cause his majesties letters pattents to be publikely read by his Lordships Secretary John Bolles, and afterwards his Lordships Commission to them. . . .[17]

Similar scenes occurred in Virginia, as when John Smith, temporarily in the office of "President," had "the letters patent" read aloud "each week" in order to bolster his authority.[18] In 1619 it was the turn of a newly met representative assembly to employ texts as a ceremonial instrument of legitimacy. The man appointed speaker, John Pory, a veteran of the House of Commons, began the meeting by reading aloud "the great charter or commission of privileges" that sanctioned the convening of the assembly. Mimicking parliamentary procedures, the assembly drafted a set of laws that were read aloud, revised, and read again before being handed on to Pory, who was to see to their "engrossing."[19]

17. Hall, *Narratives of Early Maryland*, 20. For a parallel reading aloud of "the printed Coppy of the fundamentall Constitutions lately sent here by the Lords proprietors" in South Carolina, see A. S. Salley, ed., *Journal of the Grand Council of South Carolina* (Columbia, S.C., 1907), 1:71.

18. Edward Arber, ed., *Capt. John Smith . . . Works (1608–1631)*, Parts. 1 and 2 (London, 1895), Part. 1, 150.

19. William J. Van Schreeven and George H. Reese, eds., *Proceedings of the General Assembly of Virginia, July 30–August 4, 1619* (Jamestown, Va., 1969), 25, 53, 71.

Essential as they were to the process of establishing political order, these texts and ceremonies could not keep at bay the discontents that led to armed insurrection in both Maryland and Virginia. During the life of the Virginia Company (1606–1624), the gap between expectations in London and realities in Virginia was so great that the colonists were often forced into improvising political authority.[20] Confusion resumed during the period of the English civil war and commonwealth when a "puritan" faction in each colony agitated against representatives of the king, and vice versa. A faction within Maryland exploited this situation to depose the Calverts from control in the mid-1650s, revolted unsuccessfully in 1676 and 1681, and deposed the proprietor anew in 1689. In Virginia the Royalist-Parliamentarian schism caused a change of government in the 1650s. And in 1676 the colony fell into near anarchy during the insurgency known as Bacon's Rebellion.

A class of document that loomed large in these situations was the proclamation. In the context of English political culture, the proclamation embodied the oral, the written, and the printed (this last in those versions where it reached this stage). An instrument of royal sovereignty, any English proclamation issued before 1640 had the status of statute law. Conceptually, it embodied the monarch's speech, or spoken will. Transposed into written text, the proclamation was an elaborate artifact bearing not only the royal seal and appropriate signatures but also decorative lettering. Some of this decorative lettering was carried over into the printed form, usually a single-sheet broadside. Written or printed, these sheets were commonly posted in public for everyone to read and see. The text was turned back into speech when it was read aloud, or "published," in markets or other open-air settings, a method that remained advantageous because, by this means, "the People might be informed what Acts were passed, which they were not so fully by the printing, as by proclaiming of them at their markets."[21]

As in England, so in the Chesapeake proclamations were central to the process of governing, used by governors in lieu of statute law or as

20. See, e.g., "Wyatt Papers," *William & Mary Quarterly*, 2d ser., 8 (1928):166.
21. Robert Steele, *Bibliotheca Lindesiana (Vol. V): A Bibliography of Royal Proclamations of the Tudor and Stuart Sovereigns . . . with an historical essay on their origin and use*, 2 vols. (Oxford, 1910), I:xxxi, xiii n. 11. This equation of proclamations with statute law ended in 1641 with the abolition of the Star Chamber. See also R. W. Heinze, *The Proclamations of the Tudor Kings* (Cambridge, 1976).

the means of communicating orders.[22] Shortly after Governor Thomas Dale arrived in Virginia in 1611, he "made divers proclamations which [he] caused to be set up for the publique view."[23] In Maryland, the parliamentary commissioners repeatedly "published" what they termed "declarations" asserting their authority; in riposte, William Stone, who represented the proprietor, issued counterproclamations, one of which was "published . . . in the Church meeting." These performances accelerated in the early months of 1655, with Stone (as seen by his enemies) "publish[ing] a proclamation to deceive the amazed and distract[ed] people." Hoping by force of arms to overcome the commissioners, Stone "sent two men [before him] to publish a proclamation" of Lord Baltimore's authority. The commissioners replied in kind. Boarding a ship at anchor in the Severn, they "fix[ed] a proclamation in the main mast, directed to [the] . . . commander of the said ship, wherein he was required" to aid and assist the Parliamentarians, who ended up victorious in the "Battle of the Severn."[24]

The history of Bacon's Rebellion parallels the turmoil in Maryland, for the antagonists in that uprising, Nathaniel Bacon and the governor, William Berkeley, improvised the appropriate documents to suit rapidly changing conditions. When Berkeley learned in May 1676 that the young planter had allied himself with colonists discontented with the government's response to the incursion of a few Indians, the governor issued a proclamation, reproduced in enough manuscript copies to reach each county, denouncing Bacon as a rebel, and a second, calling for new elections to the House of Burgesses. Yet Bacon forced Berkeley to grant the one document he most wanted, a commission authorizing him to pursue military action against the Indians. Thus empowered, he sought to expand his newfound authority via scribal production. Immediately after receiving the commission in June 1676, Bacon, then in Jamestown where a session of the assembly was coming to an end, prevailed on a member of the Burgesses to "Sit the Whole Night by

22. Some early examples are included in the "Wyatt Papers," *William & Mary Quarterly,* 2d ser., 7 (1927): 247, 249, and some later ones in *Calendar of Virginia State Papers and Other Manuscripts, 1652–1781, Preserved in the Capitol at Richmond,* ed. William P. Palmer (Richmond, Va., 1875). Looking back on the governorship of Lord Culpeper, Robert Beverley complained that the governor had resorted to "the *French* Method of governing by Edicts." *History,* 90–91.

23. Alexander Brown, *The Genesis of the United States,* 2 vols. (Boston, 1890), 1:493.

24. Hall, *Narratives of Early Maryland,* 224–25, 236–44.

him filling up" a parcel of "unfolded Papers" which this temporary clerk "then Saw were blank Commissions Sign'd by the Governour, incerting such Names and Writing other matters as he [Bacon] Dictated." After Bacon left Jamestown, Berkeley once again proclaimed him a rebel and repudiated the commission. When the rebellion collapsed, the governor was challenged from another quarter when newly arrived royal commissioners, acting in the name of Charles II, sought to distribute a proclamation of general pardon they brought with them. Berkeley refused to cooperate, issuing, instead, a counterproclamation of his own, sanctioning the execution of more rebels.[25]

The handwritten proclamations that survive from the seventeenth century vary in form. Some are examples of the scrivener's art, with elaborate initial letters. Others are written in a standard hand. None of the handful that survive of the proclamations that were sent to Essex County, Virginia, shows any sign of being posted. Probably they were read aloud, for on the reverse side the sheriff has written a notation of their being published. The colony seal appears on some proclamations, but in the upper left-hand corner where the seal customarily appeared, clerks who prepared the file copies wrote in the phrase, "the seal." In size, some fill a single sheet of paper of varying width and height, the largest being approximately nineteen inches wide and twelve to fourteen inches high. Others, probably file copies, are a half sheet on the order of twelve by seven inches.[26]

These proclamations were supplemented in the workings of government by another category of document, the statute laws enacted by each session of the general assemblies that arose in Virginia and Maryland. Here too, the colonists inherited a well-established form, for English printers had issued statutes or sessions laws since the end of the

25. Charles M. Andrews, ed., *Narratives of the Insurrections 1675–1690* (New York, 1915), 32–33, 35; Wilcomb Washburn, *The Governor and the Rebel* (Chapel Hill, N.C., 1957), 64, 103–7; Morgan, *American Slavery, American Freedom,* 273; Hening, *Statutes,* 2:429–30; McIlwaine, *Journals . . . Burgesses,* 2:115. This paragraph abbreviates a much richer story of communications by rumor, gossip, proclamation, and the like, which may be followed in Washburn, *Governor and the Rebel,* and John Davenport Neville, comp., *Bacon's Rebellion: Abstracts of Materials in the Colonial Records Project* (Jamestown, Va., [1976?]), which includes materials found in M 2395, the Egerton ms (British Museum). The production and distribution of "The Declaration of the People," which Bacon signed, merits detailed study; a contemporary copy survives in the Blathwayte Papers, Colonial Williamsburg Foundation Library.

26. Colonial Records/Essex County Miscellaneous Records: Proclamations & Orders, 1692, 1700 (Virginia State Library).

fifteenth century. In English practice individual laws were commonly printed as broadsides in order to facilitate the process of notification, which, as in the case of proclamations, included the reading aloud of statutes. Another class of artifact were statute books, which brought together all the laws in force.[27] The very nature of statute law ensured that these collections fell out of date almost as soon as they were printed. Keeping up with laws that were current, or differentiating these from older laws that had been repealed, revised, or superseded, was no easy business. These difficulties were compounded in the Chesapeake, for two reasons. On this side of the Atlantic, it was never easy to keep up with the flow of English statutes. But the greater difficulty lay in the division of authority between local assemblies and agencies of the Crown, for every law enacted by the government in Virginia and Maryland was reviewed in London. This process of review, which frequently resulted in laws being suspended or revoked, made for a persistent uncertainty in the legal system in the colonies, an uncertainty exacerbated by the recurrent struggle for power between royal or proprietary governors and local assemblies.[28]

In the absence of a printing press, the one technology the colonists had at hand for producing copies of statute laws was scribal publication. The task of making these handwritten copies became the responsibility of the clerk of the Assembly in Virginia and the secretary of the colony in Maryland. It was important that these men and their assistants produce copies for the authorities back in England. It was even more important that copies reach each county court, for until this happened these courts could not function properly. Recognizing this fact, the commissioners of newly designated Somerset County on the eastern shore of Maryland asked the proprietary governor, Charles Calvert, to "Cause acts of the last Session of [the] grand assembly to be sent over to us That wee may know the better to keep ourselves in due observance of the Lawes."[29] In this instance, the county was requesting

27. Katharine F. Pantzer, "Printing the English Statutes, 1484–1640: Some Historical Implications," in *Books and Society in History*, ed. Kenneth E. Carpenter (New York, 1983), 69–114.

28. Agencies of the Crown also imposed certain obligations of record-keeping; over time, these obligations expanded, and the colonists were also requested to send over a better quality of records. See, e.g., Hening, *Statutes*, 2:512; Philip A. Bruce, *Institutional History of Virginia in the Seventeenth Century*, 2 vols. (New York, 1910), 1:403.

29. Clayton Torrance, *Old Somerset on the Eastern Shore of Maryland* (Richmond, Va., 1935), 62; in 1664 the Maryland assembly had undertaken to revise the entire body of statutes. In 1662, after completing a major overhaul of its laws, the Virginia government ordered that none should take effect until copies of the new code had reached the county courts. Hening, *Statutes*, 2:147.

a copy of all the statutes in effect, for the Maryland government had recently undertaken a complete revision of the statutes in force. For work of this length, a county customarily paid the clerk or secretary 2,000 pounds of tobacco. A copy of the laws from any particular session, a much briefer document, cost in the vicinity of 350 pounds of tobacco.[30]

All did not go well with this system of production. As the nineteenth-century Virginia legal historian William Hening discovered in preparing the early volumes of *The Statutes at Large; Being a Collection of all the Laws of Virginia, from the First Session of the Legislature, in the Year 1619,* no two versions of the laws sent out to the counties were alike. From some, entire statutes were missing, and the textual variations were many. The great struggle between Royalists and Parliamentarians in the 1650s added yet another layer of complications, for it left the colonists suspended between two sources of sovereignty. A revision of the Virginia statutes in 1652 resolved this conflict in favor of Parliament. But in the aftermath of the Restoration, the colonists had to change everything around to indicate the authority of the Crown.

Some of the statute laws produced during these decades survive in the form in which they were sent to the counties; others are preserved in archives kept by the Crown. Two different sets of "Acts for the County of Lower Norfolk" dating from 1660 and 1661 and measuring eight by twelve inches bear the signature of Henry Randolph, clerk of the Assembly, and in one instance the notation "The Precedent Acts agree with the Originall." Records of another kind survive in greater numbers, these being the folio blank paper ledgers into which county clerks copied each succeeding session's laws. To turn the pages of the Surry County ledgers from the mid-1650s is to sense firsthand the task of staying abreast of current legislation, for the words "repealed" and "revised" occur again and again in the margins of these documents.[31]

In 1660–61, the Virginia government tried a different approach

30. *Md.Arch.* 2:55; 54:274, 317, 320, 363; 60:40; Hening, *Statutes,* 2:89, 481. Early on, it sometimes happened that county clerks went to Jamestown to copy acts of the Assembly. See, e.g., Charles B. Cross, Jr., *The County Court 1637–1904 Norfolk County, Virginia* (Portsmouth, Va., 1964), 30.

31. Surry County Deeds and Wills, Book I (1652–1657), 410–65 (Microfilm, Virginia State Library); ms. Virginia State Library. Thomas Jefferson collected a number of these county compilations, some of which also formed the basis of Hening's *Statutes.* E. Millicent Sowerby, comp., *Catalogue of the Library of Thomas Jefferson,* 5 vols. (Washington, D.C., 1953), 2:242. In 1634, when counties were set up, Virginia had eight; in 1660 the number had risen to seventeen, and by 1700 reached twenty-three.

to the problems arising from scribal production of what, in essence, was a periodical. The moment was propitious, for the restoration of Charles II in 1660 ended the uncertainty about what language to use in writs. Realizing, too, that the new government in London wanted assurances that things were in good order in the colonies, the General Assembly went through the entire body of accumulated statutes, eliminating some and reaffirming others while adding new laws to the whole. In the final stages the task of fashioning a body of laws fell to the deputy governor, Francis Moryson, and the clerk of the Assembly, Henry Randolph. By prearrangement, it seems, they dispatched a copy to the governor, William Berkeley, who was then in London.[32] Berkeley turned the manuscript over to a London printer, who in the late summer of 1662 issued in folio *The Lawes of Virginia Now in Force: Collected out of the Assembly Records, and Digested into one Volume, Revised and Confirmed by the Grand Assembly held at James-City.* Berkeley gave copies to members of the newly formed Council for Foreign Plantations, reporting as he did so that the colonists intended to continue having each year's laws printed in London.[33] Presumably he also carried home with him enough copies for each county court and probably for each member of the Assembly and Council.[34]

By the early 1680s the situation was turning critical once again in Virginia. For reasons unknown, in the years since 1662 the Assembly had contented itself with scribal publication. That system yielded an interesting set of artifacts in the wake of Bacon's Rebellion, for the reformist legislation enacted by the Assembly that met in June 1676 was subsequently repealed, causing some county clerks to rip the offending pages out of their cache of manuscripts.[35] The initiative to resume the technology of printing came from a first-generation planter-merchant and sometime member of the House of Burgesses, John Buckner, who imported a press to Virginia along with an experienced printer, William Nuthead, to run it.[36] Nuthead set to work in late 1682 printing the

32. Hening, *Statutes,* 2:147–48.
33. CO 1/16 at fol. 18.
34. As was soon discovered, the printed text contained a number of errors that had to be corrected; Hening, *Statutes,* 2:189, 247.
35. Hening, *Statutes,* 2:340 n.
36. Almost certainly, Buckner's initiative was related to the complex political situation in Virginia, which included considerable agitation over the right of the Crown to review laws passed by the Assembly.

sessions laws from the Assembly that met in 1680, only to encounter the wrath of Governor Culpeper and the Council, who in February 1683, having reviewed the first "two sheets" to pass the press, halted the process on the grounds that Buckner and his printer had not been duly licensed. When further advice was sought from the Lords of Trade and Plantation, the response was an order, inserted in December 1683 into the instructions for Culpeper's successor, Lord Howard of Effingham, that he not allow any further printing.[37]

It was an unauthorized edition that gave Virginians their second statute book in the customary format of folio: *A Complete Collection of all the Laws of Virginia now in Force . . . Copied from the Assembly Records* (1684?). The intermediary was John Purvis, a London-based ship captain and merchant who came often to Virginia; laying hands on a manuscript compilation, Purvis took it back to London to be printed and returned with copies, some of which contained additional blank pages. In April 1684 the Virginia government repudiated the book on the grounds that it was published "without Licence" and directed county courts not to use it.[38] Even so, and in spite of the imperfections of the text, from which entire laws were missing, the book seems to have passed into general use, for several of the surviving copies bear handwritten notations indicating the repeal or altering of laws, or—of more importance—include substantial additions, written on the blank pages bound in with the printed text, of statutes enacted after 1682.[39]

Not until 1696 did the General Assembly in Maryland move toward having its laws printed; the actual work, done on a newly established local press, occurred in 1700. Throughout the century the colony made

37. H. R. McIlwaine, ed., *Executive Journals of the Council of Colonial Virginia*, 3 vols. (Richmond, Va., 1925), 1:493; Lawrence C. Wroth, *A History of Printing in Colonial Maryland 1686–1776* ([Baltimore], 1932), 1–2; Warren M. Billings, ed., *The Papers of Francis Howard, Baron Howard of Effingham, 1643–1695* (Richmond, Va., 1989), 42. In 1690 the Crown instructed Howard, "No printer's press is to be used without the Governor's leave first obtained" (Wroth, *History of Printing in Maryland*, 2).

38. McIlwaine, *Journal . . . Burgesses*, 2:201–3.

39. Hening, *Statutes*, 1:v. At least six of the surviving copies include handwritten additions: a copy formerly owned by Edmund Andros, who served as royal governor in Virginia in the 1690s, presently in the library of the Virginia Historical Society; a copy formerly owned by William Byrd II, subsequently acquired by Thomas Jefferson and now in the Library of Congress; three copies in the Library of Virginia, one of them formerly belonging to Nathaniel Bacon, Senior; and a copy at the New York Public Library, which has other manuscript material bound in. Neither the John Carter Brown Library nor the Harvard Law School copy contains blank pages. In some copies the blank pages were bound in from the outset, for the watermark is the same throughout.

do with scribal publication—for example, ordering in 1664, in the aftermath of a thoroughgoing revision of the laws, that the secretary of the
colony prepare a copy on parchment for each county "to the End that
all the good people of this Province may have sufficient notice of" the
laws. Recommending in the same breath the parallel technology of oral
publication, the Assembly members acknowledged—with an eye, perhaps, on Virginia, and surely with an eye on current English practice—
that the colony remained dependent on procedures of scribal and oral
publication that were customary "in England afore there was printing."[40] From time to time the Maryland Assembly responded to the
ever-growing pile of statutes by periodically repealing all existing laws,
only to reenact in the same session a nearly identical set. This tactic
helped the government get around the troublesome distinction between laws current and laws repealed or revised, a distinction that in
Maryland was overlaid with the difference, arising from the right of the
proprietor in England to approve legislation, between "perpetuall" and
"temporary" statutes.[41] Reflecting in 1676 on the situation in their
colony, the members of the Assembly were acutely aware of the problem of "knowing what Lawes are in force & unrepealed"; similarly,
they were frank in acknowledging that confusion arose from "the mul-
tiplicity of Lawes to one and the same thing which many tymes interfer
one with another."[42]

A decade later, in 1685, the first printing office was set up in Maryland when William Nuthead, thwarted by the authorities in Virginia,
moved his press to St. Mary's City and began to issue printed legal
forms. Other business was scant until the insurgents of 1689, needing to
justify the overthrow of the proprietor, hired Nuthead to print copies of
documents they were sending to the new English government. In 1693
the government ordered him to print nothing without permission but
blank bonds. After he died his widow, Dinah, moved the press to
Annapolis, where the capital had been relocated, and received permission to issue legal forms.[43] It was not this printing office, however, but a

40. *Md.Arch.* 2:54–55; see, e.g., *Md.Arch.* 57:448. At this time, Maryland had seven counties.
41. *Md.Arch.* 2:542–50; 1:468; Hening, *Statutes*, 1:vi.
42. *Md.Arch.* 2:543.
43. Wroth, *History of Printing in Maryland*, chap. 2; Wroth, "The St. Mary's City Press:
A New Chronology of American Printing," *Maryland Historical Magazine* 31 (1936): 91–III;
Md.Arch. 20:449; 19:306, 370. The insurgents' "Declaration of the reason and motive for the
present appearing in arms" was issued scribally and printed some weeks later. *Md.Arch.* 8:101–7.

new venture sponsored by the clerk of the Assembly, William Bladen, that gained the necessary approval from the government to issue the colony's laws. In 1696 Bladen proposed the establishment of a printing press in Annapolis to the end of "printing the Laws made every Sessions," and urged this step anew in May 1700, on the grounds of the evident benefit of having enough copies on hand so that "every person might easily have them in their houses without being troubled to goe to the County Court house to have recourse thereto." Guaranteed the patronage of the government, Bladen went ahead with the production of *All the Laws of Maryland Now in Force*, though he had to suffer the embarrassment of being officially informed that, when compared with the manuscript "originalls," the printed text proved to contain "many Erata's." The new press also undertook to issue a variety of printed writs, encouraged to do so by an order of the Maryland Assembly in 1700 that "noe other writts be made use of but such as shalbe printed." By 1704 the craftsman who ran the press, Thomas Reading, was issuing sessions laws.[44]

Let us return to the workings of the scribal system. That system enabled power and money to accumulate in and around the office of the colony secretary and, secondarily, in and around the offices of clerks of the Assembly and clerks of county courts. How these county clerks were recruited and what training they had received—surely some of them were clerks or scriveners by profession before entering the office— is unclear. What is certain is that their office kept them very busy during sessions of the county court and that the fees they charged for services yielded a good income. These fees were set by law: as of 1662 in Virginia, in pounds of tobacco, eight for an action, fifteen for an attachment or execution, sixty for administrations and probates, thirty for recording inventories and conveyances, and so on.[45] By the time of Bacon's Rebellion there were complaints that some clerks overcharged, and a historian who has calculated the income of clerks in Maryland at the end of the century concludes that they did very well.[46] The scope of

44. *Md.Arch.* 19:466–67; 24:22, 60, 83, 198; Wroth, *History of Printing in Maryland,* 17. As the revised code of 1699 was being completed, and a new printing office in the offing, the Assembly nonetheless ordered that the statutes be issued in handwritten multiple copies on "Large Royall Papers." *Md.Arch.* 22:558.
45. *The Lawes of Virginia Now in Force* (London, 1662), 81; *Md.Arch.* 2:532–36; 7:374–75.
46. Lois Green Carr, "County Government in Maryland 1689–1709" (Ph.D. diss., Harvard University, 1968), 492–93; Hening, *Statutes,* 2:455; McIlwaine, *Journal . . . Burgesses,* 2:108.

the archive amassed by these clerks is indicated in an inventory made in Surry County, Virginia, in 1673 when there was a change of clerks: "1 new book in folio with a leather cover 2 new books in folio covered with parchment 2 old books in folio covered with blue linnen 3 old books in folio without covers being part torne & lost 13 bundles of papers of several concernments as alsoe the printed & written acts of Assembly."[47] This inventory suggests the importance of bound unlined books measuring, most commonly, fourteen by nine inches, and described in similar inventories as "paper books" to differentiate them from those that were "printed." So too, the duties of county clerks help explain the "quires" of paper frequently noted in merchants' inventories. Much of this paper would have been used for making forms, which were needed in very large quantities.

Looking back on the interplay between scribal production and letterpress printing, our sympathies may lie with the author of the preamble to the Maryland printed laws of 1700 who felt that scribal production made it impossible for judges to obtain a "perfect knowledge of the Laws," the reason being the shortage and expense of copies, so that

> Very few gentlemen of this Province, nay not all the Justices of the Provincial and County Courts have yet had the Body of Laws by them so as to read, meditate and digest them, without which it is impossible rightly to know them, for indeed they were not to be had but at a great charge and difficult to get at any cost, and then but in a [written] hand.[48]

A parallel critique was voiced in 1730 by a Virginian in *Typographia*, a poem written to celebrate the opening of a printing office in Williamsburg. Anticipating the first locally printed edition of Virginia laws, John Markland evoked the "blotted Manuscripts" in which, hitherto, "Virginia's Laws . . . lay . . . obscur'd. By vulgar Eyes unread."[49] Yet as Hening pointed out and as the Maryland Assembly learned to its dismay in 1701, printed editions of the laws were as plagued with errors as any of the scribal copies. The advantages of printing lay, it seems, in the multiplication of uniform copies and the lower cost per copy.

There is no evidence, in any case, that the everyday workings of

47. Eliza T. Davis, comp., *Surry County Records Surry County Virginia 1652–1684* (Baltimore, 1980), 89.

48. From the anonymous dedication to William Bladen, quoted in *Maryland Historical Magazine* 5 (1910): 187.

49. [John Markland], *Typographia: An Ode on Printing* (Williamsburg, Va., 1730), 10.

justice were seriously impaired under the scribal system; whatever the confusion, local magistrates, very few of whom had been formally trained in the law, continued to issue judgments on the basis of the common law and English statutes as adapted to the needs of the colonists. The advantages and disadvantages of the various technologies may have mattered less, therefore, than the work-a-day pragmatism of these magistrates, who rarely owned law books other than of the "how-to" kind.[50] Yet the material production of colonial statutes was politically consequential in the context of the endemic tension between local rights and imperial or proprietary sovereignty. That the colonists were bothered by the supervisory privileges of authorities in England, and that scribal publication made for more confusion, seems certain; as three contemporaries remarked at the end of the century, it was "a very hard Matter to know what Laws are in Force." The situation in Maryland between the mid-1670s and the overthrow of the proprietor in 1689, as the antiproprietary forces were increasingly angered by the uncertainties of the scribal system, is a case in point.[51]

∾ 2 ∾

Printed books figured in the culture of the Chesapeake from the very outset of colonization, be they informational tracts on silkworm culture shipped there by the Virginia Company, Bibles brought by individual adventurers and servants, or personal libraries carefully transferred by men of learning.[52] Once arrived, the colonists had to make do without the network of entrepreneurial printers and booksellers who, in England, stocked the commercial marketplace with a large and ever-

50. Warren M. Billings, "English Legal Literature as a Source of Law and Legal Practices for Seventeenth-Century Virginia," *Virginia Magazine of History and Biography* 87 (1979): 403–17; Francis S. Philbrick, "Prefatory Note," in *County Court Records of Accomack-Northampton, Virginia, 1632–1640,* ed. Susie M. Ames (Washington, D.C., 1954), xi, remarking on the nearly complete absence of legal terminology in local court records.

51. *Md.Arch.* 2:543; Hartwell, Blair, and Chilton, *Present State of Virginia,* 40, 43; Lois Green Carr and David William Jordan, *Maryland's Revolution of Government 1689–1692* (Ithaca, N.Y., 1974), 15–16, 21; and chap. 1.

52. Susie M. Ames, *Reading, Writing and Arithmetic in Virginia, 1607–1699* (Williamsburg, Va., 1957), 38; David B. Quinn, ed., "A List of Books Purchased for the Virginia Company," *Virginia Magazine of History and Biography* 77 (1969): 347–60; William S. Powell, "Books in the Virginia Colony before 1624," *William & Mary Quarterly,* 3d ser., 5 (1948):177–84. The subjects I deal with in this section are discussed at much greater length in Richard Beale Davis, *Intellectual Life in the Colonial South, 1585–1763,* 3 vols. (Knoxville, Tenn., 1978).

changing supply of books. No evidence has emerged in Virginia and Maryland of merchants who maintained more than a modest inventory of books. In the absence of a retail trade, books continued to accumulate in the colonies because new immigrants brought them over, as a schoolmaster was doing shortly after the turn of the century,[53] or because a local institution deemed them necessary. A handful of the colonists added to their libraries by ordering books from London through the overseas merchants and ship captains who thronged the Chesapeake each fall exchanging goods of many kinds for tobacco.

Books were meaningful to the colonists for several reasons. Early on, while the Virginia Company was in charge, a remarkable number of educated men made their way to Jamestown. In that unfamiliar and oftentimes disruptive setting they attempted to resume the cultural practices familiar to them back in England, practices that, originating in Renaissance humanism, symbolized the condition of being "cultivated" or civilized. Thus it was that a minister wrote in 1621 that he was "no statesman nor love[d] to meddle with any thing but [his] Bookes"; that George Percy, having received writing materials and books from his brother, the earl of Northumberland, kept a daily journal and wrote "the earliest known account" of the colonizing venture; that John Pory, in a letter of September 1619 to an English friend, voiced a longing "to have some good book always in store, being in solitude the best and choicest company"; and that George Sandys, educated at Oxford and the Middle Temple and son of an archbishop, continued to work on a translation of Ovid's *Metamorphoses* published after he returned from the colony. Long after these dreams of a rural arcadia had vanished, books in Latin and Greek remained central to the identity of planters like William Byrd II.[54]

For others, the rationale for having books was rooted in Protestant-

53. Richard Shelford, who may have been a schoolmaster, died on board ship en route to Virginia in 1708. He had in his effects six testaments, six psalters, twelve primers, and six horn-books. Middlesex County Will Book A, 1698–1713, 207–208 (reference provided by Darrett and Anita Rutman).

54. Richard Beale Davis, "The Literary Climate of Jamestown Under the Virginia Company, 1607–1624," *Toward a New American Literary History: Essays in Honor of Arlin Turner*, ed. Louis J. Budd et al. (Durham, N.C., 1980), 36–53 (quotations from 37, 41, 49–50, 51–52); Louis B. Wright, "The Classical Tradition in Colonial Virginia," *Papers of the Bibliographical Society of America* 33 (1939):85–97.

ism—or, among the Catholics of Maryland, in Catholicism. Accustomed to owning and reading the vernacular English Bible, many of the Protestant colonists carried copies with them to the new world; in a similar vein, a colonist of Puritan sympathies brought over the notes he had taken on sermons preached in London by John Davenport.[55] During the period of the Virginia Company, donors in London who felt anxious about the supply of Bibles and other religious books helped out by providing extra copies; "By this Shipp the Hopewell," the Company wrote in August 1623, "you shall receaue three great Bibles, two Common prayer booke and Ursinaes Catechisme; being the guift of an unknowne person for the use of those Churches that most need them." The perception that the colonists were short of Bibles lasted throughout the century, for in 1683 the bishop of London arranged for a shipment of thirty-nine copies, to be distributed to parishes in need.[56] In order to get the Church of England up and running the Jamestown colony also needed clergymen. That men of this profession depended on books was acknowledged by the Company when it agreed to pay an allowance for this purpose to emigrating ministers. The same imperative led to the English minister Thomas Bray's initiative at the very end of the century to establish "parochial" libraries for Church of England clergy in Maryland and elsewhere.[57] The close relationship between Protestantism and books was most fully realized among the sectarians who became known as Quakers, though how they employed reading and writing will concern us in another section of this essay.

For still others, books were utilitarian. The men who practiced medicine in the Chesapeake commonly owned manuals of surgery and pharmacology, and books of "physick" also turn up in other inventories.[58] Officers of the courts relied on collections of English statutes and handbooks dealing with legal forms and procedures, which county

55. Jon Butler, ed., "Two 1642 Letters from Virginia Puritans," *Proceedings of the Massachusetts Historical Society* 84 (1972): 107.

56. Susan M. Kingsbury, ed, *The Records of the Virginia Company of London*, 4 vols. (Washington, D.C., 1906–1935), 1:589; 4:271; *Calendar of State Papers, Colonial Series, America & West Indies 1681–1685*, ed. J. W. Fortescue (London, 1898), #1329. The 1683 donation included, as well, thirty-nine copies of the Book of Common Prayer, the Homilies, the Canons, the Thirty-Nine Articles, and the "Tables of Marriages."

57. Kingsbury, *Records*, 1:575; 3:506–7.

58. A number of probate inventories are cited in Wyndham Blanton, *Medicine in Virginia in the Seventeenth Century* (Richmond, Va., 1930), 89–92.

courts ordered and paid for directly.[59] A handful of men took a broader view of the law. Wanting to align the legal system in the colonies with the English common law, yet also preferring some degree of local autonomy, these men turned to works of history, English statutes, and treatises of jurisprudence in their search for such a middle way. This sense of need was expressed early on, in 1621, by George Thorpe, a Virginia colonist who asked the Virginia Company to send "the newe booke of thabridgment of Statutes and Stamfordes pleases of the Crowne and mr westes presidents and what other Lawe bookes you shall thinke fitt," the reason being that "in the matter of our Government here wee are many times perplexed . . . for . . . wante of bookes." Near the end of the century, William Fitzhugh, a wealthy planter who was active in affairs of state, told the Virginia Assembly—frustrated by not knowing whether Charles II had assented to certain laws—that the colony should be able to enact statutes of its own when and where local "expedient" justified such action. Fitzhugh's position made him all the more concerned to keep abreast of English legislation. To this end he assembled a library of legal materials that included (as did similar libraries in Virginia) John Rushworth's *Historical Collections*. Ordering books directly from England in 1698, he specified "All the Statues made since the twenty second of King Charles the second to this year," further volumes in Rushworth's *Collections*, an English translation of a Latin treatise on government in Scotland, and three works dealing with recent or contemporary English politics.[60]

Viewed in the ensemble, the quantity of books carried to the Chesapeake in the seventeenth century was considerable. Referring only to Virginia, one historian has estimated that the total reached 20,000, dispersed among a thousand or more households.[61] The probate inven-

59. Hening, *Statutes*, 2:246. In 1661 the York County court, "finding it very necessary that a Statute booke be provided for the Courts use," sought to acquire the English statutes "out of England the next Shipping"; the acquisition cost 450 pounds of tobacco. York County Deeds, Orders, and Wills, 3:125, 134 (hereafter, DOW), transcript, Department of Historical Research, Colonial Williamsburg Foundation.

60. George Thorpe to Sir Edwin Sandys, May 15, 1621, in Kingsbury, *Records*, 3:447 (Thorpe's request is usefully analyzed in Powell, "Books in the Virginia Colony," 181–82); Richard Beale Davis, ed., *William Fitzhugh and His Chesapeake World 1676–1701: The Fitzhugh Letters and Other Documents* (Chapel Hill, N.C., 1963), 110–11, 124, 363–64. See also A. G. Roeber, *Faithful Magistrates and Republican Lawyers: Creators of Virginia's Legal Culture 1680–1810* (Chapel Hill, N.C., 1981), 57–58.

61. Bruce, *Institutional History*, 1:440–41. Bruce's several chapters (13–16) on books contain much information not carried over into this narrative.

tories that survive from three counties, Surry and York in Virginia and St. Mary's in Maryland indicate that 35 percent of the individuals whose estates were so recorded owned books. As in England, so in the Chesapeake this percentage varied with what people did for a living and how much wealth they had. Clergy and doctors invariably owned books. Gloria L. Main has estimated that for "young fathers" within seventeenth-century Maryland as a whole, 20 percent of the lowest third in terms of wealth owned books. At the opposite end of the spectrum, her figures indicate that three-fourths of the households in the top 20 percent of wealth contained books. The numbers that James Horn has worked out for four Virginia counties are roughly comparable.[62]

When we analyze the inventories from Surry, York, and St. Mary's more closely, we learn that most household libraries were tiny in size. In Surry, of forty-one inventories containing books, twenty-four had five or fewer; in only three instances is it certain that the number exceeded ten. In St. Mary's, of seventy-eight inventories that refer to books, twenty-nine cite only one or two. About one in eight of these inventories indicates a personal library that exceeded ten books. In York County, close to 50 percent of the households with books had no more than five, the few libraries of any size belonging to clergy and, in one instance, a learned physician. The story of readers and their books in the Chesapeake is properly a tale not of the few great libraries but of households more than half of which did without books, and of a large group of book owners satisfied with having only the Bible and a few other titles, most probably religious in their subject matter. Comparatively speaking, these patterns represent an improvement on the situation in some parts of England though falling behind the numbers for New England.[63]

62. Gloria L. Main, *Tobacco Colony: Life in Early Maryland, 1650–1720* (Princeton, N.J., 1982), 169, 242; James Horn, *Adapting to a New World: English Society in the Seventeenth-Century Chesapeake* (Chapel Hill, N.C., 1994), 320–21. My own calculations in this and the succeeding paragraph are based on transcriptions of all surviving inventories from St. Mary's City County (Maryland Hall of Records, Annapolis; provided by Lois G. Carr); York County (Department of Historical Research, Colonial Williamsburg Foundation); and Surry (provided by Kevin Kelly, Colonial Williamsburg Foundation). Probate inventories survive for only a certain fraction of the colonists; in the case of York County it may dip to 30 percent or less, the estimate given by Ronald Grim, "The Absence of Towns in Seventeenth-Century Virginia: The Emergence of Service Centers in York County" (Ph.D. diss., University of Maryland, 1977), 108.

63. This point is emphasized by George K. Smart, "Private Libraries in Colonial Virginia," *American Literature* 10 (1940): 33–34. Horn, *Adapting to a New World*, 320–21, provides compara-

As well as indicating patterns of ownership, the inventories inform us of the books that were commonly owned. The title cited most widely in the Surry County, Virginia, inventories was the Bible (fifteen out of forty-one); for St. Mary's the figure is twenty-nine of seventy-eight, and for York, thirty-three of seventy-one. People owned the Bible in a variety of formats, and sometimes in multiple copies.[64] Few other books are mentioned by title, the prevailing reference being to "old books," a "parcel" of books, "small books," and the like, with valuations that rarely exceed one or two hundred pounds of tobacco or the equivalent in shillings and pence. Other than the Bible, the book most often named was a Protestant work of devotion, a "steady seller" of the first two-thirds of the century, Lewis Bayly's *The Practice of Piety*, the only "small book" identified by title in a York County merchant's inventory of 1657 (two copies, out of a total stock of twelve or thirteen). Some seven of the York County inventories included Bayly's much-reprinted book, an amount that equals the total references to psalters, psalmbooks, and the Book of Common Prayer.[65] Whenever the appraisers of an estate provide a list of specific titles, the subject matter is invariably religious. It seems reasonable to assume, therefore, that religion predominated as the subject matter of the "old" or "small books" left nameless in so many inventories. Books we may lump together as "secular" are a very distant second to religious books; some of these were manuals or handbooks that taught specific skills.[66] In keeping with the importance of the commerce in tobacco, land, and servants, a sixth of the York County inventories note the presence of "writings"

---

tive data for one English region. The percentage of book ownership in the English West Indies, though not specifically indicated in Richard S. Dunn, *Sugar and Slaves: The Rise of the Planter Class in the English West Indies, 1624–1713* (Chapel Hill, N.C., 1972), seems to have been much lower; see, e.g., p. 140.

64. A woman of some means, Sarah Willoughby, owned two Bibles in quarto, a Latin Bible and two testaments when her inventory was taken in 1674; *William & Mary Quarterly*, 1st ser., 3 (1894–95): 44–45. According to James Horn, a fifth of planters' inventories in Lower Norfolk County "explicitly mentioned Bibles" (*Adapting to a New World*, 402); see also *The Lower Norfolk County Virginia Antiquary* i, pt. 3 (1893): 104–6.

65. Hugh Stamford, DOW 3:23.

66. Walter B. Edgar, "Some Popular Books in Colonial South Carolina," *South Carolina Historical Magazine* 72 (1971): 174–78, surveying 2,314 inventories dating from 1679 to 1776, found that only 438 "had titles other than Bibles, prayerbooks, or testaments" (not counting innumerable "books"). "Only a handful of men, probably fewer than 5 percent of all free white adult males, owned reading matter other than these [Bibles, psalters, etc.], such as sermons and moral treatises, or books on medicine, mathematics, history, and the law" (Main, *Tobacco Colony*, 244).

(commonly preserved in a chest or trunk), account books, and paper. Some of the colonists assembled a substantial archive of these writings or ledgers and, in the course of time, used up a great deal of loose paper.[67] In generalizing about culture or mentality on the basis of these inventories, there is little to say beyond remarking on the pervasiveness of a middle-of-the-road Protestantism. Traces of this Protestantism turn up in the pious language of a handful of wills and in occasional references to classics of the English Reformation like John Foxe's *Book of Martyrs*. That Bayly's *Practice of Piety* was owned in Virginia and Maryland by persons at almost every level of wealth supports the conclusion to which the prevalence of Bibles also points, that Protestantism was something of a common denominator in the Chesapeake.[68] Yet the common culture of the Chesapeake also incorporated a folklore or mores—manifested in the practice of burying suicides at crossroads with a stake through the heart, in the circulation of wonder stories, in outbursts of anti-Catholicism, in the large-scale consumption of alcohol at funerals, and in occasional episodes of witch-hunting—that owed little to books.[69]

In particular, the inventories suggest that the colonists went without the "cheap books" that were widely available in England by the middle of the century, and that undoubtedly played a role in the shaping and transmission of popular culture. A few inventories, but no merchant's stock, contained almanacs, which in England had become almost ubiquitous by 1650. Anticipating similar demand in the new world, the

67. *Md.Arch.* 4:75–76; Ames, *Reading,* 55 (for an inventory with twelve manuscripts); the "list of writings in a Red Trunke" inventoried after the death of James Stone of York County in 1648 specified six separate account books (DOW 2:377); Davis, *Fitzhugh,* 82.

68. Horn, *Adapting to a New World,* 403; *William & Mary Quarterly,* 1st ser., 7 (1899): 248. Intent on differentiating Virginia from New England, historians of religion and book culture in the south have frequently emphasized the presence of "Anglican" publications, though also acknowledging, with an air of embarrassment, the presence of "Puritan" or Calvinist materials. Apart from badly overstating the preponderance of Anglican materials—it is simply false to assert, as John F. Woolverton does in *Colonial Anglicanism in North America* (Detroit, 1984), that Richard Allestree's *The Whole Duty of Man* "was in nearly every Virginia library whose contents have been recorded" (p. 44)—these historians fail to take account of the broad middle ground, including, historically, much that was "Calvinist," encompassed by the Church of England. The history of the more explicitly Puritan faction in Virginia is told in Babette M. Levy, "Early Puritanism in the Southern and Island Colonies," *Proceedings of the American Antiquarian Society,* n.s., 70 (1960): 69–348.

69. *William & Mary Quarterly,* 1st ser., 15 (1906–07):181. See also Darrett B. Rutman, "The Evolution of Religious Life in Early Virginia," *Lex and Scientia: Journal of the American Academy of Law* 14 (1978):192–202; Horn, *Adapting to a New World,* chap. 9.

printing office established in Massachusetts in 1640 began immediately to issue a local series. The same demand did not arise in Virginia or Maryland until the 1730s. Well before this decade, the first printer in Pennsylvania, William Bradford, had hastened to meet the need for these calendars; in a note included in the first of his almanacs, published in 1686, the author remarked that he had "journied in and through several places, not only in this Province, but likewise in Maryland, and else where," and found "the People generally complaining, that they scarcely knew how the Time passed, or that they hardly knew the day of Rest, or Lords Day, when it was, for want of a Diary, or Day Book, which we call an Almanack." As Bradford learned, however, almanacs were a contested genre, for his attempts got him into trouble with his Quaker patrons in Pennsylvania.[70]

Altogether, the Chesapeake inventories suggest that printed books of any kind were incidental to the farmers, housewives, and servants who made up the bulk of the population. Content to own a few books, at best, ordinary people wanted these books to inform them about the obligations of being good Christians. But books could not help them master the grinding routines of raising tobacco or ease the fluctuations in what they earned from the crop. Politically, it may have sufficed to hear the statutes read aloud on court day. Two other circumstances worked to limit the ownership of books. One of these was the nearly complete absence of booksellers handling new or used books, and a second was the rate of literacy.

No one in the seventeenth-century Chesapeake seems to have specialized in bookselling. Nor does anyone seem to have practiced the trade of bookbinding, though there must have been someone with the necessary tools and knowledge who worked alongside the Bladen-Reading printing office.[71] Local merchants in the Chesapeake—that is,

70. Charles R. Hildeburn, *A Century of Printing: Issues of the Press in Pennsylvania 1685–1784*, 2 vols. (Philadelphia, 1885), 1:2. A doctor in York County, Francis Haddon, had a "Dutch Almanack" among his books in 1674 (DOW 5:99). Philip Calvert had "Gadburyes Ephemerie and others 1671" and "Ephemerie 1673" in his library (Testamentary Papers, Maryland Hall of Records, Annapolis). Bruce, *Institutional History*, 1: 417, notes an Isle of Wight inventory of 1669 that contained two almanacs. A London bookseller issued in 1685 an almanac designated for the middle colonies; Elizabeth Baer, comp., *Seventeenth-Century Maryland: A Bibliography* (Baltimore, 1949), 120.

71. In *Bookbinding in Colonial Virginia* (Williamsburg, Va., 1966), C. C. Samford and John M. Hemphill II note (p. 1) the presence of an English bookbinder in Lower Norfolk County, Virginia, in the 1640s, but it is very unlikely that he practiced his craft in the colony.

permanent residents, in contrast to the transient Dutch or English merchants who exchanged merchandise from their ships for tobacco—carried supplies of paper in their stores as well as "paper books." Most of them also had a small supply of books, chiefly primers and hornbooks of the kind used by children learning to read. The inventory of the store that Richard Willis kept in Middlesex County at the end of the seventeenth century included thirty quires of paper, twenty primers, and five hornbooks; the books must have been barely visible amid the extensive quantities of fabrics, clothes, tools, nails, pipes, and buttons.[72] An inventory made in 1675 of the store of Robert Farrar, in St. Mary's County, Maryland, listed five primers and three hornbooks. Another of 1675 from York County included eight "gilt" hornbooks and six "plain," the former valued at two pence, the latter at one, among a great mass of linens, tools, pots and pans, tapes, shoes, and the like.[73] In 1668 Jonathan Hubbard of the same county had twelve hornbooks (valued, in total, at two shillings), one testament, and one psalter in his inventory; three years later, the York County story kept by Jonathan Newell included eight hornbooks valued at one pound of tobacco apiece. So insignificant were printed books as a commodity that some merchants stocked none at all, though their stock invariably included paper.[74] Only in a single instance, the store maintained by John Sampson of Rappahannock County, Virginia, were books a significant feature of the inventory, and this because in 1685, the year Sampson died, the store goods included a chest containing ninety-one copies of the 1684 edition of the Virginia statutes.[75]

72. Middlesex County Will Book [A], 1698–1713, 55–76 (a transcription provided by Ann Smart Martin). Another Middlesex merchant, Robert Dudley, whose will is dated November 1701, had three hornbooks, one primer, and three other books (Middlesex County Will Book G Order Book No. 3, p. 105); information provided by Darrett and Anita Rutman.

73. St. Mary's City Inventories; DOW 5:113–14, possibly an inventory of goods left on account in Virginia by London merchants.

74. DOW 4:230; Warren M. Billings, ed., *The Old Dominion in the Seventeenth Century: A Documentary History of Virginia, 1606–1689* (Chapel Hill, N.C., 1975), 192–98. Newell's network of trade relations is described in Grim, "Absence of Towns," 164–71. No books: in York County, Edward Phelps (1679), DOW 6:111, though his inventory included fifteen quires of "white writing paper"; Edward Lockey (1667), DOW 4:191–92. It is suggestive that the store of Robert Slye of St. Mary's City contained one paper book, ten inkhorns, five and one half reams of paper, and but two "printed" books. St. Mary's City Inventories.

75. Inventory of John Sampson, Rappahannock County, *Deeds, Etc.* No. 6, p. 62 (microfilm, Department of Historical Research, Colonial Williamsburg Foundation); alluded to in Ames, *Reading*, 34, this inventory was traced for me by Kevin Kelly. No valuation was given for the law books; the store contained two Bibles and perhaps another eight books.

Was this absence of demand linked to the rate of literacy in the Chesapeake? In assessing that rate, we learn little from remarks that were made by contemporaries, as when the Virginia Council denounced Nathaniel Bacon's followers as "the Rascallity and meanest of the people ... there being ... very few who can either write or read," or when three observers at the end of the century noted that some of the magistrates could not read or write.[76] We learn more from the wills and legal documents to which people had to add their signature, for a good many of the colonists signed with a mark. According to one careful study of Virginia wills, the rate of signature literacy for men dying before 1650 was 45 percent and rose to about 60 percent by 1680. These and other surveys indicate that men were able to sign their names at twice the rate of women, and that relative wealth influenced the rate of male literacy.[77] Court records provide further evidence of persons who lacked the ability to write and who turned to someone else to prepare a document. Thus in a case of fornication in York County, Virginia, a woman servant testified that her lover used the excuse of needing to have a letter written to come to the house where she lived.[78]

The people who signed with a mark may have been able to read. Since there is no quantitative basis for ascertaining this skill, the evidence for reading literacy must be indirect. That evidence includes court records which capture in one way or another the presence of thousands of men and women, young and old, servants, leaseholders, merchants, and planters. Rarely do these records suggest that someone could not read, and though it may be the case that women were less literate, their participation in the world of reading is evident from the references to them as givers and receivers of books.[79] The sheer mass of written documents which both women and men handled in making

76. Horn, *Adapting to a New World,* 158.
77. Kenneth A. Lockridge, *Literacy in Colonial New England: An Inquiry into the Social Context of Literacy in the Early Modern West* (New York, 1974), chap. 2. See also Bruce, *Institutional History,* 1, 450. Based on the York County court records, my rough count of the ratio of marks to signatures among women is 3:1. Amandus Johnson, *The Swedish Settlements on the Delaware, 1638–1664* (Philadelphia, 1911), has data on literacy among Swedes (p. 28) and Finns (p. 31).
78. DOW 3:68.
79. See, e.g., DOW 4:12, for a mother willing a daughter her "Church Bible" (1665). There is also evidence to suggest that, in willing books to the next generation, fathers assigned far more books to sons than to daughters, and sometimes provided *only* for sons; when gifts and bequests were made to wives and daughters, these were typically Bibles and books of devotion. See, e.g., Davis, *Fitzhugh,* 379; will of John Catlett, *Virginia Magazine of History and Biography* 3 (1895): 64; will of Samuel Baylly, ibid. 8 (1901): 422; for a contrary example, ibid. 5 (1897): 183.

property transactions points toward the same presumption, that most of them were capable of reading. This presumption is strengthened by the fact that children were taught to read before they learned to write; many who started down the path to literacy halted midway, never advancing to the more specialized skill of writing.[80]

To the premise of widespread reading literacy we must add another, that people who were unable to write could nonetheless participate in the workings of politics and the economy. At certain moments of high political tension, crowds gathered to sign their names to oaths or protests.[81] Administrators in the civil government were not always literate; it happened, for example, that certain burgesses and justices of county courts signed their names with a mark, and it was *very* common for the men who compiled probate inventories and appraised estates to use marks, as did many of the persons who witnessed legal documents and served on juries.[82] All this evidence of the supposedly "illiterate" acting side-by-side with the "literate" requires us to recognize that the practical significance of literacy in the Chesapeake was relative to specific situations. Moreover, the traditional method of "publishing" many documents by reading them aloud served to enlarge the possibilities for participation. Literacy was thus a two-sided situation, involving a hierarchy of skills but also open-ended in ways that sharply reduced the significance of gender and class.

As to how and when children learned to read and write in the Chesapeake, the evidence is again mostly indirect. Where they learned to read can be answered with a negative: not in schools organized or financed by the civil state. The continual flow of new immigrants to the Chesapeake, most of them indentured servants in their teens, included a certain number of young men and women who had become literate back in England. Children born and raised in the Chesapeake learned

80. Margaret Spufford, "First Steps in Literacy: The Reading and Writing Experiences of the Humblest Seventeenth-Century Spiritual Autobiographers," *Social History* 4 (1979): 407–35.
81. Edward Neill, *Virginia Carolorum: The Colony under the Rule of Charles the First and Second A.D. 1625–A.D. 1685* (Albany, N.Y., 1886), 119; Rutman and Rutman, *Place over Time*, 158–61.
82. Lois G. Carr, "The Foundations of Social Order: Local Government in Colonial Maryland," in *Town and County: Essays on the Structure of Local Government in the American Colonies,* ed. Bruce C. Daniels (Middletown, Conn., 1978), 80, 83; Carr, "County Government in Maryland," 622; Blanton, *Medicine in Virginia,* 88–90; Bruce, *Institutional History,* 1: 450. According to the satirist Ebenezer Cooke, "very few of the Justices of the Peace [in Maryland] can write or read" (*The Sot-Weed Factor; Or, A Voyage to Maryland. A Satyr* [1708], reprint. Maryland Historical Society Fund Publication #36 [Baltimore, 1900], 22n).

to read, and a smaller proportion, heavily male, learned to write, either in a household or by attending local schools so informally organized that it is hard to document their presence. One clue to these local possibilities is the preference expressed in wills that children be taught to read and write. By the end of the century the indentures of orphans and servants, both male and female, often included a provision that the master teach reading and, in some instances, writing. These indentures reflect the common assumption that children began learning how to read in a household.[83] Alternatively, or afterward, children studied under a schoolmaster. Responding individually to inquiries from the bishop of London in 1724, twelve Anglican clergy in Virginia informed him that the possibilities for schooling in their parishes included "small" or "little" schools where reading, writing, and, in some instances, arithmetic were taught.[84] Another form of school, the "free" or "grammar" school where boys learned the classical languages, existed intermittently in Virginia and Maryland; such a school was established alongside the newly founded College of William and Mary. Parents who wanted advanced training for their children seem to have improvised, as William Fitzhugh did in hiring a French clergyman to educate his two older sons, the consequence being, in Fitzhugh's words, that his second son, at age eleven, "can hardly read or write a word of English."[85]

Learned culture nonetheless survived in the Chesapeake, reconstituting itself in the aftermath of the dissolution of the Virginia Company, though never again, perhaps, as closely attached to cosmopolitan practices as in those early years. Little evidence remains of the libraries transported in the early years to Virginia. It seems probable that, under the chaotic conditions of the first decades, such collections were dispersed once their owners died. But a clergyman who lived for half a century on the eastern shore of Virginia, Thomas Teakle, enjoyed a

83. For references in wills by parents, see especially "Isle of Wight County Records," *William & Mary Quarterly*, 1st ser., 7 (1899): 221, 222, 236, 241, 244, 248; Rosemary C. Neal, *Elizabeth City County, Virginia Deeds, Wills, Court Orders, Etc., 1634, 1659, 1688–1702* (Bowie, Md., 1986), 86, 88. See also Edgar W. Knight, *A Documentary History of Education in the South before 1860*, 5 vols. (Chapel Hill, N.C., 1949), 1: 53–55.

84. William Stevens Perry, ed., *Historical Collections Relating to the American Colonial Church*, 5 vols. in 4 (Hartford, Conn., 1870), 1:283, 288, 300, and passim; Ames, *Reading*, 16. Davis, *Intellectual Life*, 1 chap. 3, overstates both the percentage of literacy and the number of schools.

85. Davis, *Fitzhugh*, 361.

library that had grown to 333 books when he died in 1697. In Maryland, the chancellor of the colony, Philip Calvert, a graduate of the English Catholic College of Saints Peter and Paul in Lisbon, Portugal, lived amidst a hundred or so books; the ten that were stored in his "office" included Coke's *Institutes,* the ubiquitous Dalton on the office of justice of the peace, a "Lattin booke of writts" and a "Treatise of Wills." The library of Henry Randolph, sometime clerk of the Virginia Assembly and one of the persons responsible for the printed laws of 1662, contained 29 titles in folio out of a total of some 160. Books relating to the law constituted half of the collection of 114 titles belonging to Arthur Spicer of Richmond County, who was active as an attorney. Ralph Wormeley of Middlesex County, Virginia, owned 410 titles according to an inventory made in 1701; broken down by subject, 86 of these were works of history and biography and 123 pertained to religion and morality. In 1686 Henry Willoughby, a doctor, had 74 books described by the appraisers of his estate as "divinity," another 38 characterized as dealing with the law, and 44 on "physic." By the turn of the century, the largest personal library in the Chesapeake was probably that of Francis Makemie, a Presbyterian clergyman and planter; when he died in 1708 he owned 992 titles.[86]

Much more common were collections in the range of twenty to one hundred titles. Robert Slye of St. Mary's County had "forty printed Bookes great and Small" when he died in 1671. The first of the Virginia Carters, John, owned some sixty titles at his death in 1659; many of these passed into the collection of his son John II, who had about the same number in his estate when it was inventoried in 1690.[87] The library of a physician and native German, George Hack, inventoried in 1665, contained some ninety books in a mixture of languages ("High German," "Dutch," Latin, and English) and formats, from folio to duodecimo; Hack must have brought the greater part of these with him to Virginia. A collection of forty-nine books belonging to Sarah Wil-

86. Jon Butler, "Thomas Teackle's 333 Books: A Great Library on Virginia's Eastern Shore, 1697," *William & Mary Quarterly,* 3d ser., 49 (1992):449–91; Calvert Inventory, Testamentary Papers, Maryland Hall of Records; *William & Mary Quarterly,* 1st ser., 3 (1894–95): 133–34; Bruce, *Institutional History,* 1: 419; *William & Mary Quarterly,* 1st ser., 2 (1893–94):169–74; subject analysis from Bruce, *Institutional History,* 1:426; Ames, *Reading,* 39.

87. St. Mary's City Inventories; *William & Mary Quarterly,* 1st ser., 8 (1899–1900):18; Louis B. Wright, "The Gentleman's Library in Early Virginia: The Literary Interests of the First Carters," *Huntington Library Quarterly* 1 (1937):2–61.

loughby of Lower Norfolk County was inventoried by title in 1673; aside from two testaments and four Bibles, one of them in Latin, the collection included another ten or so books in Latin as well as a potpouri of history, religion, travel, and how-to manuals.[88] Where such books were stored—in a bedroom "closet," a chest, a hall, or the infrequent "study"—varied from one house to the next.[89]

How it was the colonists added to or acquired their stock of books once they reached the Chesapeake is largely unknown. Early on, the Virginia Company advised a clergyman that he could assemble a decent library in Virginia out of the collections of his predecessors.[90] Some books passed as gifts within families or to a circle of friends, or in acknowledgment of another's professional needs—a surgeon bequeathing his Latin and English books and instruments to another would-be doctor or, in a separate instance, designating a folio Greek Testament as a gift to a much-admired minister; a man bequeathing a Bible and sermon books to a godson and goddaughter; a county clerk willing each of his executors "a booke as they Shall Choose for their reading."[91] Arriving in Virginia relatively late in the seventeenth century, a clergyman-naturalist, John Banister, was given a copy of Descartes' *Meditations* (an Elzevir) by one of the Blands. There is some evidence that the learned borrowed from each other, as William Fitzhugh did from Ralph Wormeley in 1682 when he wanted to use Rushworth's *Historical Collections* and the latest statutes.[92] English correspondents sent books; George Calvert was grateful in 1664 to receive the latest printed "news books, which are a great divertisement to us," from his father; one of John Banister's patrons sent him books; and William Fitzhugh asked overseas friends and in another instance, a

88. *William & Mary Quarterly,* 1st ser., 8 (1899–1900):237; ibid., 3 (1894–95):44–45.
89. *William & Mary Quarterly,* 1st ser., 3 (1894–95):246; Davis, *Fitzhugh,* 379; Main, *Tobacco Colony,* 163.
90. Kingsbury, *Records,* 2:506–7. Powell, "Books in the Virginia Colony before 1624," brings together much information on the ordering of books and about what was available.
91. Blanton, *Medicine in Virginia,* 90; Neill, *Virginia Carolorum,* 406; Augusta B. Fothergill, *Wills of Westmoreland County, Virginia 1654–1800* ([n.p.], 1925), 80, 97; Noel Currier-Briggs, *Virginia Settlers and English Adventurers: Abstracts of Wills,* 3 vols. (Baltimore, 1970), 1:401; and see in general Bruce, *Institutional History,* 1, chap. 13.
92. John and Nesta Ewan, *John Banister and His Natural History of Virginia 1678–1692* (Urbana, Ill., 1970), 131, and, in general, chap. 11: "Books of Banister's Bearing His Signature"; Davis, *Fitzhugh,* 124, 233.

brother, to send him "printed News" and other "newest" items of their own selection.[93] It was also possible to order specific titles, as Teakle must have done in building up his library. In the early 1630s William Claiborne of Kent Island was buying "bibles and bookes of prayers" to use in church services. Later in the century, George Hack received copies of the *London Gazette*, which he probably acquired from a transient tobacco merchant. William Byrd I relied on the Reverend John Clayton, who spent two years in Virginia, to act as his intermediary in securing items of natural science, and Fitzhugh ordered schoolbooks for his sons, along with political and legal books, from a London bookseller.[94] Aside from individuals, orders for books from England came from vestries in Virginia needing copies of the Bible and the Book of Common Prayer.[95] Quakers had their own system for acquiring and distributing books.

Learned cultured in the Chesapeake was like popular culture in being linked to Protestantism. Invariably the larger collections included the Bible and examples of the literature of devotion. More telling than the proportion of such books is the importance they had for their owners, an importance revealed in three specific legacies that involved women readers. In 1659 John Carter willed his wife three works of devotion, one of them a "steady seller" of Anglican devotion, Richard Allestree's *The Whole Duty of Man* (he also specified that his wife should retain "her own books"). In 1673 the widow of Colonel John Catlett divided up her late husband's library, giving each of her two daughters "a small Bible" and leaving the rest to be shared equally between her sons. In 1701 William Fitzhugh's widow, Sarah, made a selection of books from his library that she wished to keep for herself: four of the six titles were the Bible, the Book of Common Prayer, *The*

93. Ewan and Ewan, *John Banister*, 134; Davis, *Fitzhugh*, 286, 288, 353; *The Calvert Papers*, Maryland Historical Society Fund Publication No. 28 (1889), 236; see also 244–50.
94. Lawrence C. Wroth, "The First Sixty Years of the Church of England in Maryland, 1632–1692," *Maryland Historical Magazine* 22 (1916): 4; Bruce, *Institutional History*, 1: 432 n.; Davis, *Fitzhugh*, 271, 333, 341; Ewan and Ewan, *John Banister*, 51–52; Marion Tinling, ed., *The Correspondence of the Three William Byrds of Westover, Virginia, 1684–1776* (Charlottesville, Va., 1977), 61. See also Elizabeth Donnan, "Eighteenth-Century English Merchants: Micajah Perry," *Journal of Economic and Business History* 4 (1931): 74, 75.
95. See, e.g., C. G. Chamberlayne, trans., *The Vestry Book of Kingston Parish Mathew County, Virginia* (Richmond, Va., 1929), 2.

Whole Duty of Man, and *The Practice of Piety*.[96] These were the same books that so many middling-status English readers preferred, books deemed of "practical" significance (as they advertised themselves) in teaching the reader how to set things right with God. No less utilitarian were other sections of these learned libraries—notably, books on navigation, horticulture, surgery and medicine, the law, and scriptural exegesis, this last category constituting a third of Teakle's books. Books of a different kind altogether, the romances, miscellanies, plays, satires, and collections of epigrams that constituted the light reading of English gentlemen and gentlewomen, were thinly represented.[97]

It seems certain that learned readers were unable to re-create the social practices that characterized the world of learning in England. Nowhere in the seventeenth-century Chesapeake was there a theater or college, bookstore, club, or religious convocation where these readers could enjoy the sociability of their own kind or display to others the fruits of a specialized education; the one Virginian of this century to be elected to the Royal Society and himself English educated, William Byrd II, citing the dispersal of settlement and the paucity of ministers, noted the obvious, that there were no places "whereunto the better sort of persons do resort."[98] "Society that is good & ingenious is very scarce, & seldom to be come at except in books," William Fitzhugh remarked to an English correspondent in 1687. Lamenting in the same letter the weakness of the institutional church, Fitzhugh provided a second rationale for solitary reading: "but that which bears the greatest weight with me, for now I look upon my self to be in my declining age, is the want of spirituall help & comforts, of which this fertile Country in every thing else, is barren and unfruitfull."[99] What was true for persons of Fitzhugh's status and wealth was true more generally. Every other

96. Louis B .Wright, "Pious Reading in Colonial Virginia," *Journal of Southern History* 6 (1940): 389; George R. Catlett, *The Catlett Family in Virginia and Illinois and Related Families* ([n.p., n.d.]), 207; Davis, *Fitzhugh*, 101 n.

97. T. A. Birrel, "Reading as Pastime: The Place of Light Literature in Some Gentlemen's Libraries of the 17th Century," in *Property of a Gentleman: The Formation, Organisation and Dispersal of the Private Library 1620–1920*, ed. Robin Myers and Michael Harris (Winchester, England, 1991), 113–31. Like the argument concerning "Anglican" culture, the kindred assertion of "gentlemen" libraries and readers severely distorts the uses of literacy in the Chesapeake. But see the inventory of Captain Thomas Cocke (1697), *William & Mary Quarterly*, 1st ser., 4 (1895–96): 15.

98. Kenneth A. Lockridge, *The Diary, and Life, of William Byrd II of Virginia, 1674–1744* (Chapel Hill, N.C., 1987), 47.

99. Davis, *Fitzhugh*, 203.

kind of evidence, from legacies to the subject matter of the books most widely owned, bears out the association between reading and religion, or as the literary historian Louis B. Wright once observed, between reading and utilitarian purposes. Reading was no leisurely pastime but something undertaken to meet specific needs.[100]

At the end of the century, the first real counterweight to the dispersal of learned culture in the Chesapeake emerged in Williamsburg with the founding of the College of William and Mary. Thirty years before this, in the aftermath of the Restoration, the Virginia government, noting "the want of able & faithfull ministers," envisioned a college, as had the Virginia Company in its heyday. Not until the appointment in 1689 of James Blair, a Scotsman, as commissary of the clergy in Virginia did these long-nurtured hopes begin to ripen, with a charter in hand by 1693 and the first students enrolled by 1694. This time around, the colonists organized a two-tier institution: not only a college, but also a grammar school to train would-be scholars in the classical languages. Like the founders of Harvard before them, the founders wanted their new college to function as "a seminary of ministers of the gospel" capable of providing a sufficient supply of native-born clergy.[101]

The new college needed books, which came to it mainly through private donations. Back in 1619, when the Virginia Company entertained the project of a college, an anonymous donor responded with a gift of a three-volume folio set of William Perkins's works and Augustine's *City of God*. In the mid-1690s, the key figure in the making of the college library was Francis Nicholson, a soldier turned administrator who served as lieutenant governor of Virginia and then as governor. Initially he gave seven books, and shortly thereafter, probably in connection with his term as governor, donated the remainder of a personal collection of more than two hundred volumes, the majority of them relating to religion. Other donations arrived from England in response to solicitations James Blair made in person. Certain bishops of the church gave generously, for a student speech of May 1699 thanks two bishops for "makeing a noble present of well chosen bookes to our

---

100. Louis B. Wright, "The Purposeful Reading of Our Colonial Ancestors," *English Literary History* 4 (1937): 85–111.
101. John Melville Jennings, "Notes on the Original Library of the College of William and Mary in Virginia, 1693–1705," *Papers of the Bibliographical Society of America* 41 (1947): 242; Hartwell, Blair, and Chilton, *Present State of Virginia*, 68–69.

Library, intending hereby to take care that our Youth be well seasoned with the best principles of religion and Learning that can be taught by the most sound & Orthodox Divines." Some English patrons made gifts of money, including £ 50 received from the charitable body known as "Dr. Bray's Associates." Only two examples of expenditures for "books Mapps & papers" are noted in the surviving records, and in only one of these is a title specified, a history of the Bible.[102]

Since William and Mary remained a grammar school for its first two decades, the library, which was stored in a second-floor room in the main college building, may not have seen much use, especially if Blair, the first president, refused to let the books circulate. For sure, only the college faculty, not the students, had access to the collection. When the college building burned in 1705, the library went up in smoke. The story of the prolonged process of rebuilding would carry us far into the eighteenth century. But it is appropriate to suggest that in size and breadth the college library never equaled the great personal collections formed early in that century by William Byrd II and Landon Carter, and in the 1760s by Thomas Jefferson.

∾ 3 ∾

From the outset of colonization, people who came to the Chesapeake colonies as transient observers or to stay were eager to share their impressions of the new world. Most of these reports ended up in family papers or the cache of administrative records maintained by the church and the Crown,[103] though some, like John Rolfe's "A true Relation of the state of Virginia," circulated in the colonies and England in hand-written copies.[104] Others appeared in print, frequently abridged or

102. Kingsbury, *Records,* 1: 247, 248, 421; Jennings, "Notes on the Original Library," 239–67. The information in the succeeding paragraph also comes from this essay, which is incorporated into Jennings, *The Library of the College of William and Mary in Virginia, 1693–1793* (Charlottesville, Va., 1968). A catalogue of Nicholson's books, based on a manuscript inventory of 1695, is included in Jennings's essay.

103. A full listing of these texts lies beyond the scope of this chapter. To cite but a single example, Thomas Mathew's narrative of Bacon's Rebellion, written after the turn of the century at the request of Robert Harley, remained in manuscript in the Harleian Library until it somehow passed into the book trade and thence into the hands of Thomas Jefferson. Howard Mumford Jones, *The Literature of Virginia in the Seventeenth Century* (1946; Charlottesville, Va., 1968), 107 n. 23; much useful information is provided in this short study as well as in Davis, *Intellectual Life.*

104. Francis Berkeley, Jr., Introduction, in John Rolfe, *A True Relation of the State of Virginia* (New Haven, Conn., 1951), 24–25.

recast by someone else's hand, as parts of a compilation, a tradition exemplified in Samuel Purchas's four-volume folio *Purchas his Pilgrimes* (1625). The political crises that erupted from time to time in Maryland and Virginia drove certain colonists to write and publish, notably in the mid-1650s and a second time in response to Bacon's Rebellion. Much of the casual work has not survived, like the almanac contradicting "judicial astrology" that John Catlett wrote in 1664 and a play entitled "the Bare and the Cubb" acted by three men in 1665.[105] Augustine Herrman, an enterprising merchant who was born in Prague and reared in the Netherlands, and who became a naturalized resident of Maryland, prepared a map of the Chesapeake that was engraved and published in London in 1674; Herrman earned the reward of a large land grant for his cartography, which served the political purposes of Lord Baltimore.[106]

Our literary historians have commonly approached these seventeenth-century writers wanting to know which of them to credit for composing the "first American book," or asking which texts fit within the category of "American literature."[107] From the standpoint of book history the more appropriate task is to examine the meaning and practice of authorship in the context of the times. As a series of individual examples will make clear, no single system of rules prevailed in the Chesapeake or in the metropolis of London. In general, authors had little control over what they wrote once their material was passed on to intermediaries. To be a writer was to enter into a relationship of dependence. For some, this relationship was with a patron, for others with a bookseller, for still others with a coterie or (as in the case of the Quakers) with a religious community. Certain forms of writing—most specifically, letters, but also texts that were deliberately withheld from the marketplace—were deemed "private," though it often happened that such texts were published. Anonymity, as in the use of initials on a title page, was a means of combining privacy and publication. To enter the public realm was to encounter the possibility of censorship by the

---

105. Colonel John Catlett to Thomas Catlett, 1 April 1664 (Colonial Williamsburg Foundation Library Transcripts, 1); Neill, *Virginia Carolorum*, 315.
106. James Grant Wilson, *A Maryland Manor*, Maryland Historical Society Fund Publication, No. 30, pt. 2 (Baltimore, 1890), 32.
107. Davis, *Intellectual Life*, 1:12. For a thoroughgoing critique, see William Spengemann, *A New World of Words: Redefining Early American Literature* (New Haven, Conn., 1994), chap. 2.

civil state or ecclesiastical authorities. The sensible response to this situation was to engage in self-censorship. Alternatively, critics would write a "libel," a genre that, because it lacked the attributions of author, printer, and bookseller, often spurred the civil state into searching for and punishing the libelers.[108] Perhaps the most crucial fact that bore upon authorship in the Chesapeake was the paucity of local patrons, including much by way of a reading public. Almost without exception, to become an author in these two colonies could only be accomplished by looking overseas, to England.

The literary career of Captain John Smith is revealing of how someone who was neither learned nor a "gentleman" exploited the possibilities for patronage. Before Smith signed on with the Virginia Company of London to take part in the founding expedition of 1607, he had not thought of himself as a writer. He became one accidentally (though he surely knew of the market for travel narratives) when a long letter-narrative "to a friend of his" sent back by ship in June 1608 passed through the hands of the Virginia Company to a member of the Stationers' Company, who registered *A True Relation of such occurrences and accidents of noate as hath hapned in Virginia since the first planting of that Collony* for publication as a quarto in August. The text, a seemingly frank account of dissension and disease in Jamestown and of Smith's negotiations with the Indians, was less frank than it might have been because someone in the employ of the Company edited out certain information; justifying the abridgment, the editor invoked the distinction between private and public, noting that "somewhat more was by him written, which being as I thought (fit to be private) I would not adventure to make it publicke." Initially the printer attributed the text to "a Gentleman," then to a "Th. Watson Gent," and only in the third version of the title page to Smith himself, identified as "Coronell of the said Collony."[109]

This casualness about the author's name and text, with the printer playing a large role in deciding the spelling of place names and an

<hr>

108. The several such incidents include *Md.Arch.* 1:427–31; Davis, *Intellectual Life,* 1:354. John Hammond "fixed my name" to *Leah and Rachel* (London, 1656) to "prevent the imputation of a libeller" (Hall, *Narratives of Early Maryland,* 307).
109. Philip L. Barbour, ed., *The Complete Works of Captain John Smith (1580–1631),* 3 vols. (Chapel Hill, N.C., 1986), 1:5–6, 124; Arber, *Smith . . . Works,* pt. 1, 1–4. Whether the Virginia Company deliberately sponsored this publication is unclear.

editor—someone unknown to Smith—intervening as censor, gave way
to a different set of circumstances once Smith began to publish reg-
ularly after he returned from Virginia. The longest of his books was
The General History of Virginia, Summer Isles, and New England, published as a folio in 1624 and reprinted four times by 1632. The origins of
the *General History* lay in the embattled circumstances of the Virginia
Company. Even though its self-interest was crucially involved in shaping the flow of news from Jamestown, the Company was unable to
prevent negative reports from appearing. Almost immediately, therefore, the Company had to improvise a program of literary patronage,
sponsoring sermons and travel narratives that offered a more encourag-
ing view of Virginia's prospects as a colony. In 1621, with the success
of the venture much in doubt and its finances tied to raising money
through lotteries aimed at a broad public, a leading member of the
Company proposed that it sponsor "a faire and perspicuous history,
compiled of that Country, from her first discouery to this day." The
Company agreed, and, after joining forces with John Smith, probably financed the printing of a four-page prospectus advertising the
contents.[110]

Money is the subject of the very first sentence of the prospectus,
money Smith himself had invested, together with the "eighteene yeeres
of time" he had given "gratis" in and to the enterprise of discovery.
Now he needed money from some other source, for the book would be
a long one (by far the longest he would ever write or compile) of "eighty
sheets, besides the three Maps," the whole requiring a subsidy of "neere
in an hundred pounds, which summe I cannot disbursse." Who would
patronize the work and provide this sum? Smith addressed himself to
members of the nobility and the gentry, "humbly entreat[ing]" them
"either to adventure [i.e., invest in the hope of getting some return] or
give me what you please towards the impression." In the event, the
duchess of Richmond responded with a subsidy; nothing, it seems, was
contributed by the hard-pressed Company. And who would recom-
pense him as author? Here Smith shifted his voice, no longer representing himself as someone "accountable and thankful" to a great pa-

110. Kingsbury, *Records*, 1: 451–52; Arber, *Smith . . . Works*, pt. 1, 622. I accept the argument of
David Quinn that the "Smith" who came before the Company was not John, the explorer, but
John Smyth of Nibley. Quinn, "List of Books," 352.

tron, but speaking to the members of the Stationers' Company as a experienced writer sensible of the value of literary property: "nor shall the Stationers have the copy for nothing."[111]

In a single paragraph Smith thus tried out two alternative possibilities for financing a book and earning money as an author: disinterested great patrons or booksellers intent on making money themselves. By implication, booksellers drove hard bargains and were unpleasant to deal with. Yet to seek out great patrons involved another kind of unpleasantness, of admitting the difference in rank between sponsor and writer and embodying that difference in flattery. Addressing "the illustrious and most noble Princess, the Lady Francis, Duchesse of Richmond" in the dedication, Smith contrasted the inadequacy of his prose—"poore ragged lines" written by a "rude military hand" wielding a "rough Pen"—with the "Judicious" discernment seemingly intrinsic to persons blessed with a "glorious Name":

> If therefore your *Grace* shall daigne to cast your eye on this poore Booke, view I pray you rather your owne *Bountie* (without which it had dyed in the wombe) then my *imperfections,* which have no helpe but the shrine of your *glorious Name* to be sheltered from censorious condemnation.[112]

According to this scheme, noble patrons were a writer's ideal readers— that is, if they chose to read at all.

The reference to "censorious condemnation" points us toward another complication, the contested situation in which Smith as author found himself. That situation was generic to authorship in the period, as the Maryland writer George Alsop indicated some decades later in imagining the fate of his manuscript once it entered the public realm:

> Farewell, poor brat! thou in a monstrous world,
> In swaddling clothes, thus up and down art hurled;
> There to receive what destiny doth contrive,
> Either to perish or be saved alive
> Good fate protect thee from a critic's power.[113]

But the situation was also specific to the genre of travel narrative or history, and especially to any retrospective account of the Virginia

---

111. Arber, *Smith . . . Works,* pt. 1, cxxvi.

112. Ibid., 275–77.

113. George Alsop, *A Character of the Province of Maryland* (1666), quoted in Moses Coit Tyler, *A History of American Literature during the Colonial Time,* 2 vols. (New York, 1897), 1: 67.

Company, which, long since, had found itself immersed in a sea of "calumnies and slanders" that "run (like wilde fire) from man to man,"[114] in part because of the large discrepancies between Company-sponsored travel narratives representing Virginia as a veritable paradise and the stark reports reaching England of disease, starvation, and death. Moreover, Smith's own reputation as an explorer and adventurer was open to challenge. Was he telling the truth? This insistent question lay behind Smith's oft-repeated assertion that he had "observed" much of what he wrote about, as it did behind the apparatus of testimonials professing admiration for him as "Author." Was he not also invoking the authority of the patron to whom he dedicated the *General History?* If the position of such patrons (who for an earlier work included the Prince of Wales) in the hierarchies of culture allowed them to stand above the fray, could he do likewise by associating his work with their names?

But we must set these circumstances and Smith's quest for authority in a broader context. Here, the tension involved in going public as an author arose out of the assumption, common to the times, that anyone who published merely for the sake of earning money was certain to lie. John Hammond, a Maryland colonist who wrote in defense of the proprietor in 1656, voiced this assumption in representing himself as "not [having] written for profit, for it is known I have given away the copy, and therefore am the less to be mistrusted for a deluder, for popular applause I did it not."[115] A parallel assumption was that persons of "gentle" status, surely not in need of money, preferred to remain anonymous, or even not to publish, rather than allow their handiwork—and their persons—to become soiled in the commercial marketplace. In the very years in which Smith was fashioning his career as writer, the clergyman-poet John Donne, reacting to the "stigma of print," limited himself to the medium of scribal publication. Colonial writers and editors also had to wonder, as George Alsop did, if going public was worth the cost to personal reputation; although the editor of the English-language edition of the explorer John Lederer's *Discoveries*

114. [Alexander Whitaker], *Good Newes from Virginia* (London, 1613), sig. A2 recto.
115. Hall, *Narratives of Maryland,* 307. Closer to Smith in time, the author of *Newes from Virginia. The Lost Flocke Triumphant* (London, 1610), declared, "Reader: Thou dost peradventure imagine that I am mercenarie in this busines, and write for money (as your moderne Poets use) hyred by some of those ever to be admirered adventurers to flatter the World. No; I disclaim it" (Brown, *Genesis,* 1:421).

reasoned that "the printing of these Papers . . . might prove a service to the Publick," he had to reassure himself that their publication "was no injury to the Author."[116]

John Smith wanted the best of both worlds, that of court or aristocratic patronage and that of the bookseller. Eager to be recognized as a man of civic virtue selflessly using his "best abilities to the good of my Prince and Countrey," he also wanted to make money. That he was no gentleman but a bargainer tainted by the market is evident from the final words of the prospectus for the *General History*.[117]

Here, at the beginning of the seventeenth century, we see authorship involved in dilemmas that will recur for colonial writers right up to the American Revolution, and beyond. Not in every instance were the circumstances this complex, but the undertones persist, as did the basic problem of how to remain detached from the marketplace while negotiating with booksellers. A case in point was William Fitzhugh's effort to secure the publication of a "short description of Virginia & a methodicall Digestion of the Laws thereof." In 1694 he sent a copy of the manuscript, based on a revision of the Virginia statutes he had recently supervised, to a London merchant with whom he had business dealings, accompanying it with a letter advising that he "would not have the Impression neither in my name nor at my charge" and offering the encouragement that, since his friends expected "every one that can read both here & in Maryland would have one," the bookseller who published it could anticipate selling "some thousands," and that "suddenly." This being the case, was it not appropriate that Fitzhugh be paid "liberally for the Copy of it," more even "than is given for the Copy of the ordinaryest Play book, which is twenty shillings a sheet"? As it happened, no one bit. Three years later, Fitzhugh was providing detailed instructions to the London bookseller Hugh Newman on how additional laws should be incorporated and certain information highlighted, in part to compensate for the loss of "the fairest & best Copy" to French privateers. Reluctantly admitting that "some small Erratas will happen," yet hoping that "if this Impression sells well [these] will

116. William Talbot, trans. *The Discoveries of John Lederer, In three severall Marches from Virginia, To the West of Carolina . . . Collected and Translated out of Latine from the Discourses and Writings* (London, 1672), sig. A2 recto, verso; J. W. Saunders, "The Stigma of Print: A Note on the Social Bases of Tudor Poetry," *Essays in Criticism* 1 (1951): 139–64.

117. Arber, *Smith . . . Works*, pt. 1, 178.

be easily corrected in the next," he left to Newman the decision as to format (the bookseller had suggested octavo). What concerned him more was his own presence as author—or rather, the suppression of his presence, for he wanted Newman to "write a . . . new preface . . . as from your self, the Printer giving an account of the Casuall meeeting with the Copy," to the end of suggesting that "it were an accidentall Copy & no Author known thereto." Fitzhugh may have wished to remain anonymous in keeping with the conventions of the amateur or gentleman writer, though as an officeholder in Virginia he may also have wished to shield himself from criticism of the kind that Purvis and Buckner had encountered. Yet like Smith before him, he framed his relationship with the world of London booksellers as a business transaction, willing by 1697 to accept an offer of £20 (contingent on Newman's finding "a chapman that . . . would take off five hundred of them"), to be rendered not in cash but in books. As it happened, the manuscript never passed into print, possibly because the bookseller thought the risk of earning back his investment too great.[118]

Authorship had a somewhat different meaning for two men, both of them college educated and ordained clergy, who came to Virginia to undertake scientific studies. After spending two years in the colony (1684–86), John Clayton returned to England, where he wrote a series of letters that were published in the *Philosophical Transactions* of the Royal Society. John Banister came in 1678 and stayed, living long enough to begin a "Naturall History of Virginia," parts of which were incorporated into the work of other English naturalists. Each of these men depended on a newly emerging community of scientists for the funding that brought them to Virginia. It was this community, based partly in the Royal Society (founded in 1660) and partly in coffeehouse culture, that defined the program of research these naturalists should follow. It was also this community that provided a means of making public new discoveries—means that included an elaborate network of correspondents, the *Philosophical Transactions* (begun in 1665), and the publishing of books by subscription. These modes of publication offered two advantages to men like Banister and Clayton. The first was a certain distance from the religious and dynastic politics of the period, for, early on, the members of the Royal Society refused to be drawn

118. Davis, *Fitzhugh*, 326–27, 345–49.

into the great conflict between Puritans and Anglicans. The second
was a certain distance from the marketplace. In proposing to publish by
subscription his "Naturall History" (had the project come to fruition,
he would have been the first writer in America to use this method),
Banister acted in the awareness that (as his fellow English naturalist
John Ray complained in 1686) "the greatest part of Natural historie has
been starved and abused by the Avarice of Stationers who have beat
down the Artist." To be sure, Banister worried about the consequences
of publishing the History in parts as a serial in order to reduce the
expense to those who subscribed. But at least he could count on a
patronage that was sympathetic to his ends.[119]

In the case of one other writer, the planter John Cotton, we must
guess at the circumstances of production and distribution, for little is
known beyond the fact that, in the immediate aftermath of Bacon's
Rebellion, he wrote a sardonic history of the event that remained in
manuscript in his own day. It seems likely that Cotton wrote "The
History of Bacon's and Ingram's Rebellion" for a coterie of readers,
possibly members of a coffeehouse set in London, among whom it
circulated in a small number of handwritten copies. The members of
this circle may have shared other related texts, for Cotton included in
the History two examples of the "many copp[i]es of verses made after
[Bacon's death]." More so than any other text from the Chesapeake in
this period, the style of the History was based on the satirical and jest-
book culture that was wholly opposite to the literature of religious
devotion.[120]

Colonial writers contributed to the last of these genres as well. Here,
the meaning of authorship shifted yet again. The title page of *A Song
of Sion*, written in Virginia by John Grave, a transient Quaker, and
printed in London in 1662, immediately suggests one major difference:
the author is described as a "Citizen" of "Sion," and we do not learn his
name until the end of the tract-poem, where he signed himself "your
fellow-friend." Grave preferred this quasi-anonymity not because he

119. Raymond P. Stearns, *Science in the British Colonies of America* (Carbondale, Ill., 1970), chap.
6; Michael Hunter, *Science and Society in Restoration England* (Cambridge, 1981), 36, 41, 49–50, 52,
and chap. 3; Ewan and Ewan, *John Banister,* chap. 5.

120. The text is included in Andrews, *Narratives of the Insurrections,* 47–98. I have accepted
Howard Mumford Jones's critique of previous interpretations of the authorship and distribution
of this text; Jones, *Literature of Virginia,* 108 n. 25.

wanted to pass as a gentleman writer, but because his worldly identity could only get in the way of his goal of conveying divine truth. And although we know nothing of his dealings with the bookseller who issued *Song of Sion*, it is certain that Grave regarded the spiritual truths he rhymed in ballad metre as no one's private property, but as the voice of God: "O mind you all, these words most true, / proceeding from above. . . ." As author, Grave was merely a faithful yet appropriately self-effacing intermediary.[121]

These case histories are revealing of the ambiguities that encompassed the meaning and nature of intellectual property: to whom or to what did a text belong? They underscore the paradoxical relationship between authenticity and the marketplace, for a literary work that rejected the taint of the market, by doing so, may have made itself more attractive to patrons and readers. These examples also underscore the mutual dependence between writers in the old world and writers in the new: colonial authors depended on patrons in the metropolis, but in their turn cosmopolitan writers and patrons were needy for information from the colonies.

∾ 4 ∾

Throughout the seventeenth-century Atlantic world, authority remained contested in matters of religious practice and belief. Only in Maryland did that contest involve the deep antagonism between Catholics and Protestants, with the consequence that the civil government eschewed the conventional insistence on religious conformity, preferring, instead, a policy of toleration intended to benefit the Catholic minority. Everywhere else but in Pennsylvania, the civil government aspired to create uniformity in the face of fractures within English Protestantism. A lasting legacy of this turmoil was the Society of Friends, or Quakerism, a faith that Quaker missionaries transplanted to the Chesapeake and the West Indies well before Quaker grandees came into possession of West New Jersey in the 1670s and founded the colony of Pennsylvania (1682). Immigrants from other parts of Europe carried their versions of Protestantism across the Atlantic—the Dutch

---

121. [John Grave], *A Song of Sion* ([London], 1662).

Reformed who founded New Netherlands (1624), Huguenots who left France after the revocation of the Edict of Nantes (1685), German and Dutch sectarians attracted to Pennsylvania, Swedish Lutherans who initiated the colony of Delaware (1638), Scotch-Irish Presbyterians who arrived in enough numbers in the Chesapeake by 1680 to warrant the appearance of missionary clergymen from Scotland. The Church of England, which became the strongest institution in all of the Chesapeake and middle colonies except Pennsylvania, also has a place in the story.

Each of these groups brought to the new world its own assumptions and practices in relation to speech and reading, books and writing. Most of them linked the well-being and perpetuation of the church to the presence of a learned clergy. For the Church of England, in particular, the task of providing enough of these clergy for an ever-expanding network of parishes in the Chesapeake was never fully completed. Another task, imposed from the other side of the Atlantic on local clergy, was to provide regular reports on the state of ecclesiastical affairs. One such series of reports was the annual "letters" written in Latin and sent by the Jesuits in Maryland to the head of the English Province, who in turn communicated them to the head of the order in Rome.[122] Little has survived of what was preached and written by the scores of Protestant and Catholic clergy who served in the Chesapeake—for example, not a single page from the forty-year ministry of Thomas Teackle. No one seems to have expected that the Nuthead press would issue sermons. When the Anglican minister Duell Pead preached a sermon in Jamestown in 1686 on a ceremonial occasion, Governor Effingham dispatched a copy to London in the hope, which proved false, that it might be printed.[123]

Catholics in Maryland were always a minority; relative to the population of the colony, the number who were of this faith steadily declined

122. English versions of these letters are printed in Henry Foley, S.J., ed., *Records of the English Province of the Society of Jesus* (London, 1878), vol. 3. A full history of the practice of self-censorship in seventeenth-century America would have to encompass the Jesuits' sense of vulnerability; Hall, *Narratives of Early Maryland*, 115–16.

123. Richard Beale Davis, ed., "A Sermon Preached at James City in Virginia the 23d of April 1686," *William & Mary Quarterly*, 3d ser., 17 (1960): 371–94. In 1696 the upper house of the Maryland Assembly voted to print a sermon by Peregrine Coney, but nothing seems to have come of it. *Md.Arch.* 54:573. A sermon Francis Makemie preached in New York was published in Boston in 1707.

and in 1689 constituted a mere 8 percent of the population. How these Catholics acquired Bibles, service books, and memoirs like the *Life of Thomas More*, owned by one of the colonists, is uncertain, though the source was probably a Catholic press on the continent. On the whole the Catholic colonists kept to themselves and refrained from pros- elytizing, though in one instance Protestant servants complained that their books were taken from them by a Catholic master. Together with the Catholic gentry, the Jesuits dreamed of establishing a college at St. Mary's City, for a brief period accomplishing the lesser goal of a free (Latin) school. By the end of the century, members of the gentry were beginning to send their sons to Catholic colleges on the continent.[124]

A quite different set of practices prevailed among the Friends who emerged in the 1650s in the Chesapeake and elsewhere in the British colonies. A movement largely of lay people, most of them unlearned though long familiar with the vernacular Bible, Quakers located re- ligious authority not in the printed Bible but in inward experience of the Word. For them, truth was received directly, in ecstatic experience, as though it were a form of light. Thus transformed, these lay people rejected all ordained ministers as "lifeless" apostates from the Chris- tianity of the New Testament.[125] Taking on the role of preachers, some of these converts became "Publishers of the Truth," prophet-preachers who proclaimed the present moment as marking an apocalyptic trans- formation. This sense of the times drove these Quakers (as their critics called them) to perform extraordinary feats of preaching and writing. George Fox and his fellow itinerants undertook to "Let all nations hear the sound by word or writing." In attempting this evangelism, Quakers invaded every space where news was customarily transmitted—fairs, markets, church services, taverns, courts. Here they "published" orally the truth. Some also wrote "papers." One June evening in 1652, Fox, while sitting in an alehouse, drafted a manifesto "concerning . . . how Christ was come to teach people himself by his power and spirit," which he handed over to "the man of the house" to distribute "up and down" to others. In form these papers were commonly represented as

124. *Md.Arch.* 4:35; St. Mary's City Inventories (a volume that was printed in Paris); Michael Graham, "Meetinghouse and Chapel: Religion and Community in Seventeenth-Century Mary- land," in *Colonial Chesapeake Society*, ed. Lois G. Carr et al. (Chapel Hill, N.C., 1988), 242–53.

125. William Braithwaite, *The Beginnings of Quakerism* (London, 1912), 103, 101; John L. Nick- alls, ed., *The Journal of George Fox* (1952; London, 1975), 7–9, 11.

proclamations claiming to embody the voice of God and, in keeping with the genre, put on display in a public space. One by Fox concluded with the charge, "Let this stand where it is stuck up . . . and you that can read, read it to the people." At other moments, and especially while imprisoned, the itinerants turned to writing letters, some of protest to local authorities or to Parliament or Oliver Cromwell, others (the larger share) to fellow converts telling of the presence of God with the persecuted. Many of these letters circulated through Swarthmore Hall in Yorkshire, the manor house of Margaret Fell. Copied and recopied, the currency of these letters was extraordinary.[126]

No less remarkable was the rapidity with which Quakers turned to the printing press and, availing themselves of Andrew Sowle and Giles Calvert, two members of the Stationers' Company of London who were sympathetic to radical Protestantism and willing to run the risk of state censorship, began to issue brief, unbound pamphlets, a third of them in the genre of proclamations, to go with what was "published" orally or through handwritten texts. The first text to be printed appeared near the end of 1652; by 1660 the total had risen to more than a thousand, and in the 1660s, Quaker imprints constituted 13 percent of the output of the English press. The cost of printing these books was largely born by contributions to a special fund; some were sold, but many were given away.[127]

Quaker texts rested their authority not on the presence, overt or implied, of aristocratic patrons and academic learnedness, and certainly not on success in the commercial market, but on the presence of the Holy Spirit. Invoking the distinction between "letter" and "spirit" that the apostle Paul employed in his first letter to the Corinthians, the early prophets regarded themselves as the medium through which the

126. Rufus M. Jones, *The Quakers in the American Colonies* (London, 1911), 78; Nickalls, *Journal of George Fox*, 104; Geoffrey Nuttall, ed., *Early Quaker Letters from the Swarthmore Mss. to 1660* (London, 1952); Hugh Barbour and Arthur O. Roberts, eds., *Early Quaker Writings 1650–1700* (Grand Rapids, Mich., 1973), 31–32. According to Barbour and Roberts, one-third of Quaker publications in the 1650s consisted of proclamations.

127. Thomas P. O'Malley, "The Press and Quakerism, 1653–1659," *Journal of the Friends Historical Society* 54 (1979): 169–84; Luella M. Wright, *The Literary Life of the Early Friends 1650–1725* (New York, 1932), chap. 6; David Runyon, "Appendix: Types of Quaker Writings by Year 1650–1699," in Barbour and Roberts, *Early Quaker Writings*, 567–74; David J. Hall, " 'The fiery Tryal of their Infallible Examination': Self-Control in the Regulation of Quaker Publishing in England from the 1670s to the mid-19th century," in *Censorship & the Control of Print in England and France 1600–1910*, ed. Robin Myers and Michael Harris (Winchester, England, 1992), 59–86.

"Light" that was Christ passed by spiritual means into the hearts of readers. One of the itinerants thus likened himself to "a white paper book without any line or sentence"; what he wrote or spoke was that which was "revealed and written by the Spirit," a truth he only "administer[ed]." This suppression of the authorial self is evident in the hesitancy of Quaker evangelists to speak—and presumably to write—until and unless the Spirit moved them to do so. Characteristically, these evangelists claimed not to know in advance what they would say until this near-mystical event occurred: "I seldom knew what I would say," William Caton wrote in his journal, "till I came there; yet behold when I was to speak I never wanted words or utterance, to declare *that which the Lord gave me to publish.*"[128] Consistent with this understanding of authorship, Quakers represented printed texts as transparent, living expressions of the divine will. The act of reading as performed by the "eye of faith" was not engaged with the materiality of the text but involved the "mirrour"-like correspondence between the Word as light and an inward "eye." The Bible was the great model for such texts—not in any literal sense the printed, historical Bible but the living (ongoing) revelation and witness of the indwelling Christ for which the material text was the vehicle. At their most daring, the Quakers saw themselves as reenacting the role of the "prophets and apostles" of Scripture, receiving in the same manner "a command or word immediately from the Lord."[129]

In the 1650s Quaker missionaries carried these assumptions and practices to the West Indies and the mainland colonies. As communities of Quakers in the new world came into being, a network of production and distribution arose with them. In the early years, the making of this network was the doing of English-based itinerants. Elizabeth Harris arrived in Maryland in the mid-1650s and immediately made converts among the colonists; after she returned to England, she continued to send letters, which were copied over and dispersed in multiple copies. By the end of the 1650s Harris and other Friends were also providing books to the Marylanders, enough "so as

---

128. Isaac Pennington, *The way of Life and Death Made manifest and set before men* (London, 1658), 111; Braithwaite, *Beginnings*, 199, 85; *Journals of the Lives and Gospel Labours of William Caton and John Burnyeat* (London, 1839), 11 (emphasis added).

129. Braithwaite, *Beginnings*, xxxix–xl; Nickalls, *Journal of George Fox*, 11; Wright, *Literary Life*, 71, and chap. 5.

that all p[arts] are furnished, soe that eney one that desires may have benifit by them."[130] In the wake of other itinerants more letters and donations followed, enough by the mid-1670s for the Third Haven Monthly Meeting in Maryland to have a lending library.[131] The flow of Quaker publications ran in both directions; arriving in Jamestown in 1661, George Wilson put pen to paper (both of which he probably carried with him) to issue three manifestoes, copies of which reached the community of Friends in England.[132] Another of the transatlantic missionaries was George Fox, who traveled in the West Indies and North America in 1671–72. Ever active as a writer, Fox was accompanied by a secretary or scrivener who wrote out what he dictated and prepared multiple copies for distribution far and wide. By this decade, and for many years thereafter, Quaker agencies in London were assuming much of the responsibility for keeping in touch with, and regulating, communities of Friends in the new world.[133] Accustomed to producing their own books, Quakers also transplanted this practice to the new colony of Pennsylvania, where the Quaker William Bradford, son-in-law of Andrew Sowle, had a printing office up and running by 1686. Yet the old technology of scribal production remained in use. Friends in Pennsylvania continued to prepare book-length copies of the Book of Discipline by hand, with carefully lettered title pages, and the Monthly Meeting of Philadelphia sometimes hired a scrivener to make copies of letters for distribution.[134]

The capacity of the Quaker system to produce and distribute extraordinary quantities of printed books and handwritten letters has important implications for how we understand the workings of the book trade and the practices of writing and reading in the seventeenth century. Illiteracy and the constraints on the participation of women;

130. J. Reaney Kelly, *Quakers in the Founding of Anne Arundel County, Maryland* (Baltimore, 1963), 16–17; see also *The Books and Divers Epistles of the Faithful Servant of the Lord Josiah Coale* ([London?], 1671): "Let Copies of this be sent amongst Friends every where in the Province of Maryland, and be read amongst them in their Assemblies in the Fear of the Lord" (pp. 60–61); Graham, "Meetinghouse and Chapel," 259–66.
131. Third Haven Monthly Meeting Records (microfilm M 283, Maryland Hall of Records), [1], 3; Torrance, *Old Somerset,* 501.
132. Warren M. Billings, "A Quaker in Seventeenth-Century Virginia: Four Remonstrances by George Wilson," *William & Mary Quarterly,* 3d ser., 33 (1976): 127–40.
133. See, e.g., London Yearly Meeting Epistles (received), vol. 1, 1685–1706 (MR L68; Friends Library, Swarthmore College).
134. Ms. Collection, Friends Historical Library, Swarthmore; Marion Dexter Learned, *The Life of Francis Daniel Pastorious, The Founder of Germantown* (Philadelphia, 1908), 222.

the limitations of the local book trade; the connections between printing and constituted authority—none of these circumstances prevented
the men and women who became Friends from a remarkable level of
participation in the world of print. The will of Richard Russell, a
Virginia planter-merchant turned Quaker who died in 1667, is indica-
tive of this breadth. Expanding on the practice of gift-giving, Russell's
will included the bequest of twenty-four books to some seven fellow
Quakers, four of them women.[135] Other groups of people in the new
world did without books and letter writing. But not the Quakers.

In these same years Quakers fashioned their own system of censorship. Rule breakers, they suffered greatly at the hands of the civil state in
both England and the American colonies. In this context, the story is of
practices of subversion used by Quaker printers, booksellers, and "publishers of the truth." But the story is also one of how Quakers regulated
their own production of texts. In a movement given over to the passionate expression of ecstatic experience, the question of appropriate boundaries arose almost at once. Charged with heterodoxy by
more conventional Protestants who insisted that the Inner Light really
stemmed from Satan, and beset within their own ranks by visionaries
like James Naylor and radical iconoclasts like John Perrot, Fox and most
of his fellow itinerants gradually turned away from the language of
"wonders" and spiritual ecstasy that filled so many of the early letters.
Rereading, some twenty years later, correspondence from the 1650s
collected at Swarthmore Hall, Fox crossed out passages he now deemed
inappropriate, a procedure repeated in the 1690s by the man who edited
the first printed edition of Fox's journal. As early as the mid-1650s, Fox
had been exerting informal control over what got published, a procedure that became formalized in 1672, when the Yearly Meeting au-
thorized ten men "to see that books were carefully corrected and that no
new book or new edition was printed except by order."[136] Conflict, even
schism, became inevitable as boundaries began to harden; a learned
version of Quakerism came into being, as did a new literature of critique
from former Quakers who lamented this emerging formalism. One of
these critics put his finger on the contradiction between censorship and

135. *The Lower Norfolk County Virginia Antiquary* 4 (1904): 110–12.
136. Braithwaite, *Beginnings*, 249 n.4, 105, 134; Nuttall, *Early Quaker Letters*, 156; William C.
Braithwaite, *The Second Period of Quakerism* (London, 1919), 418 n.2, 228–43; Hall, "'The fiery
Tryal,'" 61; Wright, *Literary Life*, 98–100, 103, 106.

the assumption, prevalent in the 1650s, that what Quakers wrote and said was "Dictated Immediately by the Holy Ghost" and "of Equal Authority with the Scriptures"; on what grounds was it possible, he asked, to "chop and change the writings of their Dead Prophets, to answer the Exigency of the Times"?[137] But the apocalyptic moment had passed. With it went the textual practices of the initial years. Orthodoxy, or the imperatives of cultural and religious order, called forth a different set of practices and, in Pennsylvania, exposed the ambivalence that, in their new mode, Quakers such as William Penn felt about the press.

∾ 5 ∾

It was not only in the seventeenth century that observers fretted about the condition of the archives and wondered how anyone could know for sure which laws were in effect. Persisting long after 1700, these complaints arose in other colonies as well. Half a century later, on the heels of completing a new compilation of the laws of the Province of New York, William Smith remarked that, before its publication, "few persons could distinguish what acts were then in force." In these same years a historian of Virginia lamented that the colony's records "have been so carelessly kept, and left in such a confused and jumbled state." When Thomas Jefferson set out to collect copies, printed or handwritten, of as many of the sessions laws and statutes he could lay his hands on, he retrieved one set of manuscript county records from a tavern keeper, who was using the sheets as waste paper. Inevitably there were lapses in knowledge. Thomas Bacon, who prepared and published a new edition of the laws of Maryland in 1765, did not know of Bladen's edition of 1700 and justified his own efforts as warranted by a general state of ignorance.[138]

This chorus of complaints suggests that the underlying situation had little or nothing to do with the technology in use, be it scribal publi-

137. Hall, " 'The Fiery Tryal,' " 63.
138. Alison G. Olson, "Eighteenth-Century Colonial Legislatures and Their Constituents," *Journal of American History* 79 (1982): 550 n.13, 547 n.9; Sowerby, *Catalogue of Library of Thomas Jefferson*, 2:242; Thomas Bacon, *Laws of Maryland at Large* (Annapolis, Md., 1765), sig. b1 recto.

cation or letterpress. To be sure, the transition from handwritten to printed statute books and sessions laws that was under way by the end of the seventeenth century worked to place copies of the statutes in the hands of far more individuals than had been possible beforehand. By the 1690s a significant number of probate inventories in Virginia indicate the ownership of a printed book of laws. That a single merchant, John Sampson of Rappahannock County, had hopes of selling a stock of ninety-one copies, and that William Fitzhugh imagined selling "thousands" of such books, is further evidence of how printing had the potential to enlarge the possibilities for distribution. The more such books became available, the less necessary it was for county sheriffs to recite publicly the laws. Thus it happened that, in the course of the eighteenth century, the term "publish" began slowly to detach itself from the meaning of read aloud, or proclaim. Even among the Quakers, the intensely oral dimensions of the movement gave way to an increasing reliance on written books of discipline and printed tracts. It is not the case, however, that orality vanished from the civil and religious cultures of the Chesapeake, for as A. G. Roeber has argued, the workings of the court system remained substantially oral.[139]

To look back on the modes of production and consumption in the early Chesapeake is to be reminded anew of the hierarchies that shaped these processes—and to be reminded, also, of how these hierarchies could give way to something else. From the outset, the colonists were under the sway of metropolitan culture. The social and political benefits of learned culture were real, as were those of wealth and family connections: knowing how to write as well as read, owning useful books, having access to intellectual patronage. These forms of hierarchy were especially crucial in the making of literary culture. Would-be writers depended on the patronage of institutions of learnedness or on that of cosmopolitan individuals, chief of whom was the much-traveled royal governor Francis Nicholson; otherwise, writers had no audience and no means of getting their work out. Patronage remained important well into the eighteenth century for naturalists like Mark Catesby and, in a somewhat different manner, for the men and women

---

139. Roeber, *Faithful Magistrates and Republican Lawyers*, chap. 3.

who withdrew from the common culture of Protestantism into private clubs, libraries, and salons. The literary histories of eighteenth-century Annapolis and Charlestown are demonstrations in point.[140]

Yet the thickening influence of metropolitan culture is not the entire story. If, outside of Pennsylvania, the Society of Friends diminished in importance, a religious insurgency that had wider cultural implications remained possible, as was demonstrated in the 1740s when Presbyterians in Virginia began to participate in revivals and, a decade later, when unlearned Baptists proclaimed anew the unmediated Word. Tensions persisted between province and metropolis; after 1764, when these tensions began to dominate colonial politics, some of the contradictions and complexities of book culture in the seventeenth-century Chesapeake were reenacted as the generation of "revolutionaries" worked its way toward practices that at one and the same time constrained and opened up the possibilities for participation.

140. Bruce T. McCully, "Governor Francis Nicholson, Patron *Par Excellence* of Religion and Learning in Colonial America," *William & Mary Quarterly*, 3d ser., 39 (1982): 310–33; Stearns, *Science in the British Colonies*, 286–88, 315–26; David S. Shields, "British-American Belles Lettres," in *The Cambridge History of American Literature, I, 1590–1820*, ed. Sacvan Bercovitch (New York, 1994), 307–43.

∾

The Politics of Writing and Reading in Eighteenth-Century America

RESPONDING to a fellow minister who accused him of being too puristic in his conception of church membership, Jonathan Edwards undertook to expose the inconsistencies of his opponent. At one point Edwards paused to explain, for the benefit of those he characterized as "illiterate" readers, the expression "begging the question."[1] He had

Written for a conference sponsored by the Center for the Book and the European Division, Library of Congress, in honor of the bicentennial of the French Revolution and held at the Library of Congress in March 1989, this essay was included in *Publishing and Readership in Revolutionary France and America*, ed. Carol Armbruster (Westport, Conn., 1994), 151–66. Were it possible to rewrite this essay I would want to incorporate and make central to my discussion an argument that David Shields advances in *The Invitation: Civil Discourse & Private Society in British America* (forthcoming) about the "social organization of aesthetic experience" in England and America from the late seventeenth century onward. Shields argues that aesthetic experience was detached from didacticism in a series of spaces—notably, the coffee house, the club, and the salon—where an ethos of "civility" prevailed, together with an impulse to segregate "belles lettres" (itself a new category) from mundane and commercial activities. My essay should also have acknowledged Michael Warner's *The Letters of the Republic: Publication and the Public Sphere in Eighteenth-Century America* (Cambridge, Mass., 1990), in particular its differentiating of "the new public sphere" of "print discourse" from "religion" and its account of "republicanism" as an "ideology of print" (chap. 2); I would want to insist, however, that other ideologies of print remained critical to the "public sphere," construed somewhat more broadly. In that vein I should have cited the Wesleyan contribution as represented in John Wesley's "Advice on Spiritual Reading" and the books he chose to edit and reprint. The "Advice" is included in *John and Charles Wesley*, ed. Frank Whaling (New York, 1981), 88–89.

1. Jonathan Edwards, *Misrepresentations Corrected* (Boston, 1751), 115. Elsewhere in his writings Edwards referred to "the common people," and "the common, and less considerate and understanding sort of people" (*A Treatise Concerning Religious Affections*, ed. John L. Smith [New Haven, Conn., 1959], 210, 212).

in mind the many men and women who, in mid-eighteenth-century America, were strangers to the Latin-based world of academic learning. That world was second nature to Edwards and his opponent; both had graduated from Yale College, and in keeping with their education both writers drew on the resources of logic, rhetoric, and the classical languages in debating one another. Yet Edwards realized that the subject of church membership engaged the interests and attention of a far wider audience, the thousands of lay members who, according to the rules of "congregational" ecclesiology, were empowered to participate in church governance. Thus it happened that he found himself immersed in a complex politics of culture, a politics of privilege (the special discourse of the "literate"), and a politics of what, for want of a better term, we may term an inclusive culture that required him to reach out to the common reader.

The purpose of this essay is to reflect on this politics of culture and its relationship to the practices of writing and reading in eighteenth-century America. To simplify, I want to describe two different systems of cultural production that existed side-by-side. One of these systems presumed hierarchy and privilege: literacy in the sense of learnedness, and equivalent assumptions about writing and reading that stemmed from "genteel" culture. The other system operated quite differently, as in due course I hope to make clear.

My purpose is also to reflect on change and continuity. For a conference on the book in revolutionary France and America the question prompts itself, did a system based on hierarchy collapse as part of our war for independence? The case for France is elegantly displayed in the essays and exhibits brought together in the catalogue entitled *Revolution in Print.*[2] Some historians have argued that a "democratization of print" was occurring in postrevolutionary America.[3] I want to outline an alternative possibility, that most Americans[4] inherited a "revolution" that unfolded two centuries before the events of 1776. From this revolution sprang a literary culture premised on broad access to sacred writ-

2. Robert Darnton and Daniel Roche, eds., *Revolution in Print: The Press in France, 1775–1800* (Berkeley and Los Angeles, 1989).

3. Gordon Wood, "The Democratization of Mind in the American Revolution," in *Leadership in the American Revolution* (Washington, D.C., 1974), 68–71; Nathan Hatch, *The Democratization of American Christianity* (New Haven, Conn., 1989).

4. Especially in the middle colonies and New England; the southern colonies were less affected by the transformation I describe.

ings in the vernacular; from it followed Edwards's effort to address a wider audience.

But let us start with the distinction between "literacy" and "illiteracy." Literacy connoted cultural authority; illiteracy, cultural inferiority and exclusion. This pattern of meaning was crucial to the cosmopolitan or genteel culture that emerged to supplement learnedness in eighteenth-century America.[5] Via either of these systems, hierarchy imposed itself on the relationship between books and readers.

The colleges and the literary coteries that affirmed hierarchy as fact and value helped to convey the civilizing traditions of humanism and rationalism to a society that was prone to sectarian and interracial conflict. Hierarchy was a counterweight to decentralizing tendencies. Deferring to the authority of London, the Americans who styled themselves cosmopolitans eased the provincialism of our new world culture. They patronized what little there was of "literature" or literary activity; to the social worlds of genteel and learned culture we owe the earliest of our magazines and social libraries and the first of our writers to break free of didacticism.

Genteel culture came into being in the major coastal cities in the early decades of the century. The first such stirrings in Boston were centered on a coterie that wrote for James Franklin's weekly newspaper *The New England Courant* (1722–23). The writers who participated in this coterie specialized in verse satires on contemporary politics. Theirs was "insider" verse, made so in part by the abundance of pseudonyms and comic sallies meaningful only to those fully in the know. Not surprisingly, most of these writers were familiar with learned culture, which is to say that they were "literate" in the ancient languages and availed themselves of literary and rhetorical modes they learned from the classics. Their verse observed the conventions of the neoclassical tradition. It was customary to display a little Latin and to celebrate the ancients.[6] In these same years William Byrd (1674–1744) of Westover, Virginia, was keeping up with the classics in his private reading. Like the Bostonians to the north, he was playful in observing contemporary politics, changing every name in *A Secret History of the Dividing Line* to

5. See Richard L. Bushman, "American High-Style and Vernacular Cultures," in *Colonial British America*, ed. Jack P. Greene and J. R. Pole (Baltimore, 1984), 345–83.
6. David S. Shields, "Nathaniel Gardner, Jr., and the Literary Culture of Boston in the 1750s," *Early American Literature* 24 (1989): 196–216.

fanciful inventions that his twentieth-century editors must struggle to decode.

These practices signaled the emergence of new structures of literary production and consumption. The coterie or club, the gentlemen's library, and the periodical began to provide settings in which certain writers found a sympathetic audience.[7] In general, the persons who affiliated with these agencies thought of themselves as "gentlemen." Gentlemen writers in eighteenth-century America did not produce for the marketplace. Typically they shared their work with friends and allowed what they wrote to circulate in manuscript. Byrd was one such writer. Another was Alexander Hamilton (1712–56) of Annapolis, Maryland. Byrd circulated the *Secret History* among a handful of fellow Virginians. Not until the nineteenth century would the manuscript be "published" for a wider public. Hamilton shared the manuscript of his *Itinerarium*, a narrative of his travels from Maryland to Massachusetts and back in 1744, only with his fellow members of the Tuesday Club in Annapolis. So too the club members kept an elaborate history of them-selves that has also had to wait for publication; only now, at the close of the twentieth century, has it been published.[8]

Satire came easily to the gentlemen writers I have been describing, for it lent itself to voicing (and enhancing) the cultural distance they wished to impose between the rabble and themselves. Hence the fa-mous passages in Byrd's *Secret History* in which he described certain North Carolinians as almost wholly without civilization. Alexander Hamilton was ever ready to use satire to expose the differences between pretense and reality:

> Among the rest [in a tavern crowd] was a fellow in a worsted cap and great black fists. They stiled him doctor. Flat told me he had been a shoemaker in town and was a notable fellow at his trade, but happening two years ago to cure an old woman of a pestilent mortal disease, he thereby acquired the character of a physician, . . . laid aside his awls and leather, got himself some gallipots, and instead of cobling of soals, fell to cobling of human bodies.

7. The preceding description is indebted to Larzer Ziff, "Upon What Pre-text? The Book and Literary History," *American Antiquarian Society Proceedings* 95 (1985): 297–315. The role of the salon in eighteenth-century France was partly replicated by the "club" in colonial and revolution-ary America. (In the original version of this note, I suggested that "no women in eighteenth-century America ran a literary salon." Thanks to David Shields, I now know otherwise.

8. *Gentleman's Progress: The Itinerarium of Dr. Alexander Hamilton, 1744*, ed. Carl Bridenbaugh (Chapel Hill, N.C., 1948).

The social ineptitudes of the "lower orders" served these writers well. So did the moral code of Puritanism. Inheriting from Dryden and other writers of the Restoration the theme of anti-Puritanism, Byrd and Hamilton mocked the mores of the Yankee and his Blue Laws.[9]

Byrd's well-known frankness about sex was another legacy from the Restoration. Genteel writers had an eye for the ladies and presented themselves as eager to make conquests.

> The character of a certain Church of England clergyman in Boston was canvassed, he having lost his living for being too sweet upon his land-lady's daughter, a great belly being the consequence. I pitied him only for his imprudence. . . . As for the crime . . . it is but a peccadillo.

So too these cosmopolitans disdained "sectaries" and "enthusiastic" religion, Hamilton complaining at one point of a traveling companion who "kept poring upon Whitefield's sermons." Hamilton's own taste in writers ran to Fielding, Cervantes, Montaigne, and Rollins.[10]

In the first half of the eighteenth century coteries and clubs served as milieus in which writers exchanged work in manuscript. As David Shields has demonstrated, a substantial literary culture grew up around this apparently archaic process. Alternatively, literary culture revolved around the periodical, which drew its patrons and contributors mainly from the ranks of cosmopolitan gentlemen. When Benjamin Franklin took over the *Pennsylvania Gazette* in 1729, he appealed to "gentlemen" to send him "private letters" to print in the newspaper. Franklin was assuming that men of a certain social class would possess distinctive "Information." He wished, in other words, to link up with an existing network of exchanges that, occurring as they did among the members of an elite, bridged the public and the private.[11]

Benjamin Franklin may seem an improbable person to associate with genteel culture. Yet it was precisely the status of a "gentleman" who did not have to work for a living that Franklin adopted after handing over his printing business to his partner. He cut his literary teeth, moreover,

9. Bridenbaugh, *Gentleman's Progress*, 91; Richard Beale Davis, "William Byrd," in *Major Writers of Early American Literature*, ed. Everett Emerson (Madison, Wis., 1972), 169–171.

10. Bridenbaugh, *Gentleman's Progress*, 123, 129, 79, 75, 23, 70. "Whitefield" refers to the English evangelist George Whitefield.

11. *The Papers of Benjamin Franklin*, ed. Leonard Labaree et al., 31 vols. to date (New Haven, Conn., 1962–   ), 1: 161. See also Jurgen Habermas, *The Structural Transformation of the Public Sphere: An Inquiry into a Category of Bourgeois Society*, trans. Thomas Burger (Cambridge, Mass., 1989).

on the coterie that nourished *The New England Courant.* From them he learned to admire *The Tatler* and *The Spectator.* From them he learned as well the literary mode of burlesque and that Boston variant, the mock-jeremiad.[12]

Perhaps more crucially, these writers encouraged in Franklin an anti-Puritanism that enabled him to break with his family culture, which was authentically Protestant and Nonconformist, and start down a different road. At the age of five he was sent a poem written by his uncle Benjamin counseling him on the way of "Duty." Duty for the elder Benjamin meant something different than what it would come to signify for a man of the Enlightenment:

> Mans Danger lyes in Satan, sin and selfe.
> In vertue, Learning, Wisdome progress make.
> Never shrink at suffering for thy saviours sake . . .
> In Heart with bended knee Alone Adore
> None but the Three in One Forevermore.[13]

Young Franklin rejected both the doctrines and the cultural style of pietistic Calvinism. When he began to contribute the "Silence Dogood" essays to his brother's paper, he filled them with mockery of that "pious rhetoric and somber world-view." A characteristic subject, then as later, was the war between the sexes, treated as a cause for humor. Franklin's cosmopolitan identity was masterfully displayed in "The Speech of Miss Polly Baker," which circulated in manuscript (a copy reached the members of the Tuesday Club) before being published in 1747 in a London newspaper. In Leo Lemay's summary, "this entertaining and complex hoax satirizes New England's blue laws, protests the double-standard for women, defends prostitution, ridicules traditional Christian morality . . . and elegantly but subtly advocates deism."[14] That Franklin expected his correspondents to share the letters they received with friends—thus again making "public" what seemed "private"—is a further clue to the literary practices and assumptions that made up this system.

Let me suggest that these writers were deliberately engaged in a

12. Leo Lemay, "Benjamin Franklin," in Emerson, *Major Writers of Early American Literature*, 210 and passim.
13. Labaree et al., *Papers of Benjamin Franklin*, 1: 4–5.
14. Lemay, "Benjamin Franklin," p. 233.

politics of culture. Whatever their political allegiance in the struggle between royal government and local independence, all wanted to create a sphere that was liberated from the pulpit. The *Independent Reflector* was born in 1752 amid the intensely factionalized politics of colonial New York. Political historians regard it as signaling the transfer from England to America of "radical Whig" or "republican" ideas that would flower in an ideology of independence. But in representing themselves as friends of "free inquiry" or the "free exercise of thought," William Livingston and his fellow writers were also attempting to subvert the cultural authority of the ministry. Hence they ridiculed the discourse of theologians as consisting of meaningless "metaphysical riddles." The history of Christianity was, for them, a babble of conflicting doctrines and ideas, none of which really mattered. A much-used epithet was "orthodoxy," which they construed as a system that the clergy sought to impose on the people. Mere riddles, senseless zeal, "enthusiasm"—all these Livingston contrasted to the "rationality" and "decency" of proper religion. More bluntly, he and his colleagues contrasted the "pulpit" with the "press," labeling the former an instance of "Tyranny" and identifying the press with freedom. This way of categorizing the press has much to do with the ideology of "republicanism." But it also has to do with a specific politics of culture that, originating in the Anglican reaction to the English Civil War, deliberately misrepresented evangelical Protestantism and the relationship between the clergy and the people.[15]

This politics of culture was reprised in the 1790s as American writers turned to the genre of the novel.[16] An early example, Royall Tyler's *The Algerine Captive* (1797) extends the themes that I have been describing. The novel is a comedy of manners in which writer (a Harvard graduate) and reader amuse themselves at the expense of a naive rustic. Young Updike Underhill leaves the family farm to attempt a series of professions. His pious mother is confident that Updike will easily triumph as a minister: "she did not doubt, when he came to preach, he would be as much run after as the great Mr. Whitefield." To prepare himself for the right career Updike reads

15. William Livingston (and others), *The Independent Reflector,* ed. Milton M. Klein (Cambridge, Mass, 1963), 90, 271, 339.
16. It was also reprised as professional theater spread to cities such as Boston.

ten funeral, five election, three ordination, and seventeen farewell, sermons, Bunyan's Holy War, the Life of Colonel Gardner, and the Religious Courtship. In law, the Statutes of New Hampshire, and Burn's
Justice abridged. In physic, Buchan's Family Physician, Culpepper's
Midwifery, and Turner's Surgery.

As a doctor he turns out to be no more bumbling than his competitors.[17]

Having established that Underhill was a mere amateur, Tyler went
on to contrast two modes of reading, the one he expected of his own
readers and the unsophisticated alternative. The proper reader was
someone who, having moved from sermons to fiction and the periodical essay, knew how to recognize the special rules and implicit epis-
temology of the novel. Updike Underhill did not have that skill.
When he read *Pilgrim's Progress*, "he stuck a skewer through Apollyon's
eye in the picture, to help Christian beat him."[18] As in this example, so in general Tyler differentiated writing, reading, and learning
along an axis that at one end was labeled "country," and, at the other,
"cosmopolitan."

Did Tyler realize that the naiveté of the Underhills threatened his
own career as a novelist? His way out of this difficulty was to proclaim
that Americans were entering on a new age of reading: the novel was
triumphing over all of its rivals.

> When [Updike] left New England . . . certain funeral discourses, the last
> words and dying speeches of Bryan Shaheen, and Levi Ames, and some
> dreary somebody's Day of Doom, formed the most diverting part of the
> farmer's library. On his return from captivity, he found a surprising alter-
> ation in the public taste. In our inland towns . . . country booksellers,
> fostering the new-born taste of the people, had filled the whole land with
> modern travels, and novels almost as incredible.

Tyler continued to elaborate this tale of progress:

> with one accord, all orders of country life forsook the sober sermons and
> practical pieties of their fathers, for the gay stories and splendid impieties
> of the traveller and the novelist.[19]

17. Royall Tyler, *The Algerine Captive,* with an introduction by Jack B. Moore (Gainesville, Fla.,
1967), 32, 55.
18. Tyler, *Algerine Captive,* 32, 55. Compare the scene in Tyler's play *The Contrast* in which the
country bumpkin attending the theater mistakes a sword fight for the real thing.
19. Ibid., vi–ix.

A veritable revolution in reading was carrying cosmopolitan culture to supremacy over "sermons" and "dreary somebody's Day of Doom."

This truth was slow to dawn on the man who printed *The Algerine Captive*. Certainly David Carlisle of Walpole, New Hampshire, could not have survived as a printer-publisher on the sales of Tyler's novel, of which he issued but a single printing. The meat-and-drink of his business were ordination sermons and tales of "wonders" of a kind that Tyler would have despised, like *A Wonderful Dream of Dr. Watts.* Country printers thrived on such ephemera. When we look behind these publications and ask what they tell us about literary culture, a quite different structure comes into view, and with it a different politics of culture.

Isaac Backus, a New Light minister in the second half of the eighteenth century, was versed in a politics of culture that hinged on how to read and understand the Word of God. Backus was concerned with validating the authority of spiritual knowledge over against the authority of "learning." Were the "learned," with their esoteric knowledge of the ancient languages, the best interpreters of Scripture? On the contrary: echoing the critique the evangelist George Whitefield made of Harvard in the 1740s, Backus declared that a college education all too often introduced young men to the "corrupt principles" of "rank" Arminianism. The key qualification for interpreting Scripture was not learning, but "being internally called by the Spirit of God." Even more boldly, Backus asserted the egalitarian principle that "*every saint* now has the same way to know the truth and certainty of God's Word that his people had of old."[20]

Clergy such as Backus stepped outside of cultural hierarchy via their evangelical insistence on reversal. Whether Samuel Davies was preaching to the students of the College of New Jersey or to farmers and their families in Hanover County, Virginia, where he played a major role in inaugurating an important revival, he contrasted "the irreligious world" and "the children of God." The comparison was prelude to an act of cultural reversal:

---

20. Isaac Backus, *All true Ministers of the Gospel, are called into that Work* (1754), reprint. in *Isaac Backus on Church, State, and Calvinism*, ed. William G. McLoughlin (Cambridge, Mass., 1968), 74, 72, 77, 103 (emphasis added).

O, sinners! could you but see in all his future glory, the meanest saint whom you now contemn and ridicule, how would it astonish you! . . . You will then see those whom you now account stupid, mopish creatures, that have no taste for the pleasures of life, shining more glorious than the sun; happy as their natures can admit, and in their humble sphere, resembling God himself.

The worldly dashed from their high places, and the meek of God rewarded with eternal life—this working of the divine will undermined the authority of genteel and learned culture.[21]

Davies specified a literary consequence of this reversal. All learnedness, including his, would be displaced by the "humble language" God used in speaking to his children.[22] Humble speech was understood by everyone who felt the workings of the Holy Spirit. So too the Holy Spirit enabled the unlearned—as it once had enabled a mere carpenter—to confound the worldly wise. A process of reversal thus functioned to eliminate the problem of illiteracy: the godly knew and spoke the truths of the gospel.

Jonathan Edwards joined Backus and Davies in acknowledging this displacement. For these evangelicals in mid-eighteenth-century America, the spiritual preparation of a minister was ultimately more consequential than that person's skill in reading Greek and Latin. The true minister—and, for sure, the effective preacher—was someone who had undergone conversion, or "new birth," and who relied on the Holy Spirit in communicating the Gospel. Feeling himself infused with the Spirit, the evangelical preacher experienced a "divine power":

> The divine power seemed in some measure to attend this discourse, in which I was favored with uncommon freedom and plainness of address, and enabled to open divine truths and explain them to the capacities of my people in a manner beyond myself. . . . [And on another preaching day] the Word appeared to be accompanied with a divine influence, and made powerful impressions upon the assembly in general.[23]

This passage from David Brainerd's diary is laced with assumptions about literary production and literary consumption. Let me specify three of them.

21. Samuel Davies, *Sermons on Important Subjects*, 3 vols. (New York, 1841), 3:135.
22. Ibid., 127.
23. Jonathan Edwards, *The Life of David Brainerd*, ed. Norman Pettit (New Haven, Conn., 1985), 343–44.

1. The transparency of speech and writing. Brainerd spoke "beyond myself," and with "plainness." Once the Holy Spirit entered him, Brainerd was able to overcome the everyday limitations of speech and writing. His "people" understood him perfectly, so well that they too became infused with the Spirit. It is as though the medium by which the Spirit moved has become transparent: Brainerd the person, and the human instrumentalities of writing and speech, vanish, leaving communication to occur between pure Spirit (the living Word) and the hearts of those who believe.

2. Speech and writing as spontaneous acts. A longstanding ethic in the world of radical Protestants was that ministers should never preach from a fully written text or (at an extreme) bring written notes of any kind into the pulpit. The essential preparation consisted of meditation, a process that involved the cycle of repentance and renewed commitment to the will of God. So cleansed, the preacher rose above the corruptions of the mundane world and spoke truth directly.

3. Interpretation is figural. All acts of speech and writing referred ultimately to the grand design of God's providence, the work of redemption. The writer's task was to connect events in the everyday world to Christ's mission of salvation. This master plot was revealed in the Bible, which laid out the types or figures to which all events thereafter were but antitypes.

These assumptions were consequential for the practice of reading, the relationship between writers and readers, and, more generally, for the meaning and distribution of cultural power. One immediate result was, as Isaac Backus indicated, to minimize the importance of the learned tradition. Less obvious, but in the long run of greater consequence, was how these assumptions worked against the "literary" concepts of style and genre. Figural interpretation allowed no "description of random everyday life" or the varying of "style" to suit different occasions. Comedy became irrelevant; there was nothing to satirize, since there was but one true version of the divine will, and one essential plot, the work of redemption.[24] So too the assumptions I have outlined

24. Erich Auerbach, *Mimesis: The Representation of Reality in Western Literature*, trans. Willard Trask (New York, 1957), 39–43, 63–65. Auerbach notes that "the true heart of the Christian doctrine . . . was, as we have previously noted, totally incompatible with the principle of the separation of styles. Christ had not come as a hero and king but as a human being of the lowest social station. His first disciples were fishermen and artisans. . . . That the King of Kings was

worked against the concept of authorship. Samuel Davies and Isaac Backus participated in a wholly different system of cultural production from that of the genteel writers. Evangelicals did not retreat into a coterie that sought distance from the rabble. Nor did they elaborate a distinction between the "cultivated" and the everyday, or between the public and the private. On the contrary, the sermons they saw through the press were always public in the sense of being instruments of persuasion aimed at a general audience. Davies and Backus assumed the presence of an audience that wanted *repetitions* of a stock message—the permanent message of the gospel, not the ever-changing fashions of the moment. Consistent with this premise, evangelicals continued to recommend, and to read themselves, a stock of "steady sellers" that remained immune to the mutability of time.[25]

Notwithstanding the attention that our literary historians have lavished on the likes of Royall Tyler and his genteel predecessors, the actual production and consumption of print in eighteenth-century America was closely bound up with the religious culture I have sketched. On a strictly quantitative basis, more "religious" books were printed than those in any other category (with the possible exception of schoolbooks), and most of the persons we in retrospect deem "writers" in eighteenth-century America were clergy who wrote only sermons.[26] Within this system and its adjuncts certain kinds of books, or genres, sold consistently and widely. The better-selling religious books tended to be the work of English Nonconformists such as Isaac Watts. Some contained an element of sensationalism—say, evoking the millennium and the threat of fiery hell. The cheapest form of print may have been the tales of "remarkables" or "wonders" of the kind that David Carlisle issued from his press. Similarly inexpensive and widespread were stories of conversion or extreme religious experience. Again, it is hazardous to generalize. But the genre of spiritual autobiography (or biography) was

---

treated as a low criminal, that he was mocked, spat upon, whipped, and nailed to the cross—that story no sooner comes to dominate the consciousness of the people than it completely destroys the aesthetics of the separation of styles" (63).

25. David D. Hall, "The Uses of Literacy in New England, 1600–1850," included in this collection. On the one hand, these clergy-writers were like the genteel amateur in rejecting money as a rationale for writing. But on the other, they hoped to reach as many readers as possible.

26. This statement is based on the data in James A. Levernier and Douglas R. Wilmer, eds., *American Writers before 1800: A Biographical and Critical Dictionary* (Westport, Conn., 1983).

consistently important in eighteenth-century America, as were narratives of collective experience. A Boston minister's son established a magazine, *The Christian History* (1743–44) that filled its pages with such narratives.[27] And in keeping with the tradition, Isaac Backus inserted at the end of his pamphlet on the liberty of interpretation *An Appendix Containing Some Short Account of the Experiences and Dying Testimony* of a fellow New Light minister, a man who credited his spiritual awakening to God's "dear servant Mr. Whitefield."[28]

This genre came easily to untrained writers who may have been "illiterate" in the learned disciplines but who knew the Bible closely. The other genres to which these writers turned were the forms that Tyler mocked in *The Algerine Captive* and that Benjamin Franklin satirized in the "Silence Dogwood" essays: elegies, poems and prose describing the history of redemption, narratives of God's remarkable providence. No learning or esoteric skill was required to produce such work, which in general drew its motifs from the Bible or from a long-established set of story frameworks—deliverance from sin, the providential ordering of one's life, the passage of the saint or pilgrim to heaven from this weary world. Anyone immersed in Scripture, and who felt the stirrings of the Spirit, was apt to feel empowered as a writer. Such a writer was Franklin's uncle, and such were hundreds of others who will never figure in our literary history.

This empowerment extended to the act of reading. I have argued elsewhere that a majority of Americans became literate (in the sense of knowing how to read) in the context of a household system of instruction. Elsewhere, too, I have sketched a mode of reading that this household culture perpetuated, a mode that owed its structure and its rhythms to the practice of spiritual meditation.[29] We may trace this way of reading back to the very beginnings of the Protestant Reformation, and still further, to the medieval tradition of learning to read by memorizing a primer. As manifested in eighteenth-century America, this literacy went hand-in-hand with a limited supply of printed books.

27. It is characteristic of our secularist bias that even so great a work as Frank Luther Mott's *A History of American Magazines, 1741–1850*, 5 vols. (Cambridge, Mass., 1930–68) fails to include an entry for *The Christian History*.

28. McLoughlin, *Isaac Backus on Church, State, and Calvinism*, 123.

29. David D. Hall, *Worlds of Wonder, Days of Judgment: Popular Religious Belief in Early New England* (New York, 1989), chap. 1.

The common reader was easily satisfied; he or she owned at best but a handful of titles—perhaps a Bible, a steady seller, a psalm book—and with the probable exception of the yearly almanac, rarely added new books to this stock.

We are now in a position to appreciate more fully the politics of *The Algerine Captive*. From Royall Tyler's vantage, Updike Underhill was a naive reader, someone so accustomed to "plain" or figural interpretation that he could not differentiate the "literary" from the true or real. From this vantage Underhill was also *retardataire* in continuing to fancy the tales of "wonder" and "dreary days of doom." Interventions of the supernatural had ceased to interest the genteel writer; by the middle of the eighteenth century, genteel culture was deeply marked by the disenchantment that followed on the heels of the new science and the reaction against "enthusiasm." The final expression of Tyler's politics is his picture of a revolution in reading, as though the genres long preferred by the common reader were suddenly abandoned and fiction of the kind that Tyler wished to write prevailed. Every detailed study of country booksellers and probate inventories contradicts this fable.[30] Instead it was the genteel writer who struggled in the marketplace. As one literary historian has noted, the aspiring men of letters in the new republic were unable to discover "the appropriate form for appealing to the widest possible audience."[31]

Those who did succeed in that endeavor were the writers who owed their understanding of writing and reading to the Protestant Reformation and the inclusive culture of the Word to which it gave rise. The persistence of this culture, together with the persistence of a decentralized social system that constrained the authority of urban, professional elites, stands in sharp contrast to the situation in eighteenth-century France. Consider, as illustration, the American printer-publisher and his allies. Versatile in moving back and forth between the roles of printer, writer, bookseller, and publisher, men like Benjamin Franklin (before he retired from the business) and Isaiah Thomas regarded themselves as of the "middling classes" and articulated the values of that social formation. In France, on the other hand, the press "did not

30. I review some of this evidence in "Books and Reading in Eighteenth-Century America," *Of Consuming Interests: The Style of Life in the Eighteenth Century*, ed. Cary Carson et al. (Charlottesville, Va., 1994), 354–72.
31. Emory Elliott, *Revolutionary Writers: Literature and Authority in the New Republic, 1725–1810* (New York, 1982), 69.

routinely acknowledge [commercial expansion] or appeal to the professionals and tradespeople most affected by it. Rather, periodicals in France continued to present an aristocratic view of society."[32]

The more aggressive of our new world printers worked closely with professional writers, the most famous of them being Thomas Paine. Half a century earlier, Franklin had befriended James Ralph, who sailed with him in 1724 to England. There Ralph became a denizen of Grub Street—composing poetry and drama of his own, flourishing as a political writer in the pay of (mostly) opposition politicians, and finally being pensioned by the government in exchange for silencing his pen. Thomas Paine crossed the Atlantic in the opposite direction. Arriving in Philadelphia in 1774, he found work as a literary jack-of-all-trades, becoming the editor of the *Pennsylvania Magazine*. As Frank Luther Mott has observed, Paine was more properly a "contributing editor" who "wrote over several signatures" for the journal. His contributions included everything from "descriptions of mechanical devices" to "anecdotes, Addisonian essays, argumentative papers, and poems in some variety," the latter including "Cupid and Hymen," printed the month that the Minute Men of Lexington and Concord repelled a British expedition, and "reflections on Unhappy Marriages."[33]

Paine's versatility was in keeping with the cultural position of printer-publishers in colonial and revolutionary America and those in their employ. Such men were comfortably at home with the "popular" literary culture that encompassed almanacs, simple schoolbooks, the hoax, and certain forms of journalism. Yet they were equally at home with the modes of genteel culture. Affiliating with those who were socially superior as well as reaching out to "country" readers, these printers were uniquely situated when the movement for independence reached the point of crisis. It was at that moment that Paine wrote *Common Sense* (1776), the *only* pamphlet on the constitutional issues of the period that reached the common reader.[34] Himself a child of re-

32. Stephen Botein, Jack Censer, and Harriet Ritvo, "The Periodical Press in Eighteenth-Century English and French Society: A Cross-Cultural Approach," *Comparative Studies in Society and History* 23 (1981):490.

33. Mott, *A History of American Magazines*, 1:88–89.

34. The statistics on editions compiled by Thomas R. Adams in *American Independence: The Growth of an Idea. A Bibliographical Study of the American Political Pamphlets Printed between 1764 and 1776* (Providence, R.I., 1965), indicate a sharp drop in the number of printings (editions) after *Common Sense;* of the 220 pamphlets in the bibliography, only five had as many as seven printings and but one as many as twelve.

ligious nonconformity in England, Paine harnessed certain motifs of the culture of the Word to his attack on the British monarchy.

Protestantism, and especially the kind of Protestantism that came with the early colonists, made a difference. Yet it has been argued that in the first half of the eighteenth century the clergy in America grew apart from the people—that hierarchy imposed itself on what once had been a common culture. The remark I quoted at the outset of this essay is perhaps a case in point. Many clergy were unwilling to concede the limitations of learnedness, and some began to prefer the world of the cosmopolitans. Accordingly, it may have taken something like a "revolution" to reaffirm the premises of the culture of the Word, and especially its latent egalitarianism. Historians have pointed to the New Lights of the Great Awakening as the group that, repudiating hierarchy, moved in this direction.[35] Granting this possibility, it must also be recognized that in the long run the New Light movement was secondary or subordinate to the Reformation as a time of cultural change. Either way, we end up acknowledging a fundamental transformation that occurred prior to the movement for American independence.

The "revolution in print" that erupted in France after 1789 destroyed a centralized system of patronage for writers and a centralized system of control over the book trades. In their place the Revolution swept into power the elements of a "literary underground."[36] But our Revolution did not have these consequences. The patriots forced a few printers to stop doing business. But since most printers did not depend on the royal government for their work, and since an opposition press had operated openly for several decades, the passage from colonies to nation was marked by continuity. Like other institutions in the wider society, the business of printing was as decentralized and entrepreneurial before the Revolution as it remained in the early republic.

The agitation that preceded the outbreak of war in 1775 was innovative in certain respects, but traditional in others. In 1772 the more "radical" patriots in Boston organized a Committee of Correspondence. The goal of the committee was to sustain the momentum of the protest against British power. To this end the Committee, having com-

35. Harry S. Stout, "Religion, Communication, and the Ideological Origins of the American Revolution," *William and Mary Quarterly*, 3d ser., 34 (1977):519–41.
36. Robert Darnton, *The Literary Underground of the Old Regime* (Cambridge, Mass., 1982).

missioned and paid for a print run of 600 copies of *The Votes and Proceedings of the Town of Boston*, sent a single copy to each of the 260 towns in Massachusetts, and others to "four fifths of the Gentlemen Selectmen in the Country, the Representatives of the several Towns, the Members of his Majesty's Council and others of Note." In so doing, the Committee expected that a public reading of the text, followed by discussion, would occur in most of these communities.[37] Such moments had been characteristic of the civic culture of Massachusetts from the outset of colonization in the seventeenth century. Then as later, the government often paid the cost of distributing election sermons and codes of law to every town. Thus in Springfield when a printed copy of the code of laws of 1648 arrived in 1649, it was promptly "published," that is, read aloud to a gathering of the townspeople.[38] In this one example, as in others, the revolutionaries relied on a structure of communication that arose within the culture of the Word.

What may have made the revolution distinctive was a momentary convergence of the two cultures I have sketched. For sure, the vernacular culture entered into the making of the "myth" of American "liberty" on which the leaders of the revolutionary movement played. These leaders appropriated the Reformation motif of the freeing of the Word of God from Catholic tyranny and enlarged it into a vision of exceptionalism: Americans were entitled to liberty because they had always been distinctively free. This was the argument of John Adams's *Dissertation on the Feudal and the Canon Law* (1765–66). Adams imagined the Puritans as animated by "a love of universal liberty" that included a commitment to general education and the freedom of the press. Two centuries before him, John Foxe the martyrologist had linked the coming of the Reformation to the invention of printing. Extending that association, Adams celebrated the literacy of the colonists: "All Ranks and orders of our People, are intelligent, are accomplished—a Native of America, especially of New England, who cannot read and write is as rare a Phenomenon as a Comet."[39] In effect, the hierarchy of "ranks

---

37. The episode is described in Richard L. Bushman, "Massachusetts Farmers and the Revolution," in *Society, Freedom, and Conscience: The American Revolution in Virginia, Massachusetts, and New York*, ed. Richard M. Jellison (New York, 1976), 78–79.

38. Hall, *Worlds of Wonder*, 45.

39. L. H. Butterfield et al., *The Adams Papers: Diary and Autobiography of John Adams*, 4 vols. (Cambridge, Mass., 1962), 1:257.

and orders" gave way for the moment to the values of a different cultural system.

The same accommodation occurred in the thinking of a Maryland man who came under pressure to demonstrate his support for the patriot cause. In his own defense he quoted from a letter he had written an Englishman about the common people of America. Describing them as "a well-informed, reasoning commonality, too, perhaps the most of any on earth," this erstwhile patriot anticipated Tocqueville in saluting "the freedom and general circulation of newspapers, and the eagerness and leisure of the people to read them, or to listen to those who do."[40]

Could it be that, somehow, Americans were accustomed to a democratic world of print without having to experience a democratic revolution? To acknowledge the element of ideology in these statements, as we must, and to suggest that they partake of the mythic, does not exhaust their relevance. They underscore anew the differences between revolutionary France and revolutionary America: in the former, printing, writing, and reading were closely bound up with a centralized aristocracy; in the latter, printing, writing, and reading were far more open-ended and inclusive. It took 1789 to break open the French system. But in America, 1776 may be understood as the outcome of existing structures.

40. Peter Force, *American Archives*, 4th ser. (Washington, D.C., 1840), 3, 54. The reach and influence of the colonial newspaper is unclear. Robert M. Weir is notably reserved in describing them in "The Role of the Newspaper Press in the Southern Colonies on the Eve of the Revolution: An Interpretation," in *The Press & the American Revolution*, ed. Bernard Bailyn and John B. Hench (Worcester, Mass., 1980), 99–150.

Readers and Reading in America:
Historical and Critical Perspectives

THE HISTORY OF READING as it is pursued in the United States means different things to different people. To survey the field is to be reminded of the elasticity of the subject; for some who study it, reading has to do with literacy and thus becomes an aspect of social history or the history of education; for others, it pertains to the hermeneutics of interpretation; for still others, the distribution and ownership of printed matter, chiefly books, is the real concern. How it is we understand what reading is about, or means, depends on the nature of our inquiry—whether we are historians of working-class culture, educational institutions, religion and *mentalité*, or the politics of texts. These possibilities give energy and importance to the field even as they work against coherence and effective comparison. I begin, therefore, by noting that the American scholars who study the history of reading do not agree on the boundaries of the subject or on what its history has been.[1]

Written for a conference sponsored by the Ministry of National Education and Culture and held in Paris in January 1993. My assignment was to report on the state of scholarship in America, an assignment I interpreted generously in order to acknowledge scholarship from elsewhere that has influenced the work of Americanists. A slightly different version has been published in translation in *Histoires de la Lecture*, ed. Roger Chartier (Paris, 1995), 165–79; the version reprinted here was first published in the *Proceedings of the American Antiquarian Society* 104 (1994): 337–57.
    1. Important critical and bibliographical reflections that supplement my own are two essays by Carl F. Kaestle, "Studying the History of Literacy" and "The History of Readers," in *Literacy in the United States: Readers and Reading since 1880*, ed. Kaestle et al. (New Haven, 1991). See also

To simplify this messy situation, to cut my way through the tangle of possibilities, I have limited myself to reporting on six aspects of our scholarship. In closing, I want to reflect on the social and cultural consequences of the division of labor and on the relationship between literary theory and the history of the book.

1. *Reading as an aspect of intellectual history.* For a very long time and continuing to the present day, reading has been a synonym for the reception and diffusion of ideas. That is, describing the books that were available was important to intellectual historians concerned with mapping major patterns of thought, these being for the most part patterns within learned culture. Seeking evidence of these ideas in early America, historians have turned to lists of books that were used at colleges like Harvard and Yale or relied on the probate inventories of the Protestant clergy who constitute our first and longest-lasting learned class. Occasionally the key has been the library of an individual—for example, the remarkable collection assembled by James Logan of Philadelphia.[2]

It was such evidence that enabled Perry Miller to discern the scholastic rationalism and Ramist logic that, to his initial surprise, loomed so large in the intellectual fabric of Puritanism. Similarly, Henry May's magisterial analysis of the multiple strands of *The Enlightenment in America* relied on the contents of booksellers' stocks. Charting currents of ethical theory in seventeenth- and eighteenth-century America, Norman Fiering drew on private inventories and the contents of college libraries, and his revisionist study of Jonathan Edwards takes ac-

Robert Darnton, "First Steps Toward a History of Reading," in *The Kiss of Lamourette: Reflections in Cultural History* (New York, 1990), 154–87; Janice Radway, "Beyond Mary Bailey and Old Maid Librarians: Reimagining Readers and Rethinking Reading," *Journal of Education for Library and Information Science* 35 (Fall 1994):1–21.

2. Samuel Eliot Morison, *Harvard College in the Seventeenth Century,* 2 vols. (Cambridge, Mass., 1936); Richard Warch, *School of the Prophets: Yale College, 1701–1740* (New Haven, Conn., 1973); Edmund S. Morgan, *The Gentle Puritan: A Life of Ezra Stiles, 1727–1795* (New Haven, Conn., 1962), chap. 3; Frederick B. Tolles, *Meeting House and Counting House: The Quaker Merchants of Colonial Philadelphia 1682–1763* (1948; reprint., New York, 1963), chaps. 7–8 (with many useful references to other scholarship); Frederick E. Brasch, "James Logan, A Colonial Mathematical Scholar, and the First Copy of Newton's *Principia* to Arrive in the Colonies," *Proceedings of the American Philosophical Society* 86 (1943): 3–12; Edwin Wolf II, *The Library of James Logan of Philadelphia, 1674–1751* (Philadelphia, 1974). Another vein of scholarship, exemplified by Richard Beale Davis's *Intellectual Life in the Colonial South, 1585–1763,* 3 vols. (Knoxville, Tenn., 1978), employs these kinds of evidence to paint in broad strokes a picture of "intellectual life." Here and in all succeeding notes the references are illustrative, not comprehensive.

count of the "catalogue" Edwards kept of books he wanted to read.[3] The many possibilities for this kind of scholarship extend into the twentieth century, as Cynthia Russett demonstrated in her description of a seminar at Harvard in the 1930s devoted to reading Vilfredo Pareto's *The Mind and Society* in translation.[4]

In the centuries that lead up to our own, learned culture in America depended on books that Europeans wrote and published. How these books made their way to America has interested historians of libraries, book collecting, and the book trades. These forms of scholarship carry us beyond the history of ideas into the social history of culture, as in making evident the structure and role of certain sites—libraries, booksellers, households, salons, clubs, "circles," "connections," coteries, learned societies, and the like—where imported books were accumulated and exchanged.[5] A well-studied and important example is the circulation of books and periodicals in the 1830s among the persons who became known as Transcendentalists.[6] From another vantage, this scholarship fills in the stages in the "communications circuit" that books traverse in passing from writers to readers. The history of reading as a branch of the history of learned culture thus becomes grounded in the social and economic history of the book trades.[7]

3. Perry Miller, *The New England Mind: The Seventeenth Century* (Cambridge, Mass., 1954); Henry R. May, *The Enlightenment in America* (New York, 1976); David Lundberg and Henry May, "The Enlightened Reader in America," *American Quarterly* 28 (1976): 262–93; Norman Fiering, *Moral Philosophy at Seventeenth-Century Harvard* (Chapel Hill, N.C., 1981); idem, *Jonathan Edwards and British Moral Philosophy* (Chapel Hill, N.C., 1981). Edwards noted in the "Catalogue" (Edwards ms., Beinecke Library, Yale University) which books he was actually able to secure and read. Methodologically, there have been few sequels to Zoltán Haraszti, *John Adams and the Prophets of Progress: A Study in the Intellectual and Political History of the Eighteenth Century* (Cambridge, Mass., 1952), perhaps because the evidence, in this instance Adams's marginal comments in books he owned, survives for relatively few individuals.

4. Cynthia E. Russett, *The Concept of Equilibrium in American Social Thought* (New Haven, Conn., 1966), chaps. 7–9.

5. The literature on the history of libraries may provide the best access to this social history. See Michael Harris and Donald G. Davis, Jr., *American Library History: A Bibliography* (Austin, Tex., 1978); Michael Harris, Donald Davies, and John Mark Tucker, *American Library History: A Comprehensive Guide to the Literature* (Santa Barbara, Calif., 1989). A model study of a bookseller who catered to the learned is Elizabeth Carroll Reilly, "The Wages of Piety: The Boston Book Trade of Jeremy Condy," in *Printing and Society in Early America*, ed. William L. Joyce et al. (Worcester, Mass., 1983), 83–131.

6. Thus Margaret Fuller borrowed "volumes of Coleridge and Carlyle" from Emerson and lent him German books on Goethe, though she also depended on James Freeman Clarke for a set of Goethe's work. Charles Capper, *Margaret Fuller: An American Romantic Life*, vol. 1, *The Private Years* (New York, 1992), 201–38.

7. Studies of book production and distribution in America are summarized in the essays collected in David D. Hall and John Hench, eds., *Needs and Opportunities in the History of the*

All of this work in intellectual history and the social history of learned culture is paralleled or even pioneered in the scholarship on the intellectual and social history of *ancien régime* France: in particular, the work of Daniel Mornet, Daniel Roche, and Robert Darnton.[8]

2. *Reading as an aspect of popular culture.* In recent years historians have turned away from learned culture, where books undoubtedly mattered and where the evidence of reading and literacy seems abundant, to ask what books have meant to the lower social orders, to the working class, to those who were possibly illiterate. Should reading figure in the study of popular culture?

The way we go about answering this question is closely related to studies of the rate of literacy and of the production and consumption of printed matter. We have come to realize that, for early America, studies of literacy based on signature counts underestimate the percentage of persons who could read, but possibly not write. The distinction between the skills of reading and writing became important once it was understood that children in early America learned to read before they learned to write and, for the most part, learned to read in their households or at schools informally constituted and attended very briefly. Notwithstanding the limitations of the signature-count method, such studies suggest that by the second half of the eighteenth century, the great majority of adult males in the northern colonies or states were literate in being able both to read and to write. Surprisingly, female literacy in New England, the region for which we have the most careful studies, had reached 80 percent or higher by 1790, after rising steadily throughout the century.[9] My qualitative survey of seventeenth-century

---

Book: America, 1639–1876 (Worcester, Mass., 1987). Ronald J. Zboray carries this form of analysis a step further in *A Fictive People: Antebellum Economic Development and the American Reading Public* (New York, 1993).

8. Daniel Mornet, *Les origines intellectualles de la Révolution Française 1715–1787* (1933; Paris, 1967); Daniel Roche, "Encyclopédistes et Académiciens: Essai sur la Diffusion Sociale des Lumières," in *Livre et société dans la France du xviiie siècle,* ed. François Furet et al., 2 vols. (Paris, 1965, 1970), 73–94; idem, *Le siècle des lumières en province: académies et académiciens provinciaux, 1660–1789,* 2 vols. (Paris and The Hague, 1978); Robert Darnton, *The Business of Enlightenment: A Publishing History of the "Encyclopedie," 1775–1800* (Cambridge, Mass., 1979).

9. See Gloria L. Main, "An Inquiry into When and Why Women Learned to Write in Colonial New England," *Journal of Social History* 24 (1991): 578–89; Joel Perlmann and Dennis Shirley, "When Did New England Women Acquire Literacy?" *William and Mary Quarterly,* 3d ser., 48 (1991): 50–67. These studies alter the figures for women given in Kenneth Lockridge, *Literacy in Colonial New England: An Inquiry into the Social Context of Literacy in the Early Modern West* (New York, 1974). See also William J. Gilmore, "Elementary Literacy on the Eve of the Industrial Revolution: Trends in Rural New England, 1760–1830," *Proceedings of the American*

materials led me to conclude that more persons (men and women) were able to read, than not, in seventeenth-century New England.[10]

With illiteracy thus removed from the story, historians have turned their attention to book production and distribution and, using series of estate inventories made after death, to ownership. On the side of production and distribution, Margaret Spufford's analysis of the London booksellers who, after 1660, specialized in the chapbook and ballad trade has influenced historians like myself who go on to argue that certain "cheap books," most especially the almanac and psalm book in the seventeenth and eighteenth centuries, were produced and distributed in sufficient quantity to ensure that copies came into almost every household.[11] Bibles were also readily available in a variety of formats, some of them quite inexpensive. As for probate inventories, those for early New England indicate that half or more of all households contained books, a figure that compares favorably with English and continental percentages.[12]

Some historians have used this flow of print and the underlying literacy it presumes as the starting point for a description of popular culture, popular religion, or *mentalité*. In effect, these historians apply to the culture of ordinary people some of the expectations of intellectual history, though in the end paying less attention to the intricacies of any single text and more to the thematic structure of certain categories of cheap books, including almanacs, "wonder" stories, and "penny godlies."[13]

Antiquarian Society 92 (1982): 87–171; and for other nineteenth-century trends, Lee Soltow and Edward Stevens, *The Rise of Literacy and the Common School in the United States: A Socioeconomic Analysis to 1870* (Chicago, 1981). The importance of the distinction between reading and writing is demonstrated in Margaret Spufford, "First Steps in Literacy: The Reading and Writing Experiences of the Humblest Seventeenth-Century Spiritual Autobiographers," *Social History* 4 (1979): 407–35. There is cause for concern that the percentages in Gilmore's and Perlmann's studies that correct Lockridge's have yet to be incorporated into women's history.

10. David D. Hall, *Worlds of Wonder, Days of Judgment: Popular Religious Belief in Early New England* (New York, 1989), chap. 1. But see E. Jennifer Monaghan, "Literacy Instruction and Gender in Colonial New England," in *Reading in America: Literary and Social History*, ed. Cathy N. Davidson (Baltimore, 1989), 53–80.

11. Margaret Spufford, *Small Books and Pleasant Histories: Popular Fiction and Its Readership in Seventeenth-Century England* (Athens, Ga., 1982); Hall, *Worlds of Wonder*, passim. Not until the second half of the eighteenth century did the American book trade begin to distribute significant quantities of chapbooks and ballads of the kind Spufford describes.

12. "A Note on Book Ownership in Seventeenth-Century New England," in Hall, *Worlds of Wonder*, 247–49.

13. Spufford, *Small Books and Pleasant Histories*, chaps. 7–9; Hall, *Worlds of Wonder*, chaps. 2–3; C. John Sommerville, *Popular Religion in Restoration England*, University of Florida Social Science Monographs, no. 59 (Gainesville, Fla., 1977), with useful methodological reflections. The product that in France had attracted comparable attention is the *bibliothèque bleue*.

But can an adequate history of popular culture be constructed out of what we know about production, distribution, and ownership? One constraint is that inventories and other evidence of consumption do not provide a complete picture of the forms of print that entered households or communities. For example, we lack systematic knowledge of the borrowing of books or the sharing of newspapers and periodicals.[14] May it not be assumed that these practices served to make more, not less, available? On the other side of the ledger is the awkward fact that a significant fraction of probate inventories—the percentage varied from one locality to the next, but in early New England was as high as 40 percent—make no reference to books.[15] Does this situation lead us away from books and toward oral tradition or, at the least, impress on us the imperfect relation between the circulation of books and the popular mind?[16]

These questions become even more tantalizing when we explore the history of reading from the early nineteenth century onward. Here, as well, the broader issue is the relation between reading and social history. How are the circumstances of ethnicity, region, religion, and class reflected in patterns of production and consumption?[17] Does the data reveal sharp differences between groups, or point to the presence of a culture common to most Americans?

Let me designate the last of these possibilities the "liberal" interpretation. It celebrates an ever-mounting tide of production that car-

14. In a yet unpublished essay on the eighteenth-century New England minister Ebenezer Parkman, Ross Beales draws on Parkman's extensive diary to demonstrate the frequency of exchanges or loans in which Parkman participated. Borrowing was also crucial to the reading done by Ella Clayton Thomas of Georgia in the middle of the nineteenth century. Amy M. Thomas, "Who Makes the Text? The Production and Use of Literature in Antebellum America" (Ph.D. diss., Duke University, 1992), chap. 2.

15. Hall, "A Note on Book Ownership." See also Joseph Kett and Patricia McClung, "Book Culture in Post-Revolutionary Virginia," *Proceedings of the American Antiquarian Society* 94 (1984): 97–138.

16. In previous work I discounted oral tradition and emphasized, instead, the importance of print culture. I did so at a time when the former term was being used to signify a chasm between popular and high culture. As that exaggeration subsides, the term may regain a more limited usefulness (bearing always in mind the permeability of the two modes), as indeed it does in David Vincent's exemplary *Literacy and Popular Culture: England 1750–1914* (Cambridge, 1989). My earlier thinking is recorded in "The World of Print and Collective Mentality in Seventeenth-Century New England," included in this collection.

17. Small-scale regional differences within Windsor District of Vermont are mapped in William J. Gilmore, *Reading Becomes a Necessity of Life* (Knoxville, Tenn., 1988). On a larger scale, the differences north and south of the Mason-Dixon Line in the nineteenth and early twentieth centuries were considerable.

ried printed matter into all corners of the land. The agents of that expansion included profit-minded entrepreneurs; tract, Bible, and other moral reform societies; political parties; and the civil state, this last in conjunction with free public schooling. On the side of consumption, the longstanding barrier of price gave way as incomes rose, as the cost of production dropped sharply, and as these costs were shifted to advertisers. Enumerating the elements of expansion as they unfolded in nineteenth-century England, the literary historian Richard Altick proclaimed the emergence of a "democracy of print."[18]

Among Americanists, this equation of surging production and consumption with democracy is almost irresistible.[19] Did not de Tocqueville discover that the newspaper had penetrated the furthest reaches of the Michigan frontier and affirm that, compared to the French, Americans were much more avid in producing and reading journalism?[20] Even someone of quite different politics, the social critic Raymond Williams, employed a similar framework (though his also incorporated elements of resistance to change) in *The Long Revolution*, where the "growth of the reading public" in England, and especially the accelerating rate of growth after 1830, is linked to the "democratic revolution" and a "cultural revolution," that is, "the aspiration to extend the active process of learning, with the skills of literacy and other advanced communication, to all people rather than to limited groups."[21] The story culminates in a fresh surge of production around the turn of the century and the emergence of "mass" culture.

Yet the anomalies are many. The new Age of Reading so hopefully

18. Richard D. Altick, *The English Common Reader: A Social History of the Mass Reading Public, 1800–1900* (Chicago, 1957), 1. David Nord provides a historically specific description of tract-society readers in "Religious Reading and Readers in Antebellum America," *Journal of the Early Republic* 15 (1995): 241–72.
19. The changing structure of print culture has become an element in wider arguments about democratization: see, especially, Nathan O. Hatch, *The Democratization of American Christianity* (New Haven, Conn., 1989), chap. 5. I have criticized some versions of this scheme in an essay included in this collection, "The Politics of Writing and Reading in Eighteenth-Century America." In "Models of Literacy in the American Schools: Social and Historical Conditions and Consequences," Suzanne de Castell and Alan Luke place the transition from hierarchy to democracy at the end of the nineteenth century. de Castell et al., ed., *Literacy, Society, and Schooling: A Reader* (Cambridge, Mass., 1986), 87–109.
20. Alexis de Tocqueville, *Democracy in America*, ed. Phillips Bradley, 2 vols. (New York, 1954), 2: 119–22; George Wilson Pierson, *Tocqueville in America* (New York, 1959), 152.
21. Raymond Williams, *The Long Revolution* (1961; reprint., Harmondsworth, 1965), pt. 2, chap. 2; and chap. 11.

proclaimed at the outset of the nineteenth century never encompassed everyone.[22] A century later, when Robert and Helen Lynd surveyed reading practices in Muncie, Indiana, only a fourth of their "working-class" informants reported "expenditures for books other than school-books by members of their families during the past twelve months." Even though a remarkable and ever-increasing number of periodicals circulated in Muncie, no subscriptions whatsoever were reported among a third of the working-class families, as contrasted with a single nonsubscriber among "business" families. And but half of all families held borrowers' cards at the public library.[23]

The Lynds were interested in other forms of difference, some but not all of which were rooted in class. Working-class families mainly read one set of magazines, business-class families another. Boys preferred magazines that, for the most part, girls ignored, and vice versa. And although the "ceaseless torrent of printed matter" that deluged Muncie in the mid-1920s seemed laudable, the Lynds regretted the disappearance of certain reading practices of the 1890s, as when Sunday afternoon discussions "brought together anywhere from two dozen to a hundred people, chiefly men . . . discussing every subject from 'Books, What to Read and How to Read Them' to the *Origin of Species.* . . . No longer do a Young Ladies' Reading Circle, a Christian Literary Society (of fifty), a Literary League, a Literary Home Circle, a Literary Fireside Club meet weekly or bi-weekly as in 1890." Instead, the "culture" of reading in the 1920s consisted of "the vicarious entry into other, imagined ways of living" via fiction, a form of reading the Lynds associated with leisure, women, "constant movie attendance . . . and the prime popularity of comedy and society films."[24]

The ambivalence that marks the pages of *Middletown*—did the "torrent of printed matter" override class differences, or not? Had culture declined or advanced?—is echoed in other reports of popular reading. Observers remark that inexpensive books and periodicals were widely available, reaching, in the case of newspapers, as many as 90 percent of

22. As Zboray emphasizes in *A Fictive People,* citing, among other circumstances, the continuing limitations of cost and thus of class.
23. Robert S. and Helen Merrell Lynd, *Middletown* (New York, 1929), 229–31. For data on expenditure on reading by different income groups throughout the twentieth century, see Kaestle et al., *Literacy in the United States,* 166–79.
24. Lynd and Lynd, *Middletown,* 231–37, 240–41.

those surveyed. Yet in the same breath these reports characterize the reading habits of the people as debased. Reporting in 1880 on a New England mill town, the Unitarian minister Jonathan Harrison indicted the "story papers" that were popular among the younger workers as "vapid, silly, turgid, and incoherent." Very nearly the same language turns up in social scientific surveys of the 1930s.[25]

The liberal celebration of abundance, democratization, and, by implication, a common culture thus shades off into cultural criticism. Reacting to this tone of dismay, some historians would employ it as a datum in an alternative version of the history of reading, a version that narrates the efforts of an educated elite to shape and reshape the culture of ordinary people.[26] Another possibility is to map the reading practices among distinctive sectors of society and on the basis of such evidence to argue, for example, that the working class had its own ways of reading, its own culture. Certainly it is the case that unions, radical parties, ethnic communities, and sectarian religious groups have sponsored dissenting literary cultures.[27]

What we are to make of these differences remains unclear. In Muncie, Indiana, periodicals circulated with increasing frequency among working-class families, and by no stretch of the imagination can these periodicals be represented as embodying an alternative culture. Moreover, in that city a rapidly expanding public library system had displaced the workers' libraries of the 1890s.[28] If we can generalize from Muncie, the history of reading patterns in the first half of the twentieth

25. Jonathan B. Harrison, *Certain Dangerous Tendencies in American Life* (Boston, 1880), excerpted in Alan Trachtenberg, ed., *Democratic Vistas, 1860–1880* (New York, 1970), 166; Michael Denning, "Proletarian Literature: Reflections on Working-Class Reading in the Age of the CIO," *Lire en Amérique*, Cahiers Charles V, no. 14 (1992): 90–92.

26. Robert A. Gross, *Books and Libraries in Thoreau's Concord* (Worcester, Mass., 1988); Lawrence W. Levine, *Highbrow/Lowbrow: The Emergence of Cultural Hierarchy in America* (Cambridge, Mass., 1988), 158–60 and passim. It could also be argued that the many kinds of evidence about readers and the distribution of books reveal the perpetually contested place of learnedness or "high culture" in our society and the appeal of a middle ground—as in the lecture rooms of the lyceum—where extremes gave way to a complex process of accommodation.

27. Working-class writing and reading in nineteenth-century Britain are described in R. K. Webb, *The British Working Class Reader, 1790–1848: Literacy and Social Tension* (London, 1955) and in Martha Vicinus, *The Industrial Muse: A Study of Nineteenth Century British Working Class Literature* (New York, 1974). See also Michael Denning, *Mechanic Accents: Dime Novels and Working-Class Culture in America* (London, 1987). The "textual practices" observed within certain religious communities deserve attention of the kind that contemporary Primitive Baptists receive in Brett Sutton, "Literacy and Dissent," in *Reading & Libraries: Proceedings of Library History Seminar VIII*, ed. Donald G. Davis, Jr. (Austin, Tex., 1991), 183–98.

28. Lynd and Lynd, *Middletown*, 234 and 235 n. 21.

century would seem to demonstrate overlap and increasing homogeneity, with the real loser being learned culture and the real winner the nexus between reading and leisure, or reading and the "culture of consumption."

I want to emphasize that these are speculations. No matter what framework of interpretation prevails, we need to acknowledge that books elude, even as they also make manifest, the categories of social history. In the context of his revisionist interpretation of popular culture in early modern France, Roger Chartier has called on historians to dissolve "exclusive relationships between specific cultural forms and particular social groups" on the grounds, in part, that the consumption of cheap books or "bestsellers" extends across social lines.[29] This argument is pertinent to the history of reading in the nineteenth and twentieth centuries. A parallel observation is that affirmations of cultural hierarchy within literary culture, as when critics condemn "trash," cannot be converted into the terminology of social class.[30]

3. *Reading as "represented" in texts.* Under the influence of Wolfgang Iser, Stanley Fish, and their fellow theorists of "reader response" and "reception theory," historians have attempted to construct a description of reading drawn from the assumptions about that practice embedded in printed texts. Within the Protestant culture that I have studied, Anglo-American Puritanism of the seventeenth century, it was common for authors to address their readers in an opening statement, often headed "To the Reader." These opening statements instruct the ideal reader on how to understand and put to use the prose that follows. Since for the most part these were religious texts that describe the process of redemption, the substance of these instructions was the traditional (in the sense of dating from the early Middle Ages) advice to model the act of reading on the practice of meditation: to ingest the written word, to "chew" it, to read slowly and repeatedly. As I and others have also demonstrated, these rules encompassed an understanding of the Bible as sacred, living speech, a logocentric Word that communicated the divine will to humankind. To read the printed Bible

29. Roger Chartier, *The Cultural Uses of Print in Early Modern France,* trans. Lydia G. Cochrane (Princeton, N.J., 1987), 3.

30. That is, contrary to what is suggested in Denning, *Mechanic Accents,* we cannot infer that readers of the dime novel were necessarily lower class, or of the working class, on the basis of genteel condemnations of the genre.

was thus, by analogy, to "hear" the Word. All other godly books could similarly be represented as alive or vital, as could the act of apprehending them, which depended on the "eye of faith."

The intermingling of the oral and the printed in the logocentric Word (see 2 Cor. 3:2–3) had its correlate in the very process of learning how to read, a process keyed to reciting aloud the sounds of letters and words. Putting these parts together—representations of reading, writing, and speech on the one hand, and on the other the method of learning how to read and recorded responses to actual books—the historian can arrive at a complex description of what reading signified and possibly of how it was practiced within a particular social and historical setting.[31]

We may and should analyze the intersecting representations of reading and writing that occur throughout the past four or five centuries. Indeed, we may conceptualize a history of reading fashioned out of such representations. Crucial to this history would be the rules that inhere in literary genres. When the "historical romance" entered English literature after 1660, the genre brought with it the rule that romances were light reading.[32] As of the middle of the nineteenth century, certain novels reversed this rule and identified themselves as requiring "serious" attention. At the end of the century modernist literature imposed a rule of irony. From Rousseau's *La Nouvelle Héloise* to the present day, the sentimental novel has demanded that its readers shed a tear or two . . . or three.[33]

Equally crucial to this history would be broader ideological and social patterns that inscribe themselves in the practice of reading. One of these is the category of "useful" that was present in Anglo-American culture by the middle of the eighteenth century and that became increasingly significant thereafter. Another is the "republican" mode that

31. See, in general, Hall, *Worlds of Wonder*, chap. 1.

32. Annabel Patterson, *Censorship and Interpretation: Writing and Reading in Early Modern England* (Madison, Wisc., 1984), 160–64. As Patterson points out, the romance also represented itself as yielding a wholly different set of meanings to the serious, elite reader.

33. Louise L. Stevenson, *The Victorian Homefront: American Thought and Culture 1860–1880* (New York, 1991), chap. 2; Nina Baym, *Novels, Readers, and Reviewers: Responses to Fiction in Antebellum America* (Ithaca, N.Y., 1984); Robert Darnton, "Readers Respond to Rousseau: The Fabrication of Romantic Sensitivity," chap. 6 in *The Great Cat Massacre and Other Episodes in French Cultural History* (New York, 1984). The permeability of genres, or the problems both in theory and in practice of achieving clear definition of them, may partially offset this argument about rules.

Thomas Jefferson wanted to incorporate within a system of public schools. A third would be "leisure" in the several forms it took as of the second half of the nineteenth century: the leisure of youth imagined in a Winslow Homer watercolor of a young girl lying in the grass on a summer day reading what can only be a novel; the leisure of workers temporarily released from the rhythms of factory production, as in Jonathan Harrison's sketch of readers in a New England mill town; the leisure arising from the sharp separation between work and home. The repertory of possibilities would also have to include ideologies of opposition to literacy or reading as articulated and partially carried out with regard to chattel slaves in the southern states before the Civil War.[34]

Such a history of reading is within our reach. But let us bear in mind that this history has to do not with "real" readers but with rules within texts and ideological representations of reading.[35] It is another matter to determine whether actual readers read actual books in keeping with these rules or ideologies.[36] A further difficulty is the "ahistorical propensity" of reception theory. An American literary critic whose phrase I have just quoted has recently observed that reader-oriented criticism has "divorced" its analysis from "consideration of [how] interpretive, ideological, and material contexts governed the forms of reader activity . . . for specific historical audiences." How and why it has done so— by privileging an ideal reader (the critic's own stance) or else a particular interpretation (invariably modernist/ideological) of a given text—need not be indicated in detail in this essay.[37] Suffice it to say that

34. Janet D. Cornelius, *"When I Can Read My Title Clear": Literacy, Slavery, and Religion in the Antebellum South* (Columbia, S.C., 1991). J.-Y. Mollier provides evidence for Catholicism in "Histoire de la lecture, histoire de l'edition," in *Histoires de la Lecture: Un bilan des récherches*, ed. Roger Chartier (Paris, 1995), 207–19.

35. Kathryn Shevelow makes this distinction in *Women and Print Culture: The Construction of Femininity in the Early Periodical* (London, 1989), 201 n. 12: "I must particularly emphasize this point in regard to readers. Although the textual representations of readers undoubtedly bear upon actual reading practices, as they were intended to do . . . my focus on representation necessarily is a focus on readers as the periodicals constructed them—that is, on intended or inscribed readers."

36. Some historians of reading, myself included, have been attracted to personal narratives of reading that occur in letters, diaries, and the like. These narratives need to be understood in light of the rules (as I have termed them) that inhere in genres. Otherwise, we may grant readers a misleading autonomy and particularity.

37. James L. Machor, ed., *Readers in History: Nineteenth-Century American Literature and the Contexts of Response* (Baltimore, 1993); the quotations are from Machor's "Introduction: Readers/Texts/Contexts," viii–ix, and the entire introduction is relevant. Welcome though they are, the repeated invocations of "historically specific" by the editor and his contributors should be contrasted with the practical failure to employ the work done by historians of reading, including,

while some of us who pursue the history of reading can find common ground with literary historians concerned with the hermeneutics of interpretation, this common ground excludes the data on the production and consumption of books that is central to any social history of reading and to the history of the book.

As I indicated in previous sections of this essay, a social history of reading engages with questions of difference. So does the hermeneutics of interpretation in this respect: the rules within texts can differentiate good reading from bad, the "serious" from the facile. The hierarchy implied by these distinctions, a hierarchy that privileges learnedness and complexity, leads to a further question: was the skill of reading similarly differentiated, a matter of varying levels of ability? A commonsense response is yes. It may also be common sense to assume that these levels of ability coincide with differences of education, income, occupation, and region as these are revealed in social history. Yet another possibility is that the material form of printed texts, that is, their *mis-en-page* or typography, embodies a hierarchy of high and low (learned and unlearned). According to this argument, the form of cheap books would dictate (or anticipate) a limited capacity to read.[38]

My own preference is otherwise. If it is common sense to acknowledge that differences of ability figure in the history of reading, it also seems evident that readers in past times, as in the present, moved easily from one hermeneutical framework to another. Pious readers of the Bible in the seventeenth century readily understood secular texts, and the mill workers who devoured story papers could surely comprehend other genres. Granting always that learned culture had its distinctive modes of reading, actual readers do not seem constrained or dominated by any single set of rules or ideology, perhaps because of the "complicated, polysemic" quality of all texts themselves.[39] A history of reading

for example, any of the work of Roger Chartier, not to mention much of what has been written about reading in America. For another point of view on reader-response theory, see Jonathan Rose, "Rereading the English Common Reader: A Preface to a History of Audiences," *Journal of the History of Ideas* 53 (1992): 47–70.

38. Roger Chartier, "Du livre au lire," in *Practiques de la Lecture*, ed. Roger Chartier (Marseille, 1985), 80–85. Carl Kaestle and William Trollinger, comparing fiction in the *Saturday Evening Post* and the *Atlantic Monthly* in 1920, argue that complexity of argument and inference may have been a constraint that stratified the reading public. See Kaestle et al., *Literacy in the United States*, chap. 7.

39. The phrase in Janice Radway's, *Reading the Romance: Women, Patriarchy, and Popular Literature* (Chapel Hill, N.C., 1984), 209, where it is applied to reading. That popular or mass-produced books retain this quality is demonstrated by Radway and argued for nineteenth-century

as I have sketched it in this section would therefore have to acknowledge that readers negotiated between competing, and perhaps conflicting, interpretive strategies, and that these possibilities for negotiation
are as prominent as the boundary lines we may want to mark off
between levels.

4. *Gender and reading: the "resisting" reader.* Do women read differently from men? This is a question that has interested feminist
literary critics seeking to challenge "patriarchical" readings of high
literature and, more broadly, the patriarchy *in* high literature and the
culture that produced it. This ideological criticism becomes a call for
"resistance," the alternative being domination by the realm of the mas-
culine.[40] To any historian of popular culture, this polarity of domination or resistance has a wider resonance, for these are very nearly the
contrasting terms (the usual expressions are domination and autonomy) that theorists of popular culture, most especially Roger Chartier,
have sought to rework.

   In the case of women's reading, an adequately historical description
has taken second place to ideological criticism. Only recently have a
few literary critics realized that women in other periods of time were
not engaged in the same politics of gender that they themselves find
compelling. Jane Tompkins has insisted that a famous, and famously
problematic novel, *Uncle Tom's Cabin*, be read in keeping with the
moral and aesthetic conventions that Harriet Beecher Stowe shared
with other Protestant evangelical women of the mid-nineteenth century.[41] Yet a vein of ahistorical analysis persists in feminist literary
criticism devoted to describing women readers. James Machor, whom I
have previously quoted on the limitations of reader-response theory,
has noted that "the description of the reading experience" in Judith
Fetterley's *The Resisting Reader* is itself "a historically specific interpretive strategy: the modernist assumption . . . that the essence of American fiction is its continual fascination with the male quest for a return to

---

materials by David Grimsted, "Books and Culture: Canned, Canonized, and Neglected," in Hall
and Hench, *Needs and Opportunities*, 187–232.
   40. See in general, Elizabeth A. Flynn and Patrocinio P. Schweickart, eds., *Gender and Reading: Essays on Readers, Texts, and Contexts* (Baltimore, 1986); Judith Fetterley, *The Resisting
Reader: A Feminist Approach to American Fiction* (Bloomington, Ind., 1978).
   41. Jane L. Tompkins, *Sensational Designs: The Cultural Work of American Fiction, 1790–1860*
(New York, 1985), chap. 5.

origins."[42] Fetterley is among the feminist theorists who have argued that, for women, the experience of reading books written by women is different from the experience of reading books by male authors—books in the latter instance that must be "resisted." The historian Barbara Sicherman has pointed out, however, that women young and old in the Progressive period included "boys' books" in the near-omnivorous reading in which they indulged. She goes on to argue that these women gained a strong sense of self from what they read regardless of the author's gender; reading helped them fashion an interior space. To anticipate my fifth point, Sicherman understands reading as "appropriation" rather than as "resistance."[43]

The literary historian Cathy N. Davidson tells a different story. She links two phenomena, the increasing production and consumption of novels in America after 1790 and a presumed surge in female literacy, in arguing that women formed the primary constituency for this genre. Drawing on what is termed "ideological criticism," Davidson makes the further argument that the early novels, some of them written by women, could be read "subversively," that is, in a manner contradictory to the moral rule that novel reading was immoral. For actual women readers, the practice thus came to signify subversion and their own cultural independence.[44] The historical evidence on which Davidson relies may be more problematic than she allows, beginning with the fact that female literacy was already at a high level in the northern states a half century before novels became widely available.[45] There is the further problem that men read novels and that the official proscription of them was, like many such proscriptions, in contradiction with other values within high culture. It remains to be pointed out that a category

42. Machor, "Historical Hermeneutics and Antebellum Fiction: Gender, Response Theory, and Interpretive Contexts," in Machor, *Readers in History,* 57.

43. Barbara Sicherman, "Sense and Sensibility: A Case Study of Women's Reading in Late-Victorian America," in Davidson, *Reading in America,* 201–25; "Reading and Ambition: M. Carey Thomas and Female Heroism," *American Quarterly* 45 (1993): 73–103; and "Reading *Little Women:* The Many Lives of a Text," in *U.S. History as Women's History: New Feminist Essays,* ed. Linda K. Kerber et al. (Chapel Hill, N.C., 1995), 245–66, 414–24. Comparing male and female patrons of the New York Society Library in the mid-nineteenth century, Zboray finds no significant difference, and specifically, that each group checked out the same quantity of fiction. *A Fictive People,* chap. 11.

44. Cathy N. Davidson, *Revolution and the Word: The Rise of the Novel in America* (New York, 1986).

45. See above, note 9.

designated "women" is an oversimplification that pays little heed to social and cultural contexts, be these economic, religious, regional, racial, or the like.

5. *The reader as appropriator.* It is a truism of the new reading history that readers remake the text. In the hands of someone like Roger Chartier, this premise has rendered problematic any and all arguments concerning popular culture as the mere passive reflection of a dominant culture. Similarly, it has rendered problematic the equation of texts and social levels. Coupled with an awareness of the polysemy of all texts, this perspective has allowed historians of working-class culture to reclaim the "dime novel" as embodying the politics of "artisanal republicanism."[46] And it has enabled historians like myself to rethink the place of cheap books in the fashioning of popular religion.

The most compelling study that proceeds from both of these premises is Janice Radway's *Reading the Romance: Women, Patriarchy, and Popular Literature.* Radway analyzes yet another standardized product, the romance, that began to be manufactured in great quantities in the 1970s and to find millions of readers among women. Bringing together an ethnography of actual readers with an interpretation of the texts to which they were attracted, Radway argues that these women are able to discriminate among the romances they consume. In the end hers is an argument about function—of how readers, situated within the contradictions of a culture of consumption overlaid with an older culture of the work ethic and situated also within complicated representations of men, women, and romance, use the conventions of plot and characterization to satisfy certain emotional and social needs.[47]

6. *Was there a "reading revolution"?* This concept, made famous by Rolf Engelsing, concerns a major transformation that separates the modern period (the nineteenth and twentieth centuries) from the old regime.[48] Three American historians have implied or asserted the exis-

---

46. Denning, *Mechanic Accents.*

47. See also Radway's critique, "Reading Is Not Eating: Mass-Produced Literature and the Theoretical, Methodological, and Political Consequences of a Metaphor," *Book Research Quarterly* 2 (Fall 1986): 7–29.

48. Rolf Engelsing, *Der Burger als Leser: Lesergeshichte in Deutschland 1500–1800* (Stuttgart, 1974). *Note in 1996:* the work of two generations of German literary and social historians on the "reading revolution" and other matters is discussed in Hans Erich Bodeker, "D'une 'Histoire litteraire du lecteur' à l'histoire du lecteur': Bilan et Perspectives," in *Histoires de la Lecture,* 93–124. It is a major weakness of this essay of mine that I am unable to report in detail on this scholarship, much of it revisionist in relation to early arguments about the "revolution."

tence of such a revolution: myself, in an early essay;[49] Cathy N. Davidson in her study of women and fiction; and William J. Gilmore in a
study of Windsor District, Vermont, using as data the probate inventories that include books.[50] Davidson's is a limited case because the word
"revolution" that is in the title of her book refers obliquely to the
American Revolution and directly to the presumed greater role of
women as readers; it should be noted, moreover, that she does not
accept Engelsing's unflattering characterization of "extensive" reading.
Gilmore's study demonstrates the "commercialization" of rural life, a
quickening of the flow of goods that by the 1830s had pushed books and
newspapers into more frequent circulation. Yet his evidence from the
probate inventories is perplexing for it shows, as do other studies of
book holdings in this time period, that most household libraries were
tiny in size, did not change over time, and usually contained the Bible.
Plus ça change, plus c'est la même chose. What should be pointed out in
the American context and no doubt in the European is that the assertion of a reading revolution is also (or perhaps primarily) an assertion
about other forms of change in society and culture—for example, a
transition from the religious to the secular, or from self-sufficiency to
the "commercial," or from scarcity to abundance in material goods.
That is, the problem of determining whether a reading revolution
occurred leads immediately into a wider set of problems each involving
complex tasks of conceptualization.[51]

I myself have alluded to a change in the mode of reading, from the
devotional mode of seventeenth-century Protestants to what contemporaries in the nineteenth century regarded as superficial reading. This
argument did not take account of a point I make in *this* essay: in any
given period of time, readers had available more than one representation or ideology of reading, texts, and writing; and the proper history of
reading should thus be arranged around the multiple possibilities and
perhaps the conflicts that existed within a particular frame of time

49. David D. Hall, "The Uses of Literacy in New England: 1600–1850," included in this
collection.
50. Gilmore, *Reading Becomes a Necessity of Life.* For other studies, see Kaestle et al., *Literacy in
the United States,* 52–55.
51. Could we consider it a form of reading revolution that the coming of the railroad made
possible the integration of local centers of literary production into a national network, as Zboray
demonstrates in *A Fictive People?*

rather than exclusively around the transition from one mode to another. As we increasingly realize, the nineteenth century had its intensive readers and the seventeenth century its extensive. The conceptual question left unaddressed is whether and how changes in the system of book production and distribution, especially the changes associated with new technologies and business practices emerging in the nineteenth century, affected the practices of readers.

It is tempting to suggest an alternative reading revolution. For what follows I am indebted to the British social historian David Vincent's *Literacy and Popular Culture.* Vincent calls attention to the role of state-sponsored elementary schools and the mode of literacy or reading for which they became instruments. In England, such age-graded schools became the norm after 1870; in America the effective date varies from one region to another, but in the northern states we may say that this system was emerging by 1860. These schools had a standardized curriculum keyed to age and teachers who employed uniform methods of instruction using textbooks specially developed for the classroom. With the appearance of this bureaucracy, the place where the skill of reading was imparted shifted from household to school. Accordingly, reading and literacy developed apart from work life and the rhythms of family culture. The mode of reading instituted by these schools can be understood as flowing from and serving to create a social identity that suppressed the particulars of class, region, religion, and ethnicity in favor of a generalized public culture. Students in these "common" schools acquired the uniform language (spelling, pronunciation, vocabulary) of the center: the civil state, the classless cadre of teachers. (Whether or how differences of social identity reappeared in this setting deserves further attention.) The Bible was displaced as, to a very large extent, were whole books in favor of "readers." In the elements of this system lie, I venture to assert, a reading revolution that may also be discerned in the burgeoning production of schoolbooks in the second half of the nineteenth century.

Let me call attention to another dimension of change in the nineteenth century. As rural society yielded to industrialism, the division of labor proceeded apace and with it an ever-sharpening distinction between work and leisure that, for persons in the middle class, coincided with the difference between men and women. Certain categories of books became coded as designed for leisure; and in the course of time, since leisure was what some women had, these same books, and even reading itself, were increasingly associated with their gender. It is in and through the division of labor and the categories of work and leisure that I would incorporate much of modern social history into the history of reading, taking note, for example, that women became preponderantly the founders of public libraries, reading circles or clubs, and the teachers in elementary schools.[52]

As I look back on scholarship in America, I am struck by how it divides into two streams: one encompasses those of us who, practicing the history of the book as it has emerged out of the intersection of the histories of printing and publishing with the social history of culture, attempt to construct patterns of actual consumption by groups we conveniently name "readers"; and another encompassing those in literary studies who are primarily concerned with authorship and the hermeneutics of interpretation. For the first of these groups, studies of reading have become linked to a reappraisal of popular and mass culture and to underlining the many possibilities for "appropriation." Literary critics take a different path, for they tend to view reading and writing as practices that reveal the presence of domination, subversion, and resistance. Can we hope that some day these critics will interest themselves in the social history of production and consumption, and, conversely, that social historians will acknowledge the power of texts?

52. Elizabeth Long provides some interesting suggestions about the relations among reading, leisure, and representations of women in "Textual Interpretation as Collective Action," in *The Ethnography of Reading*, ed. Jonathan Boyarin (Berkeley, Calif., 1992), 180–211.

Index

Adams, John, 10, 28, 29, 167
alehouse, 69
Alleine, Joseph, 50, 61, 76
Allestree, Richard, 121 *n*, 129
almanacs, 3, 24, 28, 34, 46, 47, 48, 49, 60, 63, 68, 70, 74, 84, 91, 121, 122, 164, 165, 173
Alsop, George, 136, 137
Altick, Richard, 175
American Antiquarian Society, 7, 18, 19
American Revolution, 24, 29, 42, 138, 165–68, 185
Amory, Hugh, 91 *n*
Andros, Edmund, 111 *n*
Anglicanism, 49, 50, 70, 121 *n*, 129
anonymity, 133
Antinomian controversy, 93–95
archives, 101–2, 102 *n*, 114, 148
Auerbach, Erich, 161 *n*
Augustine, Saint, 131
authorship, 6, 11, 12, 44, 93, 132–41 *passim*, 145, 154, 162, 187; Cotton Mather and, 93–95

Backus, Isaac, 159, 160, 161, 162, 163
Bacon, Nathaniel (Sr.), 111 *n*

Bacon, Nathaniel, 106, 107, 107 *n*, 124
Bacon, Thomas, 148
Bacon's Rebellion, 103, 105–7, 110, 113, 132 *n*, 133, 140, 148
ballads, 47, 48, 51, 73, 79
Baltimore, Lord, 103, 104, 105, 133
Banister, John, 128, 139, 140
Baptists, 150
Baptists, Primitive, 177 *n*
Bartlett, John Russell, 18, 19
Battle of the Severn, 106
Baxter, Richard, 49, 50, 61, 62, 63, 76
Bayly, Lewis, 86, 120, 121
Beecher, Lyman, 76
belles-lettres, 91
Bennett, H. S., 81 *n*, 86
Berkeley, William, 99, 106, 107, 110
Beverley, Robert, 106 *n*
Bible, 5, 31, 42, 100, 129, 142–45, 159, 161, 163, 178–79; inventories and, 120; literacy and, 55–60, 117; Quakers and, 144–45; reaction against, 73–74, 77
bibliography, 7–9, 11, 18, 34, 41–42, 45, 62
bibliothèque bleue, 39, 46, 47, 85, 87, 88
Bishop of London, 117, 126
Bladen, William, 113, 122, 148

189